the living earth
a resource for learning

living earth foundation

Hodder & Stoughton

A MEMBER OF THE HODDER HEADLINE GROUP

Editorial and project management: Andrew Steeds

Research: Catherine Davis, Deborah Niblock, Gail Debuisser

Living Earth editorial team: Niall Marriott, Roger Hammond

Consultants: Chris Durbin, David Oakley, the Environmental Education Working Group of the Geographical Association, Cathy Watson

Living Earth and the Publishers would like to express their appreciation and gratitude to the following organisations, who have generously sponsored this publication:

Midland Bank plc for sponsorship of the Rainforest Education Programme, from which the idea for this publication grew

Ashden Trust for funding initial research on this project

Unilever plc without whose generous support this book would never have been compiled.

The paper used to produce this publication was produced from pulp derived from sustainably harvested softwood.

British Library Cataloguing in Publication Data
Living Earth Foundation
  Living Earth: Resource for Learning
  I. Title
  333.707

ISBN 0-340-56820-8

First published 1994

Impression number 10 9 8 7 6 5 4 3 2 1
Year   1998 1997 1996 1995 1994

© 1994 Living Earth Foundation

All rights reserved. No part of this publication may be reproduced or transmitted in any form or by any means, electronic or mechanical, including photocopy, recording, or any information storage system, without permission in writing from the publisher or under licence from the Copyright Licensing Agency Limited. Further details of such licences (for reprographic reproduction) may be obtained from the Copyright Licensing Agency Limited, of 90 Tottenham Court Road, London W1P 9HE.

Typeset by Wearset, Boldon, Tyne and Wear.
Printed in Great Britain for Hodder & Stoughton Educational, a division of Hodder Headline Plc, 338 Euston Road, London NW1 3BH by Thomson Litho Limited.

Acknowledgements

The Publishers and Living Earth would like to thank the following for permission to use copyright material:

ACTIONAID for photograph from *Pampagrande – a Peruvian Village* (p. 61); Aluminium Can Recycling Association for cover of *Teacher's File* (p. 113); The Advisory Unit for Microtechnology in Education, Hertfordshire, for material from *Ecosoft* (p. 26); AVP for material from *Water Pollution* (p. 27); BBC Educational Publishing for covers of *Water* and *Rainforest* (p. 66); Books for Keeps for cover of *The Books for Keeps Green Guide to Children's Books* (p. 21); Cambridge University Press for cover of *Urban Ecology* (p. 46); Cambridgeshire Software House for material from *Can You Find It?* (p. 29); Cassell Publishers Ltd for covers of *Down the Plughole* (p. 18) and *What a Load of Rubbish* (p. 19); Centre for Alternative Technology for their logo (p. 125); The 'Bizarro' cartoon (p. 138) by Dan Piraro is reprinted by permission of Chronicle Features, San Francisco, California; Civic Trust for their logo (p. 126); Council for Environmental Education for cover of *Annual Review of Environmental Education* (p. 37) and their logo (p. 122); CWDE Software for material from *The Water Game* (p. 28); Stan Eales for illustrations on pp. 174, 182, 232, 240, 253, 255 and 265, all taken from *Isn't Progress Wonderful?*, published by Grub Street; English Heritage for covers of *A Teacher's Guide to Using Abbeys, A Teacher's Guide to Using Listed Buildings* (p. 90) and *Teaching on Site: History and Geography* (p. 91); Friends of the Earth for their logo (p. 121); Gaia Books for cover of *Gaia – an atlas of planet management* (p. 17); Victor Gollancz Ltd for cover of *The Young Green Consumer Guide* (p. 21); Grisewood & Dempsey Ltd Kingfisher Books for cover of *Ian and Fred's Big Green Book* (p. 17); The Institute of Biology for cover of *Living Biology in Schools* (p. 46); ICCE Services for photographs from *It's Your World – Don't Waste It, Wildlife in Danger, British Wildlife in Danger* (p. 68) and *Acid Rain: The Silent Crisis, No Trees... No Life* (p. 74) and *Making Peace with the Planet* (p. 75); Gary Larson for illustrations on pp. 47, 227 and 236; Learning Through Landscapes for their logo (p. 124); Longman Logotron for material from *Landmarks* (p. 30) and from *Sky Hunter* (p. 30); Angela Martin for illustrations on pp. 42, 63, 104 and 285; National Association for Environmental Education for cover of *Environmental Education* (p. 36); New Scientist for posters *The Greenhouse Effect* (p. 80) and *The Tree* (p. 82); Northamptonshire Training and Enterprise Council for page from *We Have a Road* (p. 115); Futzie Nuztle for permission to reproduce the illustration on p. 152, from *Run the World: 50¢* by Futzie Nuztle © 1991, published by Chronicle Books; Optech Ltd for material from *A Dictionary of the Living World* (p. 30); Pictorial Charts Educational Trust for their logo (p. 85) and posters (pp. 86 and 87); Roma Oxford for cover of *Classroom Creatures* (p. 43); Resource material from *Spaceship Earth* (p. 27); The Rising Sun Country Park and Countryside Centre for their logo (p. 148); Royal Society for the Protection of Birds for page from *Bird Studies for Primary Science* (p. 45); Royal Society for the Prevention of Cruelty to Animals for their logo (p. 49) and for covers of *Animals in Schools* and *Small Mammals in Schools* (p. 46); School Curriculum Industry Partnership for cover of *Industry and the Environment – Friend or Foe?* (p. 110); Sherston Software Limited for material from *Viewpoints* (p. 29); Posy Simmonds for the illustration on p. 88; Ralph Steadman for the illustration 'The man who loved flowers' (p. 52); *Streetwise* for cover of their magazine (p. 35); TVE International for cover of *Moving Pictures Bulletin* (p. 64); University of Cambridge Local Examinations Syndicate for page from *Minibeasts* (p. 43); Wayland (Publishers) Ltd for cover of *Children Need Food* (p. 18); World Wide Fund for Nature for covers of *Only One Earth* (p. 55), *The Decade of Destruction* (p. 56), *Greening the Staffroom* (p. 57), *Teaching Environment: The Management of a Cross-Curricular Theme* (p. 57), *Looking into the Environment* (p. 58), *Environmental Education in Primary Schools* and *Environmental Education in Secondary Schools* (p. 67), *Stimulus Video Project* (p. 67), photographs of posters in their *Resources, Natural Regions of the World* and *Environmental Impact 2000* series (p. 79) and the use of their logo (p. 124); Worldaware for page from *Focus on Castries – St Lucia* (p. 61) and their logo (p. 123).

Contents

	Page
Foreword by John Hurt	vi
Editorial preface	1
Introduction	4
What is environmental education?	4
Exploring your own context	7
Planning a unit of work	7
Environmental education and the National Curriculum	12

Section 1 Resources

Classroom resources

Books for a greener planet *Ted Percy*	16
Computer software: nine ecological packages *E Carole Sampson*	25
Earthquest explores ecology *Bev Wight*	33
Journals and magazines *Chris Oulton and Bill Scott*	35
Some useful living resources *Michael Reiss*	42
Guidelines for the use of animals in the classroom *The Royal Society for the Prevention of Cruelty to Animals*	49
Multi-media packs *Vincent J Bunce*	54
Photographs for developing environmental education *The Environmental Education Working Group of the Geographical Association*	60
Television, radio and video *Malcolm Whitehead*	63
The answer is in the mix *John D Rogers*	72
Wall charts and posters *Jane Inglis*	78
The pictorial charts education trust *The Environmental Education Working Group of the Geographical Association*	85

Fieldwork resources

The English Heritage Education Service *The Environmental Education Working Group of the Geographical Association*	88
Using zoos for educational purposes *Malcolm Whitehead*	92
Tools and equipment *Stewart Anthony*	97

Human resources

Using the local authority in environmental education *Julian Agyeman*	101
Interview with Alan George, Unilever plc *Living Earth*	104
Industry and the environment – friend or foe? *Mary Barry*	109
How school links with business can help *Jan Hussey*	112
Links with local industry *Phil Cooper*	118
National and local environmental groups *Sophie Yangopoulos*	121
Interview with the Young People's Trust for the Environment and Nature Conservation *Living Earth*	128
Using an environmental education consultant *Julian Agyeman*	133

Section 2 The classroom toolbox

Art

We belong here *Chris Thomas*	138

Drama

Neptune and the sea people *Kate Clarke, Sarah Kemp, Malcolm Green and Dominic Ackland*	144
The wise wet-woman (or wizard) *Rosemary Linnell*	149

CONTENTS

English
A level literature and the environment *Neil MacRae* — 153
Environmental collage *John McKellar* — 160

Geography
The *Mobil Greensight Pack* video project *Martin Roberts* — 164
Examining the future development of an historic town The Environmental Education Working Group of the Geographical Association — 169

History
Historical approaches to the environment *Martin L Parsons* — 175
Teaching about survival: the volcano *Chris Kelly* — 182

Information Technology
Global environmental problems presented using IT *David J Wraight* — 189
Environmental newsday *Sally Wicks* — 193

Mathematics
Rivers *Allan Lund* — 198
Plotting the position of local amenities *Colin Semple* — 203

Modern Languages
Environment and pollution in the target language *Christiane Montlibert* — 208
Verschönung eines städtisches Wildnises *Duncan Sidwell* — 213

Music
Five musical projects on the environment *Peter Gambie* — 220

Religious Education
A three-year cycle to celebrate Easter *Valerie Pacey* — 228
A planet fit for the future? *Lorraine Rimington* — 232

Science
What's the science behind that nasty smell? *Maggie Hannon* — 237
Acid rain: how are different stone building materials affected? *Janet Cook* — 240

Special Needs
Understanding Antarctica *Lynn Stuart* — 246
Adult Basic Education and 'Third World' issues: some practical ideas *Joe Carter* — 250

Technology
The outside school environment *Carol Hughes* — 256
Litter *Sally Wicks* — 265

Section 3 Ways of working
'People, Places and Plants': an environmental education scheme *Sue Bennett* — 270
Our wildlife area – from bare earth to outdoor classroom *Ralph Slaney* — 280
'A Tree for Life' project *Richard Burrows* — 285

The Rainforest Education Programme
Rainforests OK *Chris Durbin* — 293
Index — 303

Foreword

This book is at once a record and a celebration of environmental education in the UK today. It is aimed at all teachers – from primary to tertiary – who have an interest in the environment, regardless of their level of understanding of the subject and their experience in the field. The 60 or so people who have contributed articles to the book have widely different teaching backgrounds and degrees of environmental expertise but all of them are united in their belief that the environment should inform their teaching.

The environment consistently appears as one of the foremost concerns of young people today. Teachers who make the environment the focus of their teaching will therefore discover that holy grail of all teachers – immediate pupil motivation. The environment is directly relevant to pupils' lives in a way that few areas of the curriculum can claim to be; when, additionally, the environmental focus is on the local environment and community, that relevance is dramatically enhanced.

The evidence captured in the pages of this book points to the fact that an education which is of vital importance to our futures can nevertheless be taught in ways which are stimulating, exciting and fun. What's more, it's an education which does not want for lack of resources and outside help: some of the most exciting examples of environmental education in this book are based on school/community partnerships.

What this book is *not* trying to do is to be an exhaustive or definitive guide to environmental education; as the book clearly indicates, these exist elsewhere. Rather it is an augur of the current progress and state of environmental education which, like the world it seeks to shed light on, is constantly changing. In an interview reproduced in Section 1 of this book, Alan George of Unilever declares, 'I'm not one of these people who believes that [concern about the environment] is a five day wonder; I don't think schools are going to tire of it.'

One of the convictions of this book is that schools never will.

John Hurt

Patron of Living Earth

Editorial preface

The idea for *The Living Earth – a resource for learning* came from teachers themselves. Feedback from schools with whom Living Earth had worked on earlier projects indicated that there were many teachers who would have liked to do more work on the environment but who lacked:
- the time to read about and around the subject of environmental education in order to find out what resources might be available and how to select those which would best serve their purposes and budgets;
- the confidence to make the environment a focus of their teaching at a time when the National Curriculum was defining more and more closely what they *had* to be teaching within their particular curriculum area;
- the inspiration and the motivation to work in this area.

Further research indicated that environmental education, despite its popular appeal outside schools, was still considered a specialised subject within schools, and one which many teachers felt should be left to either the Science or the Geography department. This position now shows signs of changing. Public awareness of environmental issues has increased dramatically over recent years, and when the National Curriculum was announced, environmental awareness was identified as one of the five cross-curricular themes. Far from being the concern of two defined curriculum areas, it was clear that all teachers could now legitimately introduce some element of 'environmental education' into their own teaching. The questions were 'How?' and 'What?'

In an effort to answer those questions, the Living Earth Foundation set up a three-year project, generously supported by Unilever plc, of which this publication is the end result. The project has enlisted the help, advice and actual contribution of hundreds of teachers across the country, whose generosity – at a time when every week seemed to produce a new government edict for schools to implement – is indicative both of the level of the profession's commitment and of how widespread concern for the environment has now become.

We are, however, conscious that, of the two questions mentioned above, we have answered the question 'How?' more than we have answered the question 'What?' Readers who are approaching this book with a view to finding the ultimate definition of environmental education are in for a disappointment, although they could do a lot worse than read the Introduction that follows this Foreword. Similarly, purists who *know* what environmental education is and know even more firmly what it is *not*, will, we are sure, find numerous examples of heresies here to keep their hearts warm. There is something like a common *approach* to teaching about the environment in the pages of this book – an approach which maintains that pupils learn more from doing than they do from abstract learning, and that the basis of environmental awareness involves, to use that well-worn phrase, thinking globally and acting locally – but the prime concern of the compilers of this book has been to capture the enthusiasm of teachers who have already introduced work on the environment into their teaching and to show others how they might do the same.

THE STRUCTURE OF THIS BOOK

The Living Earth – a resource for learning is divided into four main sections:

The Introduction that follows this Preface attempts to help teachers and schools define what environmental education means to them and how it should fit into their curriculum planning. These pages may be used as an INSET activity by a school or department or read by individual teachers for their own interest and information.

Section 1, Resources, is a collection of reviews designed to help teachers make appropriate selection of materials for classroom work and for fieldwork: the section also looks at the human resources available to teachers. Details of these materials and resources – which were correct at the time of going to press – have been presented separately at the end of each article and review or at the end of an appropriate sub-section within it.

The writers of these articles and reviews have, for the most part, attempted to be objective, but we hope that the brief biographical note that follows each contribution will enable readers to place the articles in some kind of context.

Section 2, The classroom toolbox, gives an account of how teachers have managed to focus on the environment from within their own subject specialism. The work in this section covers thirteen curriculum areas, most of which are represented by two separate approaches. Again, a brief biographical note follows each contribution, in order to explain the context in which the contributor wrote the article.

While the collected contributions in this section span the complete educational age range, there has been no attempt to cover all educational phases within each curriculum area. Most contributions, however, give some indication of the age range within which an activity may, suitably adapted, be used.

Section 3, Ways of working, presents five case studies of whole-school initiatives which have specifically focused on an environmental issue. Two of these are taken from secondary schools, and three from primary. Unlike the articles in Section 2, the purpose of these case studies is not to inspire other schools to undertake the same kind of project, but to show how it is possible for any school to organise a project which is a unique expression of the collective concerns of pupils, staff and parents in a specific local environment. We would hope that the articles here represent an incitement to action rather than to imitation!

LIVING EARTH AND UNILEVER

Living Earth is an environmental charity specialising in education. It was founded in 1988 with the objective of bringing about protection of the environment through the empowerment of the individual. In its five years of existence, the organisation has established national programmes in the United Kingdom, Cameroon, Venezuela and Brazil. Working largely through schools, these programmes are run by locally employed people and are designed to draw on local expertise and resources to meet the local community's needs. Support from individuals, trusts, companies and governments around the world has enabled these programmes to reach many thousands of teachers and pupils with the sort of support they need if they are actively to develop a positive relationship with the environment and its precious resources.

In the UK, projects and products have been developed in a variety of curriculum areas and at different educational levels. These cover many themes, ranging from types of habitats (e.g. rainforests) to types of resource use (e.g. industry and the environment). Professionals from a wide range of sectors actively and routinely contribute to the development process, reflecting Living Earth's commitment to the production of high quality and well balanced educational strategies and resources.

Living Earth is dedicated to working in active partnership with all the key environmental stakeholders – business, industry, science, environment and education – in the belief that the process of bringing about the sustainable use of resources is a challenge for the whole of society and that successful strategies are likely to be co-operative. Partnership enables Living Earth to harness the best available expertise in the development of its products and programmes and to account for the variety of perspectives which exist on the issues.

Traditionally, relations between representatives of the key environmental stakeholders are marked by a certain antipathy. Business involvement in education is viewed by many with suspicion, fuelled by fears of the classroom being usurped as a glorified advertising hoarding. Industrialists and environmentalists are two groups which have well documented reservations about each other's motives. By exercising complete editorial control over its materials, Living Earth aims to combine scrupulous and balanced research with a guarantee of credibility and integrity so as to satisfy both partners and audiences alike.

Unilever is one of the world's most successful international businesses, with some 500 operating companies employing nearly 300,000 people. It aims to be the foremost company in meeting the daily needs of consumers in its chosen markets. The greater part of Unilever's business is in branded consumer goods, primarily foods, detergents and personal products. Speciality chemicals is its other major activity.

In the UK, Unilever employs about 25,000 people working in 25 operating companies. It has a tradition of community involvement dating back more than 100 years to the time of William Hesketh Lever, founder of Lever Brothers and Port Sunlight village. He believed that good citizenship meant good business and that the success of the company and the welfare of the community go hand in hand.

Today, that conviction lives on. Unilever in the UK is committed to a programme of activities designed to support the community in which it operates. In 1992, this involvement was valued at around £5 million. The company has chosen particular areas in which to focus its efforts – the environment, economic regeneration, good neighbourliness and, most importantly, education and training.

On a local level, Unilever companies liaise regularly with over 200 schools. In many cases, these links are long established, although every year new projects and partnerships are undertaken. This collaborative approach is endorsed by Unilever centrally. As well as supporting the companies in their activities, it initiates national projects aimed at supporting the work of teachers.

This publication combines the environmental expertise of Living Earth with the experience of teachers to meet a need identified by teachers themselves. Unilever believes that participation in this project meets its objectives of offering direct, practical support to teachers.

Introduction

WHAT IS ENVIRONMENTAL EDUCATION?

There are many definitions of environmental education. Whether you are reading this on behalf of a school, a department or simply for your own classroom use, you need to arrive at a definition which *you* can use. A school which makes this definition will have gone some way towards developing a corporate policy statement or identifying which National Curriculum subjects, for example, have most to offer environmental education.

The questionnaire on page 5 is designed to:

- engender discussion of some of the important issues of environmental education;
- help colleagues to reach a consensus about these issues;
- identify the key points which will inform a written definition.

You should ideally complete the questionnaire individually, before discussing each other's views as a group. The aim is to reach a consensus about the key issues for environmental education which may then be incorporated into your definition.

An interpretation of the eight statements and some definitions

1. Particular teaching and learning strategies are essential if pupils are to be educated about the environment
A range of teaching and learning strategies can be used to develop environmental education, provided that they are the most suitable for the learning objectives identified at the planning stage. However, these activities should be put into the context of an environmental enquiry, in which an overall question, issue or problem is investigated (see 'Examining the future development of an historic town' in Section 2, page 169). Once you have agreed on an overall enquiry focus, you can develop a series of sequential questions. The most appropriate learning activities can emerge from these questions. The enquiry focus helps pupils to identify which are the important areas of knowledge they are to acquire and to analyse a range of values and attitudes. This helps them to clarify personal values.

2. The sciences rather than the arts are the principal contributors to environmental education
The National Curriculum has specifically identified environmental knowledge as a component of the Geography, Science and Technology Orders, but environmental education may

INTRODUCTION

Statements	Strongly agree	Agree	Neither agree nor disagree	Disagree	Strongly disagree
1. Particular teaching and learning strategies are essential if pupils are to be educated about the environment.					
2. The sciences rather than the arts are the principal contributors to environmental education.					
3. One aim of environmental education is to educate for conservation.					
4. Environmental education should examine issues relevant to people.					
5. A concentration on environmental issues will lead to feelings of 'gloom and doom' among pupils.					
6. It is impossible to teach environmental education without fieldwork.					
7. Since most people live in an urban environment, we should emphasise issues relevant to the built environment.					
8. Environmental education needs to link local environmental work to global environmental issues.					

Figure 1 What is environmental education? (questionnaire)

also be developed through the whole curriculum as a cross-curricular theme (see pages 12–14). Indeed, all subjects provide environmental contexts and opportunities for the development of environmental education, and there is a strong case for saying that, for the sake of balance, all subjects need to make a contribution.

3. One aim of environmental education is to educate for conservation
The objective of an enquiry-based approach to environmental education is to make an open-ended investigation and to consider a range of possible solutions for pupils to evaluate. The conservation of an environment may be one of those solutions, but it is by no means the only one.

4. Environmental education should examine environmental issues relevant to people
Empowerment of the learner is one of the aims of environmental education which differentiates it from environmental studies: empowerment means giving pupils the ability to understand and even to take part in decisions affecting the quality of life. The selection of relevant environmental issues is crucial to motivate and involve the learner. Environmental education ceases to be environmental studies when the learner acquires knowledge which encourages her or him to understand how decisions are made and (potentially) to take action.

5. A concentration on environmental issues will lead to feelings of 'doom and gloom' among pupils
There is no danger of this happening if the enquiry approach is adopted. The last (predictive) stages of an enquiry look forward to the planning decisions which could be implemented. The enquiry ends with an evaluation of *positive* proposals, e.g. What might be done to reduce soil erosion? What options are available for traffic planning in the city? How might they be implemented?

6. It is impossible to teach environmental education without fieldwork
Some topics may confine pupils to investigations of secondary sources, but direct experiential work in the environment is always an advantage. Fieldwork allows pupils to collect primary data and develops environmental understanding by placing them in direct contact with issues concerning the relationship of people with the environment.

7. Since most people live in an urban environment, we should emphasise issues relevant to the built environment
Pupils should begin their environmental education by investigating their own environment, whether it is urban or rural. Whatever planned programme takes place thereafter should use a range of environments as contexts and maintain a balance between the rural and the urban.

8. Environmental education needs to link local environmental work to global environmental issues
Young people are often highly aware of environmental issues, and this awareness often extends to global environmental issues. The education process tries to develop their understanding of these issues. Such understanding is helped by linking what's going on in the local environment (e.g. mineral extraction) to the relevant global issue or issues (in this case, the global use of resources).

INTRODUCTION

Some published definitions and descriptions of environmental education

'The objective of environmental education is to increase the public awareness of the problems in this field, as well as possible solutions, and to lay the foundations for a fully informed and active participation of the individual in the protection of the environment and the prudent and rational use of natural resources.'
(Council for the European Community, reprinted in *Curriculum Guidance 7* NCC, 1990)

'Good environmental education is not just about topical "green" issues; the aim is to provide children with knowledge, skills and understanding relating to nature, scientific processes and the world's resources.'
(*'This Common Inheritance' – Britain's Environmental Strategy* HMSO, 1990)

'Environmental education seeks to give individuals and groups the opportunity to develop awareness, skills, knowledge, understanding and values, in order to make informed decisions about their lifestyles and the impact they have on the environment.'
(*A Derbyshire Approach to Environmental Education* Derbyshire County Council, 1992)

EXPLORING YOUR OWN CONTEXT

Who is The Living Earth – a resource for learning *for?*

This book is for all teachers, whichever phase of education you work in and whatever your understanding of, or interest in, environmental education. The previous pages will already have given you an insight into what environmental education is and what issues arise from defining it. Once you have read through those pages, you need next to explore the context in which you came to pick up this book.

How does this book relate to me/us?

The activity in Figure 2 (over the page) is designed for you to use on your own, with a group of colleagues or with all staff members of the school: it helps you review briefly where you are and what you would like to do. Exploring each key question will help you build up a profile of your position in relation to environmental education.

PLANNING A UNIT OF WORK

This section looks at organising and planning a unit of work with an emphasis on environmental education. The process, which is known as an enquiry process, could apply to a unit of work intended to last one lesson or to an extended project. Enquiry is common to all the National Curriculum statutory orders and is particularly appropriate to the investigation of environmental issues.

What type of school do you work in?
Do you plan the curriculum as:

- a whole staff?
- groups of staff?
- an individual teacher?

How is your curriculum organised?

- single subjects?
- cross-curricular topics?
- mixture of both?

Does environmental education feature in your curriculum?

- explicitly?
- implicitly?
- in part explicitly, in part implicitly?

Have you begun to consider environmental education as a school?

- not at all?
- begun discussions?
- writing a policy?
- implementing a policy?

What is your reason for picking up this book?

- casual interest but nothing planned?
- specific interest but not sure what?
- specific interest in policy?
- specific interest in a project or task?

What options are you considering for environmental education in your school?

- environmental education project with a class?
- environmental education project with a whole school?
- a policy for a whole school?
- a review of environmental education in a core or foundation subject?
- other?

Figure 2 Environmental education – a self review

PLANNING A UNIT OF WORK

This section looks at organising and planning a unit of work with an emphasis on environmental education. The process, which is known as an enquiry process, could apply to a unit of work intended to last one lesson or to an extended project. Enquiry is common to all the National Curriculum statutory orders and is particularly appropriate to the investigation of environmental issues.

INTRODUCTION

What are the characteristics of an enquiry approach?

An enquiry approach to teaching and learning involves:

- the investigation of an environmental issue;
- a structured series of sequential questions that investigate the issue;
- an enquiry which is based on the attempt to answer an open-ended question (an open-ended question is one where the outcome is not predetermined);
- an open-ended outcome;
- an exploration of values and attitudes;
- the ability to take action.

What is the nature of an enquiry approach?

The structure of an enquiry goes through a sequence of stages:

1. Observation (attempting to answer the question, 'What?').
2. Description (attempting to answer the questions, 'Who?', 'Where?' and 'How?').
3. Analysis (attempting to answer the question, 'Why'?).
4. Prediction (attempting to answer the question, 'What might . . . ?').
5. Conclusion (attempting to answer the question, 'What should . . . ?').
6. Action (attempting to answer the question, 'What will I do . . . ?').

An enquiry may include:

- asking a question;
- collecting relevant data from primary and secondary sources;
- analysing and interpreting data;
- drawing conclusions;
- evaluating the enquiry.

Constructing the question

In using this approach, the teacher, or increasingly the pupil, designs an overall enquiry question. An example might be:

'What is the impact of out-of-town superstores on town-centre shopping?'

The teacher or pupil then designs structured enquiry questions to investigate the overall enquiry question. Such questions might be:

- What is a superstore?
- Where is it located?
- Why is it located there?
- Who uses the superstore?
  and so on through the enquiry.

The teacher or pupil devises activities or lines of research which will enable the pupil to answer the enquiry questions, draw conclusions and decide on appropriate action. (The various activities and resources illustrated in this book could form part of such an enquiry.) Since these activities are likely to draw on all subject areas, an environmental enquiry tends to be genuinely cross-curricular.

(For a worked enquiry, see 'Examining the future development of an historic town' in Section 2, page 169.)

What are the advantages of using an enquiry approach?

There are many advantages in using an enquiry approach to teaching and learning. The pupil is given the opportunity to undertake a structured enquiry and learns:

- the skills of research;
- how to formulate and make informed decisions;
- how to consider the opinions of others;
- that there is no single right answer to environmental concerns, only a preferred option.

Most importantly of all, perhaps, an enquiry approach provides motivation.

Designing an enquiry

You can use the following activity to design a unit of work using an enquiry approach.

Task

a) Obtain a copy of your local newspaper.
b) Identify an issue that concerns more than one group of people (the issue should focus on a proposed change in the local environment).
c) Identify the different groups and their particular viewpoints.
d) Design an open-ended question that would enable pupils to investigate the issue.
e) Design a series of questions that will explore the issue (see Figure 3 below, for prompt questions).
f) Design activities that will help pupils to gather information with which to answer the question.
g) Relate the activities to the programmes of study for the subjects within which you are working. (See Figure 4 opposite, for an example of a planning sheet: this planning sheet shows how an enquiry can also be designed to investigate a place.)

A series of questions designed to investigate a local issue. These questions should be altered to suit the issue chosen.

- What is the issue about?
- Where is the issue taking place?
- Why has the issue arisen?
- Who are the people involved in the issue?
- What are the views about the issue?
- How is the issue connected to global issues?
- What are the alternative solutions to the issue?
- Who has the power to make a decision?
- What do you think should be done?

Figure 3 A local environment issue

ENVIRONMENTAL EDUCATION CURRICULUM PLANNING

Year _____ Key Stage _____ Topic _____ Place emphasis _____
Question/Issue _____ Scale(s) of enquiry _____

Enquiry/activities	Issue/theme questions	Learning activities inc. community involvement	Resources	Key ideas and significant statements of attainment	Assessment-selected SOA's tasks
What is this place? What is this place like? Where is this place? What do people think about this place?					
Why is this place as it is? Why is this place here? Who used this place? How is this place connected to other places? How has this place changed?					
How might things change? Why might this be? What impacts are likely to result? Who cares about this place? Who makes a decision about this place?					
What ought to happen? Why? What can be done about it?					

Figure 4 Environmental education curriculum planning

ENVIRONMENTAL EDUCATION AND THE NATIONAL CURRICULUM

Environmental education is one of the five cross-curricular themes identified in the National Curriculum, the other four being economic and industrial awareness, health education, careers education and guidance, and education for citizenship. Environmental education also appears as a distinct subject of enquiry within the curriculum requirements for Science, Technology, Geography and History.

As a cross-curricular theme

As one of the five cross-curricular themes of the National Curriculum, environmental education has its own distinct educational objective:

> *'To help pupils make informed decisions about environmental management and identify solutions to environmental issues.'*

This objective is to be achieved by teaching a body of knowledge through specified topic areas:

Knowledge and understanding	Topics
• the natural processes which take place in the environment • the impact of human activities on the environment • different environments, both past and present • environmental issues such as the greenhouse effect, acid rain, air pollution • local, national and international legislative controls to protect and manage the environment; how policies and decisions are made about the environment • the environmental interdependence of individuals, groups, communities and nations – how, for example, power station emissions in Britain can affect Scandinavia • how human lives and livelihoods are dependent on the environment • the conflicts which can arise about environmental issues • how the environment has been affected by past decisions and actions • the importance of planning, design and aesthetic considerations • the importance of effective action to protect and manage the environment	• climate • soils, rocks and minerals • water • materials and resources, including energy • plants and animals • people and their communities • buildings and industrialisation and waste

Figure 5 Topic and knowledge areas for environmental education

INTRODUCTION

Environmental education shares common aims with the other four cross-curricular themes, promotes the same skills, attitudes and values, and may best be delivered through the same activities, opportunities and experiences.

Aims

- to provide knowledge, understanding and skills which help pupils to participate in these aspects of life beyond school
- to provide opportunities to reappraise personal attitudes and values

Skills

- communication
- problem-solving
- numeracy
- information technology
- personal skills (including study)

Attitudes and values

- respect for evidence and rational argument
- respect for different ways of life, beliefs, opinions and the legitimate interests of others
- regard for equal opportunities including the challenging of stereotypes and an active concern for human rights
- respect for non-violent ways of resolving conflict
- concern for quality and excellence
- valuing oneself and others
- constructive interest in community affairs
- independence of thought
- tolerance and open-mindedness
- consideration for others
- flexibility and adaptability to change
- enterprising, persistent approach to tasks and challenges
- determination to succeed
- self-respect, self-confidence and self-discipline
- sense of responsibility for personal and collective action

Activities, opportunities and experiences

1. Planning which:
- uses pupils' experiences and relationships as the starting point and extends to cover national, European and worldwide contexts;
- involves pupils and encourages them to plan, evaluate and record their experiences and achievements.

2. The use of a range of teaching methods which:
- emphasise enquiry, investigation and practical exercises, in lessons and other activities, which help to extend pupils' first-hand experiences, e.g. through fieldwork, direct experience of work, business and community enterprise, simulations, outdoor education

(continued)

- encourage links and personal contact with individuals, local, national and international organisations, statutory and voluntary
- enable pupils to be involved in decisions about features of life at school, to exercise responsibility and to apply knowledge and skills developed through work on the themes.

Figure 6 Common features of the five cross-curricular themes

As part of curriculum areas of the National Curriculum

The topics identified in Figure 6 above form part of the curriculum requirements of specific subjects of the National Curriculum, most notably Geography, Science, Technology and History.

Geography

Environmental education permeates National Curriculum Geography, which has one attainment target (AT5, Environmental Geography) wholly devoted to it and develops it through three strands:
- the use and misuse of natural resources;
- the quality and vulnerability of different environments;
- the possibilities of protecting and managing environments.

Science

Environmental education is particularly relevant to the following attainment targets:
AT1 Scientific investigation;
AT2 Life and living processes;
AT3 Materials and their properties;
AT4 Physical processes.

Technology

Environmental education has a particular relevance to Technology, which is concerned with using informed judgement to seek practical solutions to problems. In particular, AT1 requires pupils to 'recognise the issues and implications' associated with all aspects of Technology.

History

The statutory order for History (published in autumn 1991) demonstrated that the study of the environment has a particular part to play in the subject area, where it can be used to show how the environment has been shaped by the influence of human behaviour as well as by natural change. In this context, it is evident that historical skills may be usefully applied to interpret written sources and physical remains which might give clues to changes in the environment.

In addition to the curriculum areas mentioned above, the programmes of study for most curriculum areas offer opportunities for teachers to use the context of environmental education as a starting point for work in their own specialism. Section 2 of this book, 'The classroom toolbox', demonstrates how teachers from a range of curriculum areas and across the curriculum phases have managed to do this without deviating from their statutory requirements.

section one

RESOURCES

CLASSROOM RESOURCES

Books for a greener planet

TED PERCY

INTRODUCTION

It's taken a long time for green concerns to emerge in books for young people. Long after *The Silent Spring* and *Small is Beautiful*, somebody, suddenly, in the early 1980s must have realised that the burgeoning green philosophy should influence what young people know and believe – indeed, that the decision-makers of the future were a more important audience for the articulation of such thought than their elders. From the mid-1980s, green books began to spring up in publishers' lists. By the beginning of the present decade – its growth assisted by the presence of environmental education as a cross-curricular theme in the National Curriculum – these lists were growing greener than St Andrew's. This survey is an attempt to evaluate that growth.

The range of green information books is bewildering in its width, and it is important to establish the features that distinguish the truly helpful green book, for many titles with 'green' marketing labels display none of these features. To be truly helpful, a green book must supply:

- information about our planetary environment, the threats to it and ways of improving it;
- inspiration to help readers counter environmental decline;
- instruction in courses of individual action to befriend our environment.

Many books provide all three of these, but the most elusive and most precious quality is inspiration – it provides the surest test of the author's and publisher's intentions and the surest means by which any work may rise in estimation above its fellows.

The Silent Spring, Rachel Carson, Houghton Mifflin, 1962
Small is Beautiful, E F Schumacher, Penguin, 1973

General introductions

Let us start with a look at introductions to the concept of environmental concern and the overall background of environmental change. If there is a starting point it must be *The Gaia Atlas of Planet Management*. This remarkable publication puts its hand firmly on our time and, with ingenious statistical maps and an expert author-base, has become a touchstone of green attitudes. Doing the same sort of job, but in a way more accessible to middle and secondary age groups, come Nick Middleton's two Oxford *Atlases*. Each presents 28 spreads dissecting and amplifying leading issues from *Noise* through *Famine* to *Education*: the explanation of general principles is spectacular. On the same tack and age level, David Flint's *Europe and the Environment* brings the area of concern tellingly nearer home.

The status of the green book for younger readers was immeasurably advanced by the bestowing of the TES Senior Information Book Award upon *Ian and Fred's Big Green Book*. This giant volume by Fred Pearce and Ian Winton does a fine job of interpreting the tenets of global warming to a junior/middle audience. Two contributions to Watts's 'Green Issues' series show their author, Alexander Peckham, to be worth watching: *Changing Landscapes* and *Resources Control* highlight humankind's responsibility for the environment.

The Gaia Atlas of Planet Management, Pan, 1986
The Oxford Atlas of Environmental Issues, Nick Middleton, OUP, 1988
The Oxford Atlas of World Issues, Nick Middleton, OUP, 1988
Europe and the Environment, David Flint, Wayland, 1992
Ian and Fred's Big Green Book, Fred Pearce and Ian Winton, Kingfisher, 1991
Green Issues: Changing Landscapes, Alexander Peckham, Franklin Watts, 1991
Green Issues: Resources Control, Alexander Peckham, Franklin Watts, 1990

The population explosion

It is the human world which causes – and suffers from – population explosion, famine, drought, energy waste and shortage, health dangers, war and genocide and which needs self-administered aid and education. Books on the difficulties and problems are easier to assemble and more picturesque than those with solutions, so there are lots of them. Dennis and Jeremy Leggett's *People Trap* explains the population problem squarely for middle school pupils and concludes that the answer lies in education and improving living standards. In his outstanding book, *Children Need Food*, Harry Undy shows that food is health, religion, community and culture as well as physical fuel, and that famine is consequently far more than plain starvation. This is a book for juniors, as is Gill Standring's *Food for Thought*, which emphasises the value of organically grown vernacular foodstuffs. These get a good airing, too, in *Food for the World*, which is aimed at middle and secondary ages. Clint Twist has written the excellent *Feeding the World* for the same age group. This book gives as straightforward an account as any can of the way in which, despite the fact that we regularly produce more food than we eat, millions regularly starve.

>   *People Trap*, Dennis and Jeremy Leggett, Heinemann, 1991
>   *Children Need Food*, Harry Undy, Wayland, 1987
>   *Food for Thought*, Gill Standring, A & C Black, 1990
>   *Food for the World*, Su Swallow, Evans Cloverleaf, 1990
>   *Feeding the World*, Clint Twist, Wayland, 1990

Water

If we are not to be short of water we must learn to use less and clean it better before re-use. No book explains this more effectively than Thompson Yardley's *Down the Plughole*. This delightful book is part of the publisher's wackily commonsensical 'Spaceship Earth' series, which uses an abundance of comedy to illustrate its cardinal points to a wide age range. Philip Parker's *Water for Life* stresses the need for clean water throughout the world and sows seeds of doubt about the long-term benefits of dams and barrages. This is good for middle and secondary ages, while *Water Cycle* simplifies, without gutting, the water situation for infants.

>   *Down the Plughole*, Thompson Yardley, Cassell, 1990
>   *Water for Life*, Philip Parker, Simon & Schuster, 1990
>   *Water Cycle*, Joy Richardson, Franklin Watts, 1992

Energy

Books about energy conservation and 'alternative' sources are legion. Alan Collinson has done a splendid job for older children with *Renewable Energy*, in which he clearly shows that conservation is itself a fuel and that nuclear sources are a long-term non-starter. Spurgeon and Flood's *Energy and Power* was on the TES shortlist for 1990, and its illustrations of national energy uses in relation to national populations are well within a middle school pupil's grasp, to whom the typical Usborne 'corn-flake packet' style of presentation may also appeal. It is strange how primary energy sources like sun and wind are now dubbed 'alternative'; Wayland's 'alternative energy' series makes a good job of explaining the harnessing of these and other natural sources, perhaps the best being Graham Houghton's *Bioenergy*.

> *Renewable Energy*, Alan Collinson, Evans Cloverleaf, 1991
> *Energy and Power*, Richard Spurgeon and Mike Flood, Usborne, 1990
> *Bioenergy*, Graham Houghton, Wayland, 1990

Waste

'The main thing wrong with rubbish is that most people think it's rubbish,' says Steve Skidmore in his richly original *What a Load of Rubbish*. While this is true, no single green activity has grabbed individual ambition quite as effectively as the recycling of waste. It's something even very young children can do and appreciate, so it's heartening to see that, although we're still desperately short of green information books for infants, publishers have seized on recycling as an opportunity to redress this age bias. Simon and Schuster's uneven 'Take One' series, for instance, contains the excellent *Rubbish*. Equally applicable to under-eights, the same publishers' 'Why Waste It?' series introduces *Plastic*, *Aluminium*, *Glass* and *Paper*, which are simple, practical and have been widely welcomed. The same materials are dealt with more comprehensively for juniors upwards in Watts's series 'Just Rubbish?' which itself uses recycled paper.

> *What a Load of Rubbish*, Steve Skidmore, Cassell, 1990
> *Take One: Rubbish*, Simon & Schuster, 1991
> *Why Waste It? Plastic*, Sally Morgan and Pauline Lalor, Simon & Schuster, 1992
> *Why Waste It? Aluminium*, Sally Morgan and Pauline Lalor, Simon & Schuster, 1992
> *Why Waste It? Glass*, Sally Morgan and Pauline Lalor, Simon & Schuster, 1992
> *Why Waste It? Paper*, Sally Morgan and Pauline Lalor, Simon & Schuster, 1992
> *Just Rubbish? Recycling Glass*, Judith Condon, Franklin Watts, 1990
> *Just Rubbish? Recycling Metal*, Joy Palmer, Franklin Watts, 1990
> *Just Rubbish? Recycling Paper*, Judith Condon, Franklin Watts, 1990
> *Just Rubbish? Recycling Plastic*, Joy Palmer, Franklin Watts, 1990

Greenhouse effect, the ozone layer, loss of habitat and rainforests

The greenhouse effect and the thinning ozone layer have also caught the public imagination and are well served by explanatory texts. But there is a numbing sameness about most of them, and an easy winner is Lawrence Pringle's *Global Warming*. Here is an expert and able writer whose gentle unravelling of our atmospheric complexities makes engrossing reading for middle school pupils upwards. For younger or less able readers, Simon Bishop's illustrations in *The Greenhouse Effect* by M Bright are very helpful, as are they in *Acid Rain*.

The loss or spoliation of habitat, often insidious and always as a result of human intervention, is an emotional business and was one of the first symptoms of environmental decline to attract public attention – television wouldn't be the same without it. Twelve years ago, Eric Thomas and John White produced, out of the blue, the influential *Hedgerow*, which, as well as celebrating this great and diverse form of wildlife habitat, alarmed us into realising that one fifth of Britain's hedges had disappeared since the end of the Second World War. Thanks to publishers Dorling Kindersley, this wonderfully illustrated magnum for the whole family is still in print.

We have come to accept the stunning photography that is a feature of so many picturesque habitat books as the norm, but drawing, painting and penmanship are the potent agents in Barbara Bash's *Tree of Life*, which shows why the baobab tree, a community in itself, is so respected a member of the larger community of the African Savannah. Richard Mabey's seminal *Oak and Company* does the same for the English tree. Both these books are suitable for all ages.

'If you buy a hardwood hi-fi, your hand is on the chainsaw,' says Lawrence Williams in *Conserving the Jungles*, a thoughtful book aimed at secondary-school pupils. Despite its textbook appearance, this offers a very readable appraisal of the rainforest dilemma. More eloquent even than this – and suitable for all ages – is Anna Lewington's *Antonio's Rainforest*, a superb book in which we join a rubber-tappers' co-operative in the Amazon basin and learn at first hand the vital importance of the rainforest habitat in enabling the low-impact, high-efficiency lifestyle of its inhabitants to continue.

Loss or erosion of habitat leads inevitably to the endangerment of living species. Threatened animals get all the press, and it is sad to have to record that among the plethora of books on the subject there is not one about endangered plants – presumably the pictures are less marketable. In *Noah's Choice*, David Day tells stories of extinction and survival, producing not only a memorial to human folly but plenty of hopeful messages for today: the text reads like a novel and is suitable for middle-school pupils upwards. Jane Goodall and Oria Douglas-Hamilton are *the* experts on chimpanzees and elephants respectively. Their lucid *Chimpanzee Family Book* and *Elephant Family Book* transcend the ordinary: full of loving involvement, they introduce us to their communities. It's a fine way to learn the language.

Global Warming, Lawrence Pringle, Hodder & Stoughton, 1990
The Greenhouse Effect, M Bright, Franklin Watts, 1991
Acid Rain, M Bright, Franklin Watts, 1991
Hedgerow, Eric Thomas and John White, Dorling Kindersley, 1980
Tree of Life, Barbara Bash, Little Brown, 1989
Oak and Company, Richard Mabey, Viking, 1983

Conserving the Jungles, Lawrence Williams, Evans, 1989
Antonio's Rainforest, Anna Lewington, Wayland, 1991
Noah's Choice, David Day, Viking, 1990 (Puffin, 1992)
Chimpanzee Family Book, Jane Goodall, Picture Book Studio, 1989
Elephant Family Book, Oria Douglas-Hamilton, Picture Book Studio, 1990

Guides to action

So far we have looked at the major – and popular – areas of environmental concern and some of the texts that deal with them. The question remains: 'What do we do about this?' We could just, in the words of the old song, 'put out the lights and go to sleep' – at least the power stations would produce less pollution – but there must be something more positive besides going to the bottlebank. Luckily there are plenty of sensible 'going green' books to encourage us to positive action. A milestone in such achievements was set up by the publication of the *Young Green Consumer Guide*. It immediately garnered awards and critical acclaim, being reviewed in one paper as 'the single most effective contribution to young peoples' understanding of green issues and green living'. The guide talks directly to juniors and upwards, as does Thompson Yardley's *Buy Now, Pay Later*, a thoughtfully crazy polemic on careful shopping. For a different kind of consumption, those young people interested in finding out more about vegetarianism – and there are more and more of them each year – could find no better introduction to the subject than that offered in Jane Inglis's *Some People Don't Eat Meat*, a text readily accessible to juniors upwards.

The *Green Guide to Children's Books* bemoaned the lack of an organic gardening book for young people, but Thompson Yardley has come to the rescue again with *Grow Your Own*. The garden as habitat has inspired several books from the School Garden Company, for instance Nigel Matthews's *Garden for Birds* and Shirley Thompson's *Bats in the Garden*. This modest company specialises in producing sensible, practical and cheap books to improve our environment, starting with gardens. Their enterprise is commendable, and their mail

order catalogue should be sought by all serious green-going teachers (PO Box 49, Spalding, Lincolnshire, PE11 1NZ).

> *Young Green Consumer Guide*, Gollancz, 1991
> *Buy Now, Pay Later*, Thompson Yardley, Cassell, 1990
> *Some People Don't Eat Meat*, Jane Inglis, Oakroyd Press, 1987
> *Green Guide to Children's Books*, Books for Keeps, Harper Collins, 1991
> *Grow Your Own*, Thompson Yardley, Cassell, 1992
> *Garden for Birds*, Nigel Matthews, School Garden Company
> *Bats in the Garden*, Shirley Thompson, School Garden Company

Series on the environment

So far this has been a ramble through the landscape of green books, noting some of the landmarks by the way. This way is, of course, paved with good intentions – there is a great mass of broadly helpful books, most of which appear as part of a publisher's series. The series is, of course, a marketing device, but it can also be a useful buying device, provided that the series' members show sufficient quality and consistency to be worth buying individually anyway.

A look at some reliable series may be a help. 'Last Frontiers for Mankind', the dramatic title chosen by Evans, has articulate and expert writers like Alan Collinson and Lawrence Williams who give the series a cutting edge that its dreary-seeming production doesn't immediately display. A good example is Williams's *Defeating the Deserts*. The same publisher's Cloverleaf imprint has gone on to give us 'Ecology Watch', of which Collinson's *Grasslands* is the most significant member, and 'Repairing the Damage' which is exemplified by Basil Booth's *Earthquakes and Volcanoes*. All these are aimed at secondary and middle schools. The team behind Cassell's 'Spaceship Earth' series is extremely successful at punching across simple digestible messages: their leading writer, Thompson Yardley, produces consistently excellent radical and humorous texts, with pictures to match. In addition to titles already mentioned, juniors and upwards will benefit hugely from his *Get Switched On*, which turns the series' unique style towards energy-saving.

Ever in the vanguard of information texts, Franklin Watts provide some of the most reputable lines. Their secondary/middle 'Issues' and 'Survival' series are now undergoing updates, and it's good to see Michael Bright's *Pollution* and *Wildlife* being given another run and to be able to count John McCormick's *Acid Rain* among the updated issues. Lower down the age range, the same publishers' 'Save our Earth' series goes on with a consistency bordering on sameness; recent additions include Jo Gordon's *Recycling* and Tony Hare's (the series' leading writer) *Polluting the Air*. At this level, too, Franklin Watts's 'Just Rubbish?' series deals with recycling waste, and the appearance of Joy Palmer's *Recycling Plastic* was timely and valuable.

Late, but effectively, on to the green scene, Simon & Schuster's 'Caring for Environments' uses able ecologist Brian Knapp to examine, among other subjects, *Grasslands* and *Temperate Forests*. These are both areas where information is especially welcome; here it is suitable for middle and secondary school level. The same publishers do well for infants with their 'Why Waste It?' series, which has been previously listed.

> *Last Frontiers for Mankind: Defeating the Deserts*, Lawrence Williams, Evans Cloverleaf

Ecology Watch: Grasslands, Alan Collinson, Evans Cloverleaf, 1992
Repairing the Damage: Earthquakes and Volcanoes, Basil Booth, Evans Cloverleaf, 1992
Spaceship Earth: Get Switched On, Thompson Yardley, Cassell, 1992
Survival: Pollution and *Wildlife*, Michael Bright, Franklin Watts, 1991
Issues: Acid Rain, John McCormick, Franklin Watts, 1990
Save our Earth: Recycling, Jo Gordon, Franklin Watts, 1992
Save our Earth: Polluting the Air, Tony Hare, Franklin Watts, 1992
Just Rubbish? Recycling Plastic, Joy Palmer, Franklin Watts, 1990
Caring for Environments: Grasslands, Brian Knapp, Simon & Schuster, 1992
Caring for Environments: Temperate Forests, Brian Knapp, Simon & Schuster, 1992

A final word on selecting books

One of the main difficulties with series books seems to be that (with the exception of the 'Spaceship Earth' series) they cannot be produced without enormous teams of planners and designers, and time and again the end result, though initially attractive, lacks textual consistency and narrative punch. Bibliographies are omitted in order to accommodate copious photo-credits, indexes are squeezed on to end-papers: these are but two symptoms of this unhelpful trend. Additionally, before buying any information book, the buyer, all too often, can only inspect it under such conditions that purchase is an almost inevitable consequence. In authorities where they still exist, School Library Services can be of the utmost help towards constructive purchasing. Not only do these agencies select books objectively, but the experience their staffs gain in doing so makes them uniquely able to advise and recommend the best titles for any particular need. This advisory capacity is as much a part of any School Library Service's job as the supply of books. In times of financial straitness, this information and expertise must not be undervalued. Many services maintain specially composed exhibition stocks where the essential inspection can be done, and even compile bibliographies to make it easier for teachers to select books.

It is up to every teacher to find out what the local School Library Service can offer: one of the things it is most able to do is to recommend good booksellers. From a school's point of view the most effective booksellers are those with the best stock, namely those which style themselves 'library suppliers' and hide well off the High Street. It will be from these specialists that the Schools Library Services' books come, although it may be the case that schools are only able to benefit from a reduction on books ordered if they order these through a supplier approved by the local authority. The advantage of dealing with library suppliers is that their stocks are usually vast, quickly replenished and housed in self-selection showrooms staffed by people whose book knowledge is profound. And the people who know the local (and more distant) library suppliers are those who run the School Library Service.

We are not short of green books and many of them are excellent. It is up to educators of all kinds, from parents to publishers, to make sure that the well-expressed messages are available – and heeded.

Ted Percy has spent 25 years as a professional children's and schools' librarian, the last 15 of them with Buckinghamshire County Library, from whose service he has recently retired. He reviews science information books for Books for Keeps and compiled the information bibliography for the Books for Keeps Green Guide to Children's Books, *published in 1991.*

Computer software: nine ecological packages

E CAROLE SAMPSON

GENERAL POINTS ON THE USE OF COMPUTERS

Using a computer can help to bring many aspects of the environment into the classroom. The computer can be used to record findings, illustrate patterns in data and enhance and supplement fieldwork.

Introducing the computer into the classroom as another means of study, recording or enquiry can be challenging and rewarding. The class teacher should, however, feel confident with the computer equipment and the software to be used, and the software chosen should readily fit into the scheme of work planned for the class.

There are a number of small manageable steps that may be taken to ensure teacher confidence and the pupils' successful use of the computer as part of the whole learning experience. Begin by taking an interest in the pupils' use of, and experience with, the computer at home or in school. Read the accompanying teacher's and pupils' books carefully: they may in themselves provide springboards for new ideas and approaches. The very fact that the computer is being used may also offer ways of structuring the topic in an interesting and varied way.

Planning is crucial. Plan for three stages:

- the work which needs to be done before the computer is approached;
- the work to be accomplished on the computer;
- the desired outcomes of the work.

Build into the scheme of work the vocabulary and understanding necessary to operate the machine and negotiate the software. If this is done, the software will be experienced in a meaningful way when it is used.

Do not abandon the pupils who are using the computer. The computer should not make you feel redundant: you should be busy bringing to bear on this situation all teaching skills necessary to capture what is being achieved. You can be reflecting on: whether the software chosen is adequately covering what has been planned as outcomes of the lesson; whether the pace of work is suitable or too demanding; whether the depth of coverage is correct for the range of pupils in the class or whether perhaps some pupils need more guidance about the topic away from the computer. Listening to pupil discussion around the computer can also provide you with valuable points of information which can be woven back into the lesson to enhance the topic as a whole or help to formulate next steps and future strategies when the computer is to be used again.

When using the computer to introduce a theme, develop a single topic or highlight an issue, the approach is basically the same: prepare and plan well in advance of the lesson, review critically what has happened during the lesson and praise everyone concerned when the outcome is successful.

Ecosoft

Main application: To process and display graphical information collected during fieldwork
Subjects: Environmental education, Science, Geography, Maths
Suggested age: 13–18 (although it has been used above and below this age range)
Systems: Archimedes, RM Nimbus, BBC Master

A two-disc package, plus a booklet. Disc One has programs which draw bar and pie charts and deal with calculations. Disc Two has programs which allow the user to record findings and display them in many forms. The booklet explains how to enter data, use data, and how to print results. There is also advice from teachers who have used the software.

Spaceship Earth

Main application: A simulation of global disaster in which the human race must leave Earth and locate another suitable planet
Subjects: Environmental education, Science, Geography, Drama, Art
Suggested age: 10–16
Systems: BBC Master, RM Nimbus

The software contains data on 400 imaginary planets with detailed information on 23 of them. The simulation offers a context in which major issues can be explored and discussed, issues such as: suitable environments, atmosphere, resources and all aspects of survival and the quality of life for all who travel to the new planet. (A copy of Find, Junior Find or Quick Find is needed to run this program.)

Water Pollution

Main application: Role-play. Pupils take the role of the Environmental Committee of a large town as planners and decision-makers.
Subjects: Environmental education, Geography, Science, Drama, Maths, Information Technology
Suggested age: 13–16
Systems: Archimedes, RM Nimbus, BBC Master

There is scope here for a wide range of activities, using the role-play as a springboard. Pupils are set the task of choosing a sewage treatment site and determining the level of treatment. Industrial waste and its treatment are also featured. The implications of these activities in human terms and with regard to fresh water organisms are also explored. Visits from guest

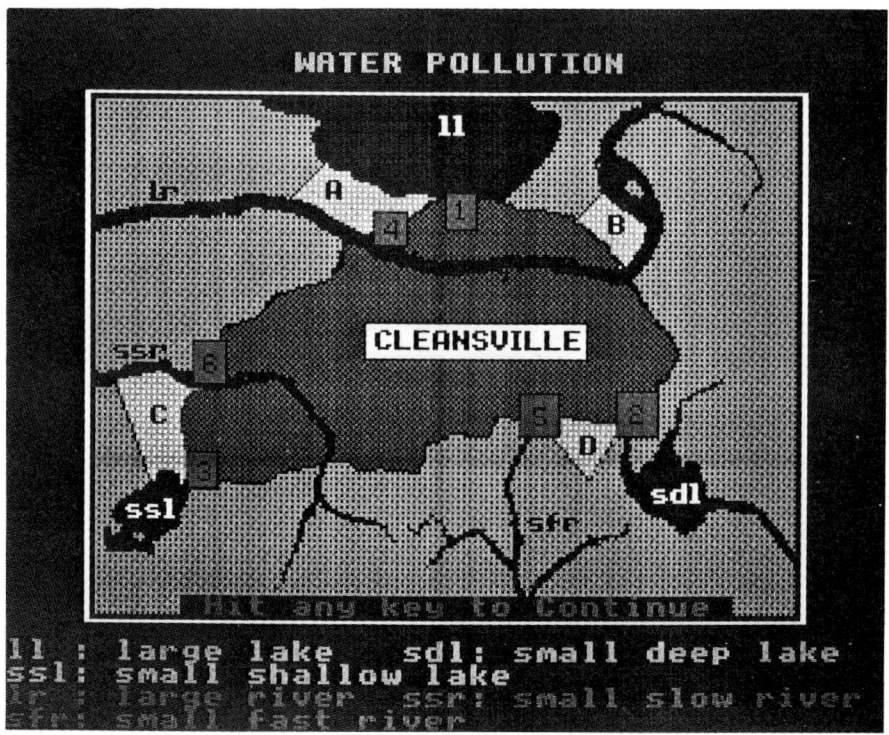

speakers, investigations, project work and report-writing could be co-ordinated to explore this topic fully.

The Water Game

Main application: Topic-based computer simulation, where pupils have to estimate the water needs of humans, animals and crops over a period of time
Subjects: Environmental education, Science, Maths
Suggested age: 8–13
Systems: RM Nimbus, BBC Master

The setting is a country cottage which has no running water. The challenge is to estimate the water requirements of all concerned, and to bring the water from the river/lake or to use hand-pumps. After several days, during which time events such as pollution and other mishaps can occur, the consequences of the decisions taken are given in a report. Subjects covered in the report include water pollution, contamination and shortages of water.

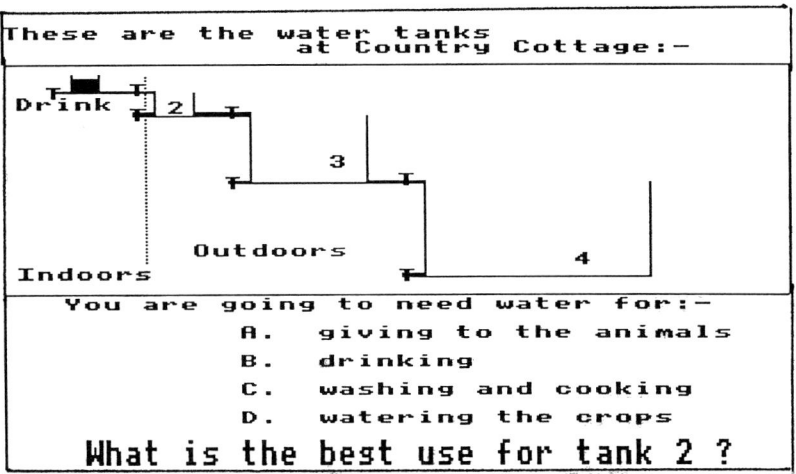

Viewpoints

Main application: An interactive environment which includes coastline, rivers, woods, a small town to explore – photographs of discoveries can be taken along the way and used later
Subjects: Environmental education, Geography
Suggested age: 8–14
System: Archimedes

This software encourages pupils to watch and wait for discoveries in the countryside – the essence of an environmental study. Based around a simple map and database program, pupils explore the terrain and set out to find locations or animals. Activities and ideas for classroom use, a set of illustrated animal cards, maps and a teacher's book are included.

David J Wraight (see Section 2, 'Global environmental problems presented using IT') adds:
The teacher's book for 'Viewpoints' provides a wealth of information to allow easier understanding of the software for hard-pressed teachers. The best ideas featured are four simulation exercises which will stretch the more able pupils.

The only drawback to the software is the movement around the map: this does not always

COMPUTER SOFTWARE: NINE ECOLOGICAL PACKAGES

follow exact directions. The scale of the map is perhaps too large to encompass the topography of the land as featured in the program.

Can You Find It?

Main application: A content-free simulation, with environmental resources which help to create an environment or habitat
Subject: Environmental education
Suggested age: 6–13
Systems: Archimedes, RM Nimbus, BBC Master

A software package which is very easy to use. There is one screen display for young pupils and another for older pupils. There are two files based on Brownsea Island and Fossils. Resources include line drawings of animal and insects, with brief notes on their preferred habitats.

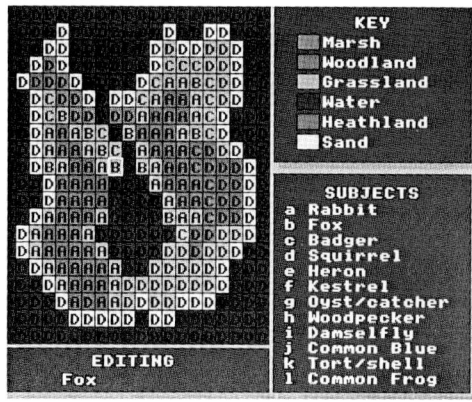

Landmarks – The Rainforest

Main application: An observational simulation
Subjects: Environmental education, Science
Suggested age: 9–14
System: Archimedes

This simulation allows pupils to explore an environment without changing it in any way. Betumi is a young girl living with her family in a small village deep in the South American rainforest. Life has remained unchanged for thousands of years, as the communities live in complete harmony with their environment.

A Dictionary of the Living World (CD-ROM)

Main application: A multi-media encyclopedia of the Life Sciences on CD-ROM
Subjects: Environmental education, Science, Geography
Suggested age: 11–16
Systems: CD-ROM, Archimedes

A large database with a search, export and replay facility. Complete with excellent still photographs, moving pictures and sound.

Sky Hunter (reviewed by David J Wraight)

Main application: This program, ostensibly concerned with issues of preservation of bird species, is in fact more involved with language work, logical thinking and observations.
Subjects: Environmental education, English
Suggested age: 11–14
System: Archimedes

This program is linked to the BBC series, 'Look and Read'. In the program, the pupils act as detectives, tracking down the villains who are stealing and trading wild birds. Pupils are taken through a series of exercises, many of which are 'environmental' in only the broadest sense. The major activities are concerned with language work, logical

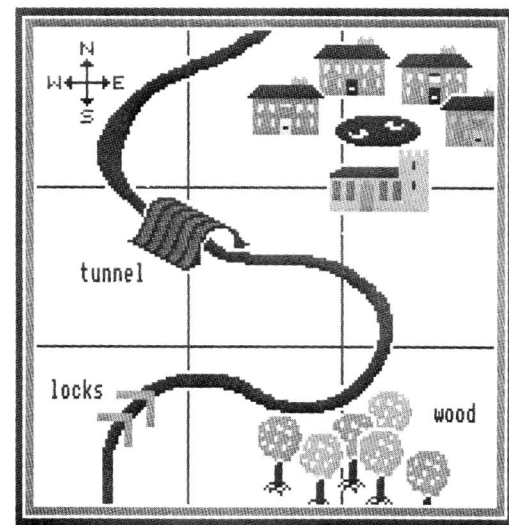

thought and observations. Although the overall theme is concerned with the theft of birds, the program does not develop this to any great extent.

The teacher's book provides a wealth of ideas for the development of extension activities. The active teacher will be able to use the program as the starting point for a range of environmental activities which might involve the pupils in work on birds and care of the environment.

Details of software referred to in this article

Ecosoft
£35.00 (Arch and RM Nimbus)
£25.00 (BBC Master)
from Advisory Unit for
Microtechnology in Education
Endymion Road
Hatfield
Hertfordshire
AL10 8AU
Tel: 0707 265443
Fax: 0707 273651

The Water Game
£21.45 (incl. VAT and postage and packing)
(RM Nimbus and BBC Master)
from WORLDAWARE CWDE Software
1 Catton Street
London
WC1R 4AB
Tel: 071 831 3844
Fax: 071 831 1746

Spaceship Earth
£30.50 (RM Nimbus and Arch)
from Resource
Exeter Road
Wheatley
Doncaster
South Yorkshire
DN2 4PY
Tel: 0302 340331
Fax: 0302 328735

Viewpoints
£35 (excl. VAT) (Arch)
from Sherston Software
Swan Barton
Malmesbury
Wiltshire
SN16 0LH
Tel: 0666 840433
Fax: 0666 840048

Water Pollution
£35.00 (Arch and RM Nimbus)
£29.50 (BBC Master)
from AVP Computing
School Hill Centre
Chepstow
Gwent
NP6 5PH
Tel: 0291 625439
Fax: 0291 629671

Can You Find It?
£34.00 (excl. VAT and carriage)
from Cambridgeshire Software House
7 Free Church Passage
St Ives
Huntingdon
Cambridgeshire
PE17 4AY
Tel: 0480 67945
Fax: 0480 496442

Landmarks – The Rainforest
£24 (excl. VAT)
from Longman Logotron Ltd
124 Cambridge Science Park
Milton Road
Cambridge
CB4 4ZS
Tel: 0223 425558
Fax: 0223 425349

Sky Hunter
£24 (excl. VAT) (Arch)
from Longman Logotron Ltd
124 Cambridge Science Park
Milton Road
Cambridge
CB4 4ZS
Tel: 0223 425558
Fax: 0223 425349

A Dictionary of the Living World
£205.63 (incl. VAT)
from Optech Ltd
East Street
Farnham
Surrey
GU9 7XX
Tel: 0252 714340
Fax: 0252 711121

E Carole Sampson was Advisory Teacher with Cleveland Education Computing Centre in 1990-91 and is currently the computer specialist at Eston Park Comprehensive School, in which capacity she reviews software across the curriculum for all levels of ability. She looks out for software which challenges the able, offers guidance and support to the less able and empowers all to become independent learners.

Earthquest Explores Ecology

BEV WIGHT

This review looks at a software package for the Apple Macintosh. It will work with System 6 and System 7 machines. One megabyte of memory is acceptable, although two megabytes is a more realistic configuration. 'Earthquest Explores Ecology' requires Hypercard version 2.0 (or higher) which is provided with the software. For sound and colour facilities a hard disc is required, but for all other purposes the software will run on any machine with two 800K floppy drives. Installation is straightforward although, in common with many software manufacturers, the names of the files have changed slightly from the instruction book to the disc.

EARTHQUEST EXPLORES ECOLOGY (EARTHQUEST INC.)

Main application: A voyage of exploration with games, tests and quizzes based on the rainforest simulation provided. A variety of routes through and around the software are available as it is produced as a series of Hypercard stacks. The sound is good (I cannot comment on colour as I reviewed this on a black and white machine)
Subjects: Geography AT2, AT3 and AT5; Science AT2. The language and concepts involved indicate KS3/4 pupils
Suggested age: 11–18

Strengths

Individual pupils can make their own voyage of discovery through the rainforest flora and fauna. The software enables them to identify ways in which we can use and develop the rainforest and ways in which we are exploiting and destroying it. It is easy to obtain print-outs of each screen.

Weaknesses

This is very much a package produced for the USA market, so much of the supporting documentation and addresses for action are based in that country. It has little to offer whole-class or group work.

This is an interesting program which would perhaps have been better produced on a CD-ROM (although this would have raised the price). Despite this limitation, it is an interesting and motivating way for pupils to learn about the rainforest. It is well illustrated, and the sounds add considerably to the atmosphere. The program represents a useful addition to the classroom compendium for exploring ecological issues, but one which is insufficient to base a unit of work on. Some pupils will be motivated to explore further, and others will just play at it. Individual pieces of material are provided in small amounts as and when pupils require them. They are also under pupil control, as they need to click the mouse to access them. For pupils with control problems, the almost total use of the mouse to access all levels of the program means that they can use this with their specially adapted keyboards with minimum alteration or help. There is a workshop where pupils can work within Hypercard to create and add their own cards to the program. I do not think that many British pupils will wish to take up this option, unless they are in a school already heavily into Hypercard programing, but teachers may wish to use it to customise or personalise the program for their pupils and their local environment.

Conclusion

This package will find adherents among both staff and pupils. I feel that it would be most suitably placed in a library or resource centre as it is essentially a voyage of discovery. Provided the price is right, and you can wrench control of the Apple from the DTP brigade, then it would be a useful addition to any school software library.

> *Earthquest Explores Ecology*
> £47.00 (excl. VAT)
> *from* MacLine
> Mill House
> Mill Lane
> Carshalton
> Surrey
> SM5 2WZ
> Tel: 081 401 1111
> Fax: 081 401 1112

Bev Wight spent 19 years in the classroom before becoming advisory teacher for Information Technology and Assessment in an outer London borough, where she works with teachers from all key stages and in most subject areas, developing ways in which IT can be used to support learning and improve motivation and interest in pupils of all abilities.

Journals and magazines

CHRIS OULTON AND BILL SCOTT

OVERVIEW

This review examines four journals which are readily available to people active in environmental education. Of all the publications we might have chosen for review, these have been selected because they represent, between them, a variety of strands of environmental activism and involvement, and because they approach the issues from a range of perspectives. They are also all readily affordable and of interest to a wide range of people. However, it is also true that our final selection was to some extent arbitrary, and the absence of any publication from this review should not be taken to mean that it does not meet the criteria listed above.

Streetwise

Streetwise is the quarterly bulletin of the National Association for Urban Studies (NAUS). The length of each issue varies but averages around 40 A4 pages.

The aims of NAUS are, first, to develop an understanding of the urban environment as an integral part of our environment; secondly, to encourage and enable people of all ages and in all sections of the community to play an active part in improving their urban environment; and, thirdly, to promote the use of the urban environment as an educational resource. *Streetwise* is devoted to the achievement of these aims, and sets about this task through a mixture of special reports, feature articles, 'street teacher' case studies, conference reports, resource and book reviews, and a notice board illustrating forthcoming events.

Recent editions have included a very full (58-page) conference report on the 'Sustainable City' featuring contributions from a number of European countries, features on drama and local studies, community arts programmes and city farms, explorations of links between Art in the National Curriculum for England and Wales and environmental education, and between the built environment and environmental education, and special features on map work, energy education and town trails.

The involvement in urban studies which frames the work of *Streetwise* is obvious in every edition, but the contents are likely to be of interest to anyone involved in environmental education, whether or not they come from a geographical, architectural or planning background. It is equally important to note that *Streetwise* focuses on issues *across* the environmental spectrum, and makes strong links between environmental education and most of the other cross-curricular themes in the National Curriculum – most notably, economic and industrial awareness, and health education. This has been exemplified recently through features on energy management in schools, fuel use at home, the economics of sustainability, and health issues in an urban community.

Streetwise is habitually internationalist in outlook, generally strikingly illustrated and, at times, acutely provocative.

Environmental Education

Environmental Education is published by the National Association of Environmental Education (NAEE), and is published three times a year. The length of each issue varies, but averages around 31 A4 pages.

The journal's claim to importance lies in its focus on school curriculum issues, although not every contribution sets out to be something of *direct* use to teachers. There is, rather, a clear desire to inform, stimulate and challenge. In the recent past there have been articles on *Curriculum Guidance 7* from the NCC (National Curriculum Council), environmental education audits, cross-curricular fieldwork, and the role of outdoor and field study centres in educating for the environment. In addition, a variety of international perspectives are taken; these take the form of articles describing environmental education in different parts of the world, and looking at a variety of developmental issues relating to environmental education.

One feature of the journal is an eight-page pull-out section titled 'News and Views'. This is used as a formal means of communicating with NAEE members and contains features which bring readers up to date with developments and forthcoming activities across the various local branches of the Association. One 1992 edition, for example, contained material as varied as: a profile of UNEP, details of resource material from various sources including ESSO and the Health Education Authority, adverts for in-service programmes, and details of exhibitions and conferences. A constant feature is a list of Association publications, and membership details.

Few articles come from classroom teachers; authors are more likely to be advisors, administrators, Higher Education lecturers and study centre tutors. This is not to be critical of the crucial contribution which such people can make, but merely to note that the journal does not make it easy for school practitioners to speak to each other. Members and other readers are invited to write to the Editor, and the journal's 'News and Views' section contains many items received from readers.

Annual Review of Environmental Education

The *Annual Review of Environmental Education (AREE)* is published at the turn of each year by the Council for Environmental Education (CEE). *AREE* superseded CEE's *Review of Environmental Education Developments (REED)* in 1987. Each issue now averages around 50 A4 pages.

AREE has as its purpose to 'report, evaluate, encourage and help to guide progress in environmental education, particularly as it relates to school and non-formal education'. It sets out to: provide information on important initiatives and developments and comparative international developments; give a critical overview of the progress of environmental education in the UK, and use the evidence of the past to identify issues and priorities for the future.

There has been a remarkable consistency of approach over its issues. In *AREE* you will find an editorial, sections on research, international issues, educational developments and environmental education, and case studies, *inter alia*, of practice in schools, local authorities and youth groups. In addition, AREE contains a 'Soundings' section, where prominent people such as politicians, internationally-known environmentalists, and academics offer their views on particular issues. There is also an 'Issues and Reflections' section where a similar set of people seem to do much the same.

It is clear that *AREE* does not set out to cover the ground in a uniform fashion, to provide, as it were, a detailed landscape or panoramic view of environmental issues; its strategy is to eschew wide angles, preferring selective portraiture and a focus on particular features. The power of this approach lies in the way that important issues can be examined and particular lines of development explored. A good example of this in action was the 1991 concentration on National Curriculum developments. The problem with this approach, of course, is that a number of notable and distinctive features do not necessarily hang well together, and very occasionally there is a lack of coherence. There is also the sense that the journal inevitably feels it has to be 'all things to all groups'; this can lead to brief articles which, no matter how well they are arranged around the plate, can lead to the same lack of satisfaction associated with much nouvelle cuisine.

But this is to dwell too much on the negative; the strength of *AREE* lies in its professional and personal authority. This authority comes partly from its parent, CEE, but more from the wide range of prominent people who contribute to it. Although it might not much like the notion, it does tend to constitute a regular outlet for the environmental education establishment, and many people who are looking for the views of opinion-formers and opinion-leaders within the movement turn eagerly to *AREE*.

Green Teacher

Green Teacher is a non-profit making journal which is published six times a year. The length of each issue averages 40 A4 pages.

Green Teacher is a journal for 'teachers, teacher educators and curriculum developers'. As well as providing 'a networking centre for education in ecological concern, energy studies, alternative technology, and peace and development education', the journal's producers claim that it 'relates the latest green movement debates to practice in education for the environment' and 'provides materials directly usable with teaching groups'. It is this broad approach to environmental education and the commitment to providing practical help for its readers that determine the journal's character.

Each edition is an eclectic mix of articles, worksheets and ideas for projects. Activities may relate to all age ranges and come from a wide range of subject areas. There is a strong international contribution in each edition. A recent edition included: worksheets on recycling; a report on a project to develop story telling from the landscape; a Canadian story about learning from our environment; an evaluation of the 'green credentials' of the UK political parties prior to the 1992 election; an Australian short story about experimenting with worms; ideas for pupils to carry out green shopping surveys; an article on reflective learning and green education; practical tips for experimenting on water power in the classroom, as well as the regular section reviewing resources and the 'Noticeboard' of information.

The strengths of *Green Teacher* are that it provides clear evidence of and practical support for the notion of environmental education as a cross-curricular theme. There is also a clear commitment to the notion of education *for* the environment through its encouragement of individuals to take action. As such, it is an excellent publication for schools and other organisations where groups of individuals wish to develop environmental education on a number of fronts. Paradoxically, the broad base of the publication may reduce its appeal to individuals who are working from a particular viewpoint. For example, a teacher of a particular subject in a secondary school may not find anything of specific interest for a number of editions.

Green Teacher is an appealing journal, full of cartoons and illustrations. This should not fool the potential reader into thinking that it is lightweight. *Green Teacher* functions at the deeper and darker end of the green spectrum and has a serious and important contribution to make to environmental education generally.

CONCLUSIONS

For teachers in schools, local authority advisors and inspectors, and people working in NGOs (non-government organisations), agencies and pressure groups, there is much of value to be found in the publications highlighted here which impinges directly upon their work. The publications are, in their quite distinctive ways, potentially effective means of dissemination across the wide environmental education movement; they have the capacity both of stimulating the sharing of activities between practitioners and also of affecting and *effecting* practice on the ground.

What these journals cannot do is have much effect on the dissemination of fundamental *research* outcomes outwards to schools and the wider community. This is no criticism of these particular publications, as it is not their prime purpose. It points, rather, to an important gap in provision which can only be filled by an international research journal devoted to environmental education; a journal which each of these publications would find useful as a source of ideas and data. The Carfax publishing company has recently announced the advent of such a journal, *Environmental Education Research*. The first volume will appear early in 1994.

Details of journals referred to in this article

Streetwise (ISSN 0 0957-6517)
Editor: Richard Welsh
c/o National Association for Urban Studies
Lewis Cohen Urban Studies Centre
University of Brighton
68 Grand Parade
Brighton
BN2 2JY
Tel: 0273 673416
Free to members of the Association (current subscription for individuals, schools and voluntary organisations £25), and to non-members (individuals, schools and voluntary organisations) at an inclusive cost of £15.50 per annum.

Environmental Education (ISSN 0 309-8451)
Editor: Phil Neal
c/o National Association for Environmental Education
University of Wolverhampton
Walsall Campus
Gorway
Walsall
WS31 3BD
Tel: 0922 31200
Available free to members of the Association (current individual subscription £8.50), and to non-members at an inclusive cost of £3.00 per annum.

Annual Review of Environmental Education (ISSN 0 953-0428, ISBN 0 906711 21 5)
Editor: Stephen Stirling
c/o The Council for Environmental Education
Faculty of Education and Community Studies
University of Reading
Reading
RG1 5AQ
Tel: 0734 756061
Available at £10 per copy, plus £1 postage and packing.

Green Teacher (ISSN 0 953-3028)
General editor: Damian Randle
Green Teacher
Machynlleth
SY20 8DN
£12 per annum inclusive (for six issues).

Other journals not mentioned in the article, but worthy of attention

- *Acid News*

Newsletter from the Norwegian and Swedish NGO Secretariat on Acid Rain
Box 245
S-401 24 Göteborg
Sweden

- *The Ecologist*

- *English Nature*

English Nature
Northminster House
Peterborough
PE1 1JY

- *The International Journal of Environmental Education and Information*

(University of Salford)

- *Journal of Biological Education*

(Institute of Biology)

- *Learning Through Landscapes Newsletter (E-Scape)*

Learning Through Landscapes
3rd. Floor
Southside Offices
The Law Courts
Winchester
Hampshire
SO23 9DL
Tel: 0962 846258 (10.00-16.30)

Chris Oulton and Bill Scott are co-directors of the Environmental Education Unit in the School of Education at the University of Bath. Chris Oulton is a lecturer in the School of Education and has responsibility for the environmental science pre-service teacher education programme. Bill Scott is a senior lecturer in the School of Education, with responsibility for the school-based PGCE in Partnership programme. Chris Oulton and Bill Scott have, at various times, written for each of the publications they have reviewed in this article, either individually or together, by virtue of their work within environmental education.

Some useful living resources

MICHAEL REISS

INTRODUCTION

This review concentrates on resources (mostly published) which use animals and plants in a school setting (rather than on field trips). Some of these require organisms to be brought into classrooms from the wild; others require organisms to be kept in captivity. Teachers, technicians and pupils must, of course, be aware that appropriate care needs to be taken with living organisms and, specifically, that:

- animals should not be caused to suffer;
- natural habitats should not be damaged (for instance, plants should not be uprooted, and organisms which are collected from the wild, like woodlice, should be returned to the wild unharmed).

Jan Stewart's *Minibeasts* is a teacher's book (54 pages) with an accompanying children's workbook (16 pages). The materials were developed as part of the Authentic Assessment Project funded by the Shell Centre, University of Nottingham and the University of Cambridge Local Examinations Syndicate.

Minibeasts is an excellent publication for use with 5-7 year olds. Fully referenced to relevant Statements of Attainment at levels 1, 2 and 3 of the English, Mathematics, Science and Technology National Curriculum, it includes such activities as: finding and describing spiders' webs; using a simple key to identify spiders

SOME USEFUL LIVING RESOURCES

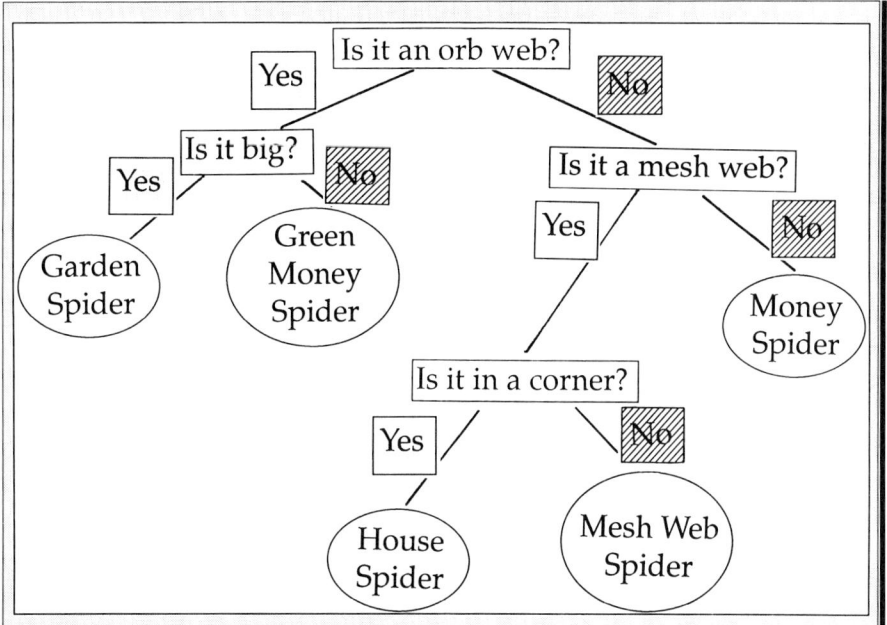

A page from *Minibeasts*, Teacher's Book

(house spider, mesh web spider, garden spider, green money spider, money spider); making a mini-beast finger puppet. The book covers many useful skills, like organising data, constructing graphs and caring for living creatures. As a bonus, there is a lovely selection of short poems on insects, snails and spiders by Christina Rossetti, Roald Dahl, William Wordsworth and others.

Classroom Creatures is a pack of 30 A4 pages, written by Roma Oxford, which contains eight units: spiders, snails, tadpoles, stick insects, ladybirds, worms, ants and a mini-beast safari pack. It is an invaluable publication for Key Stages 1 and 2 Science. For example, the unit on snails contains carefully written and appropriate advice on how to keep and breed snails in a classroom. The unit contains activities which range from looking at the variation between individuals in size, shape, pattern and foot colour to working out how much food snails eat each day.

Roma Oxford also runs a mobile environmental education service. For approximately £15 (plus petrol) she visits schools in the North Yorkshire and Humberside area. She brings a van filled with such creatures as tarantulas, crickets, beetles, earwigs, stick insects, slugs, hedgehogs and bats. (The bats and hedgehogs are rescued animals which are either being restored to health before return to the wild or are unable to survive in the wild. Roma Oxford holds all the necessary animal-handling licences.)

The Science and Plants for Schools (SAPS) programme is a major curriculum development project in the UK. Its basic premise is that good teaching of the life sciences depends for its success on the use of suitable living plant material. Recent legislation, together with public concern about the use of living organisms in laboratories, has placed some restrictions on the use which Science teachers can now make of living material. For example, the Wildlife and Countryside Act (1981) makes it illegal to collect wild plants indiscriminately.

Teachers are therefore increasingly turning to plants which can be grown easily and quickly in school laboratories. One such example is a rapid-cycling variety of *Brassica rapa* (syn. *campestris*), which will reliably flower two weeks after sowing the seed and which will complete its life cycle, from seed to seed, in just five weeks.

The aim of the SAPS Programme is to promote and to support exciting teaching of plant science in schools and thereby to dispel the view, widely held among young people, that plants are boring. This is particularly appropriate at a time when the importance of the plant kingdom in the global economy is increasingly being realised.

The SAPS programme:

- is working with Science teachers to develop practical investigations in plant science for the National Curriculum, at A level, and for Scottish Standard and Higher Grade courses;
- runs workshops for teachers which show, through hands-on practical work, how they can use plants to support exciting Science teaching;
- offers secondments to suitably experienced teachers so that they can help to develop curricular material for plant science. The seconded teachers also help to organise and run workshops;
- has developed educational kits for practical investigations with rapid-cycling brassicas;
- sponsors selected schools which, in exchange for a grant towards the cost of building a light bank and a free kit for growing rapid-cycling brassicas, are asked to work on specific areas of interest in plant science and to provide feed-back to SAPS;
- is forging links with universities, colleges and other plant science research institutions in order to provide a channel through which Science teachers can have access to information on the very latest discoveries and techniques in plant science;
- produces a highly useful newsletter, *Osmosis*, which is circulated free of charge to any school that registers with the programme (recent issues of this newsletter have included articles on investigations with rapid-cycling *Brassica campestris*, growing carnivorous plants and using discarded plastic (soft drinks) bottles to make model ecosystems).

SAPS believes that, in addition to rapid-cycling brassicas, many other plants make good experimental material for use in schools. They are anxious to hear from any teachers who have developed interesting and stimulating practical work in plant science.

Bird Studies for Primary Science in the National Curriculum is an extremely useful 'guide to practical studies' (39 pages), produced by the Royal Society for the Protection of Birds. The publication contains detailed and helpful advice about a large number of ways in which birds may be studied in primary schools. For Key Stage 1, four themes are introduced: Caring for wild birds; Getting to know wild birds; Investigating wild birds; Birds and seasonal changes. For Key Stage 2, six different themes are introduced: Identification of birds; Studies at a birdtable or in the school grounds; Evolution and extinction; Adaptation; Predator-prey relationships; Human influences.

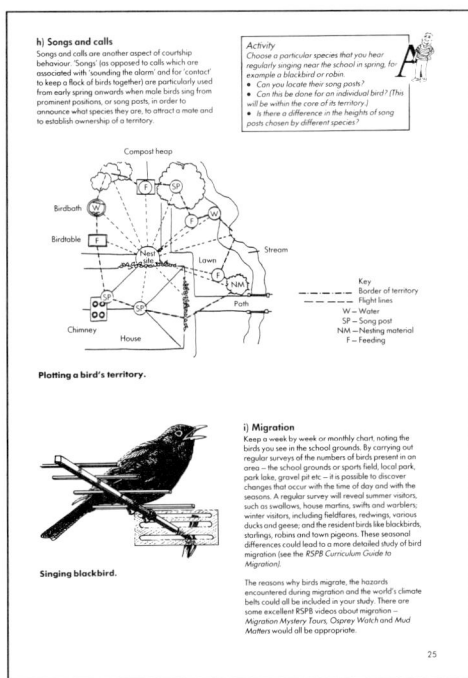

A page from *Bird Studies for Primary Science*

The guide uses these themes to give teachers further ideas about studies to be undertaken. For example, at Key Stage 1, under the theme 'Caring for wild birds', the guide suggests that a birdtable, a birdbath or nest boxes could be set up in school grounds and that pupils could then take turns to be responsible for looking after these devices. At Key Stage 2, there are a variety of possible activities described in the theme, 'Studies at a birdtable or in the school grounds', one of which is the observation of 'feeding behaviour'.

Urban Ecology: A Teacher's Resource Book by Martin Collins is a most valuable book (143 pages) for teachers who want to provide field investigations in Biology in towns and cities. Some ten years old, it is already something of a classic. (See overleaf.)

The book contains a number of useful suggestions, a flavour of which may be gained from some of the sections in Chapter 2 (Urban habitats): walls, pavements, stony paths, asphalt surfaces, lawns, sports fields, weedy areas, vacant land, cemeteries, commons, refuse tips, compost heaps and buildings. In addition, the book suggests a large number of possible projects, including:

- a comparison of the crevices between the paving stones of streets subjected to different degrees of trampling;

- colonisation by plants of a school playground;
- the ecology of a heap of decaying vegetation;
- the fauna of moss cushions and root gutters;
- determining human age-specific mortality from tombstone dates.

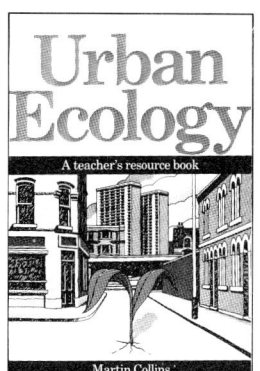  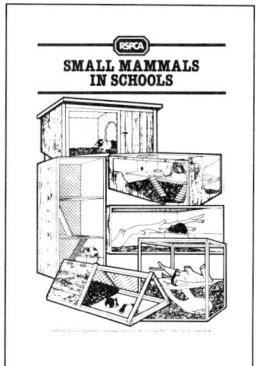

There are also keys to the major groups of terrestrial invertebrates found in urban areas, a detailed section on ecological methods and a comprehensive list of further reading.

The Royal Society for the Prevention of Cruelty to Animals (RSPCA) has a large Education Service: the service produces a variety of very reasonably priced publications and offers other services to schools. Among its publications are:

- *Animals in Schools,* which provides guidelines on how suitable animals may be kept in schools (see above);
- *Small Mammals in Schools,* which provides more detailed advice on keeping gerbils, guinea pigs, hamsters, mice, rabbits and rats, together with a number of suggested projects such as finding out how much time an animal spends on its various activities (e.g. grooming, feeding, drinking, exploring, digging and sleeping) (see above);
- *Visiting Animal Schemes,* which is a guide to good practice for schools, local education authorities and visiting animal schemes operators.

The RSPCA Education Service also deals with over 60,000 enquiries a year from pupils and teachers on various aspects of animal welfare. It provides in-service training and development programmes for teachers and runs a junior award scheme called CARE.

Living Biology in Schools is a 64-page book written by members of the Institute of Biology and edited by Dr Barbara Tomlins, the ex-Education Officer of the Institute of Biology. The book consists of nine chapters: Scope and aims; Why use living organisms in schools?; Microbiology; Plants; Animals (excluding humans); Pupils as a resource; Legalities; Safety; Moral and ethical issues.

CONCLUSION

Recent research has shown a worrying tendency for many schools to cut down on the amount of work that their pupils do with living organisms (Reiss, MJ and Beaney, NJ, 1992, 'The use of living organisms in secondary school Science', *Journal of Biological Education*, 26, 63-66). However, as this review has indicated, the last few years have also seen an encouraging increase in the number of publications outlining non-invasive ways in which living organisms can be studied in schools. It is to be hoped that school education will increasingly introduce 5–16 year olds to the natural environment and to organisms around them in a responsible manner.

Details of resources mentioned in this review

Minibeasts, Jan Stewart, Authentic Assessment Project, 1991, £8.50 (teacher's book with one children's workbook) or £25 (teacher's book with 30 children's workbooks)
Details from: Ron McClone, UCLES, 1 Hills Road, Cambridge CB1 2EU.

Classroom Creatures, Roma Oxford, 1991, £4.00 (incl. postage and packing)
Available from: Roma Oxford, 519 Huntingdon Road, York YO3 9PY.

Science and Plants for Schools (SAPS)
For further information, teachers in England and Wales should contact SAPS at: Homerton College, Cambridge CB2 2PH. Teachers in Scotland and Northern Ireland should contact SAPS at the Royal Botanic Garden, Edinburgh EH3 5LR.
The Science and Plants for Schools programme is currently funded by the Gatsby Charitable Foundation, which is one of the Sainsbury Family charitable trusts.

"An excellent specimen ... symbol of beauty, innocence and fragile life. ... Hand me the jar of ether."

Bird Studies for Primary Science in the National Curriculum, Royal Society for the Protection of Birds, 1991, £1.25
Available from: RSPB, The Lodge, Sandy, Bedfordshire SG19 2DL.

Urban Ecology: A Teacher's Resource Book, Martin Collins, Cambridge University Press, 1984.

The Royal Society for the Prevention of Cruelty to Animals publications:
Animals in Schools, 1986 (4th edn), *Small Mammals in Schools*, 1989 (2nd edn) and *Visiting Animal Schemes*, 1988.
Full details are available from: Head of Education, RSPCA, Causeway, Horsham RH12 1HG.

Living Biology in Schools, ed. Dr Barbara Tomlins, Institute of Biology, 1993
Further details from: The Education Officer, Institute of Biology, 20 Queensberry Place, London SW7 2DZ.

The Reverend Dr Michael Reiss is a lecturer in the University of Cambridge Department of Education. His teaching, research and writing interests are in the areas of science education, health education, environmental education and ethics. He is a Fellow of the Institute of Biology, Chair of the Education Division Committee of the Institute of Biology, a Chief Examiner at S level and a Moderator at A and AS level.

Guidelines for the use of animals in the classroom

ROYAL SOCIETY FOR THE PREVENTION OF CRUELTY TO ANIMALS

INTRODUCTION

The National Curriculum requires children to derive a grounding in animal husbandry. Moreover, valuable experiences in terms of the way children regard animals with both respect and sensitivity can encourage a more responsible treatment of animals in the environment and at home.

An understanding of basic responsibilities for the physical and mental well-being of animals, in terms of accommodation, food and medical treatment is essential to ensure the correct treatment of animals kept in schools. Teachers must consult adequate in-depth manuals before obtaining any animals.

The kind of animals kept in the classroom will very much depend on what points the teacher wishes to emphasise, and the advantages and disadvantages of different species must be weighed up. At the same time, teachers must consider the level of commitment involved. Can the care of the animal be fitted into an already busy day? Will there be sufficient funding to ensure that proper facilities are made available for keeping the animal?

HEALTH PRECAUTIONS

These range from the basic daily hygiene methods (such as cleaning food bowls and bedding) which must be undertaken to reduce the risk of disease, to the necessary veterinary arrangements which the teacher in charge should sort out. The LEA may provide financial aid for veterinary accounts. If not, such provisions should be allowed for in the annual budget.

Schools should advise parents that their pupils should be immunised against tetanus if they are to handle the animals. It will also be necessary for teachers to recognise the symptoms of infections, so that infected animals can be removed from possible contact with children. The two commonest infections are Ringworm, which is a skin infection, and Salmonella, which is a gastro-enteric illness.

CARE AND ACCOMMODATION

To ensure perfect care for animals, the proposed housing area must be in line with their actual needs. In other words, the welfare of the animals must be put before convenience to the school. Schools must therefore ensure that a suitable environment is available in terms of heating, ventilation and lighting. The ideal arrangement is for there to be a separate animal room. Schools must also select suitable accommodation and be aware of such considerations as what kind of cage, and what size, is most appropriate for the animal concerned.

During holidays and weekends, the animals must be suitably looked after, either by the teacher or by pupils who have parental consent. Lack of proper care can cause considerable stress to the animal. Arrangements must be made to ensure that parents know the name, telephone number and surgery times of the veterinary practice used by the school.

If an animal has, for reasons of illness, to be put down, a vet, or another qualified person, should be asked to do so, so that the procedure may be carried out quickly and painlessly.

CHOOSING A HEALTHY ANIMAL

Only reliable suppliers, such as laboratory suppliers and reputable breeders, should be considered. Pet shops are generally not good sources for animals. It is a good idea to arrange a veterinary inspection of the animal before it is introduced into the school.

When choosing an animal, schools should follow basic guidelines, including looking for positive signs of good health, cleanliness, confidence and alertness.

LEGAL CONSIDERATIONS

There are six main Acts of Parliament relating to the use of animals in schools which teachers need to be aware of: The Protection of Animals Act, 1911; The Abandonment of Animals Act, 1960; The Pet Animals Act, 1951; The Animals (Scientific Procedures) Act, 1986; The Wildlife and Countryside Act, 1981; The Dangerous Wild Animals Act, 1976 (for further information, teachers should consult *Wildlife, the Law and You*, NCC).

GUIDELINES FOR THE USE OF ANIMALS IN THE CLASSROOM

The RSPCA considers the following animals suitable for schools:

Small mammals
Gerbils, mice, rats all require indoor housing. Guinea pigs and rabbits should be housed outdoors.

Large mammals
Farm animals such as cattle, goats and sheep require a great deal of care. Financial factors must therefore be weighed against welfare considerations.

Birds
Chickens, geese, quails should have suitable pens. For canaries or finches, aviaries are preferable to cages.

Amphibians
Native species should only be kept temporarily, while non-native species may be kept permanently in schools. Conservation of the species can be enhanced by the controlled collection and later release of spawn by the children.

Reptiles
Slow-worms are suitable reptiles for schools.

Fish
Freshwater or marine species are the easiest to care for and show the fish in a near natural environment. Tropical marine aquaria can be expensive to look after (requiring heating equipment, pumps, tank). Schools should bear in mind that the use of electricity (for the pumps, etc.) imposes more stringent safety considerations.

Invertebrates
Stick insects, locusts and American cockroaches (on a long-term basis); earthworms, woodlice, slugs and snails (on a short-term basis). Some invertebrates are protected by law (the British Entomological Society has a code of conduct on this matter, to which it is worth referring). Invertebrates tend to be easier to look after, and their life cycles can be easier and more interesting to study. However, they must be treated with the same respect as vertebrates.

Native animal species
Butterflies, spiders and slugs. These demand just as much care and attention as other animals and should be returned to their natural habitat.

The RSPCA considers the following animals unsuitable for keeping in schools:

Wild mammals and wild birds
This category includes abandoned fledglings. These wild animals can transmit disease. It is also necessary to keep in mind any infringements of Acts of Parliament concerning wild animals.

Carnivores
These creatures need to be fed with live vertebrates; this may cause problems, if not considerable distress, in class.

Primates
A licence is required for these animals.

Amphibians
Some species are protected by law, for example the Natterjack Toad and the Great Crested (Warty) Newt. If these species are to be collected, they should never be collected in autumn. They should also be released during the summer term.

Reptiles
Tortoises and terrapins are difficult to look after in school environments and can carry Salmonella. The importation of lizards and snakes can cause conservation problems, and some reptiles are totally protected by law.

Birds
The Department for Education advises against the use of certain members of the parrot family, including the budgerigar (as well as recently imported birds), which are highly likely to carry disease.

Involvement and projects

It is important to maintain pupils' interest in the animals throughout the year; all too often, the initial enthusiasm with which their arrival is greeted gives way to boredom. Schools should formulate various projects which look at the way in which the animals behave: for example, in relation to their natural environment. Also, while it is best to keep actual handling of the animals to a minimum, class rotas can be used to ensure that each child has a certain degree of responsibility for the welfare of the animal.

Teachers can encourage responsible attitudes towards pet ownership, and these positive attitudes may be an important link in the future reduction of animal suffering.

References

> *Animals in Schools*, 1986 (4th edn)
> *Small Mammals in Schools*, 1988 (2nd edn)
> Full details are available from: Head of Education, RSPCA, Causeway, Horsham RH12 1HG.

Additional notes from the Institute of Biology

The Institute of Biology produces guidelines on the obtaining of animals, and their subsequent use in the classroom, which broadly parallel those given above by the RSPCA.

Pupils should be taught how to handle the animals properly in order to avoid bites or scratches. Immediate medical attention should be sought if a pupil receives a wound which is judged sufficiently serious. Teachers should bear in mind that some people are susceptible to allergic reactions which may take the form of runny eyes or wheezing or a more serious case of asthma. Pupils affected by such conditions should have minimal contact with the animal. This is another reason why it is best to keep animals housed out of the classroom, to decrease the time that such pupils are exposed to allergens.

Growing plants for classroom use

In its publication, *Living Biology in the Classroom*, the Institute of Biology advises on the selection of species which pupils can easily propagate and suggests that schools could grow a specimen of each Phylum in the classroom or garden.

Children like to grow plants which can be eaten, such as cabbage, broad beans or calabrese. Common annual flowering species, such as busy lizzies, cornflowers or sunflowers, are also popular, as are wheat, oat and barley, which can be used for various experiments and valuable lessons on pollination.

Some plants may cause irritating symptoms, and teachers must take precautions to prevent pupils coming into contact with these plants. Particular care is needed when dealing with berries and fungi.

Reference

Living Biology in the Classroom, Institute of Biology, 1993. Available from: Institute of Biology, 20–22 Queensberry Place, London SW7 2DZ.

Multi-media packs

VINCENT J BUNCE

Multi-media packs have become an increasingly common response to shrinking departmental budgets and the need for more flexible resource provision. A small but growing number of agencies – not, on the whole, the larger commercial publishing houses – provide these resources. Perhaps the most prodigious provider is the World Wide Fund for Nature (WWF UK), which has a vast repertoire of packs and videos. Also involved are other charities like Living Earth, broadcasters like BBC TV (supported by the International Broadcasting Trust) and specialist units like Team Video. A more recent trend is for packs to attract sponsorship from large multi-national companies, perhaps keen to salve their consciences over past (and present?) environmental misdemeanours. There is only room here to look at a few of the best materials available. The materials have been divided into three sections: those aimed mainly at youngsters; those aimed at teachers and governors; and those aimed at other adults.

RESOURCES FOR THE CLASSROOM

For a good general introduction to a range of environmental topics, you could do no better than to consider using *The Global Environment*. This is a series of ten 20-minute programmes made by the International Broadcasting Trust for BBC Schools Television. Each programme gives a clear exposition of a major environmental issue. Topics covered include urbanisation, air pollution, waste disposal and energy conservation. The programmes are entertaining and informative and should hold the interest of most pupils at both lower and upper secondary school. *The Global Environment* provides examples from developed and developing world contexts. It examines some of the planet's major problems without unduly depressing the viewer, and always looks at sustainable solutions. Also available are a set of teachers' notes and a free-standing pupils' textbook, both strongly activity-orientated.

Only One Earth is almost as wide-ranging as *The Global Environment*. This package comprises a wall chart, a video and several booklets. The video features films made for a general audience and broadcast to mark the publication of The Brundtland Report in 1987. A booklet is provided on the theme of each film (urbanisation, desertification, tropical forests, industrial pollution and ocean fisheries), which includes extra material for teachers and activity sheets and readings for pupils. The level of the print material is quite high and, in general, would be best reserved for Year 11 pupils and those studying in the sixth form.

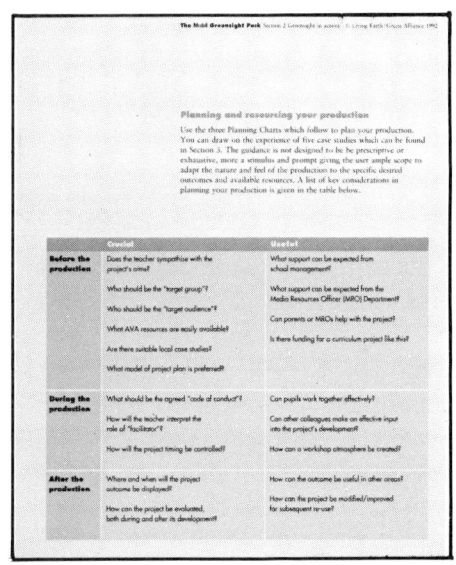

(*above*) *Only One Earth*, book and video
(*right*) A page from *The Mobil Greensight Pack*

The Mobil Greensight Pack is rather more focused in its objectives. This pack is designed to support pupils who are producing their own 'Greensight' video film about the relationship between a local industry and its environment. This local focus is to be commended, and the video contained in the pack presents a thorough overview of the processes by which a television documentary is made, from investigating the jobs of researcher and sound engineer to portraying different types of camera shots. The handbook provides information on environmental problems and printed support sheets on video production techniques, as well as case studies of 'Greensight' productions made by schools who helped in the pilot phase of the project. While only a few schools have easy access to the technical equipment necessary to allow the use of this pack, it is certainly thorough and well designed and encourages high standards of excellence from pupils engaged in the task it sets.

Team Video is a company specialising in integrated video resource packs. Their productions are consistently good and they include four in a series entitled 'Choices for the Planet', which are worth mentioning here. Each takes the form of a series of short (typically one to six minutes) chunks of film footage, usually from a television documentary, often supplemented with specially shot material. These clips have been carefully chosen for their relevance to the theme and their ability to provide a stimulus or to highlight a particular point. Each is linked to one or more activity sheets (photocopiable) which are stored in a ring-binder. There is also guidance for the teacher.

Another pack with a single clear task is *The Greenhouse Effect* pack for Key Stage 3. A lively 30-minute video called 'Can Polar Bears Tread Water?' interweaves interviews with academics, farmers and politicians with maps, graphs, computer-generated weather sequences and news footage. The result is an attention-grabbing and thoughtful film, which is ably supported by a book of copyright-free pupil activities. These can be directed at classes of mixed ability with confidence. The pack also encourages pupils to consider action that can be taken to reduce the greenhouse effect, on both an individual and a global level.

Food Production and our Environment examines the choices involved in food production: the debate between chemical and organic farming is highlighted, as is the cash crop versus food crop argument. Perhaps inevitably, farming the rainforest also makes an appearance. Energy use in a developing country, acid rain and the woodfuel crisis are among the issues featured in *Energy and our Environment*. *Safari* examines the impact of tourism on the environment and people of Kenya, and *Pollution* looks at acid rain, industrial pollution and river ecosystems. These four video resource packs are thoughtfully put together and can greatly enrich the classroom if used sensibly. They also help to develop visual literacy and a critical awareness of the media of film and television.

Some brief mention needs also to be made in this section of other material worth considering. *The Decade of Destruction* is the story of the Amazonian rainforest during the 1980s. The video, which is derived from award-winning documentary material filmed by

Adrian Cowell and originally nationally broadcast on the ITV network, presents some powerful and stimulating images. Some film clips with sound effects but no voice-over are included and these provide scope for experimental classroom use. Copious classroom material is provided in booklets for Science, Geography, English and Media Studies. The material is good but its readability, style and presentation pitch it perhaps at too high a level ... and there is too much of it! The video, OHP transparencies and printed sheets contained in another resource called *Understanding our Environment* make for a truly multi-media pack. Designed for the 10–14 age range, this pack comes in a large ring-binder and is very comprehensive. Lastly, a number of useful slide-sets with cassette commentaries (also available on VHS video-tape) are produced by the International Centre for Conservation Education (ICCE).

> *The Global Environment* (The International Broadcasting Trust for BBC Schools Television)
> *Only One Earth* (WWF UK, 1988)
> *The Mobil Greensight Pack* (Living Earth/Green Alliance, 1992)
> *The Greenhouse Effect* (Hodder & Stoughton/WWF UK, 1990)
> *'Choices for the Planet': Food Production and our Environment, Energy and our Environment, Safari* and *Pollution*, Team Video
> *Decade of Destruction* (WWF UK/Central Television, 1992)
> *Understanding our Environment* (Du Pont/Conoco, 1992)

RESOURCES FOR TEACHERS AND GOVERNORS

Much of the multi-media material about environmental education designed for teachers derives from the World Wide Fund for Nature (WWF UK). *Greening the Staffroom* would make an ideal base around which to develop a staff development day at either secondary or primary level. It comes with a video cassette, activity sheets, background notes and materials designed for copying on to OHP transparencies. The pack presents its case forcefully and provides examples of how staffrooms can be 'greened' as well as a series of varied and

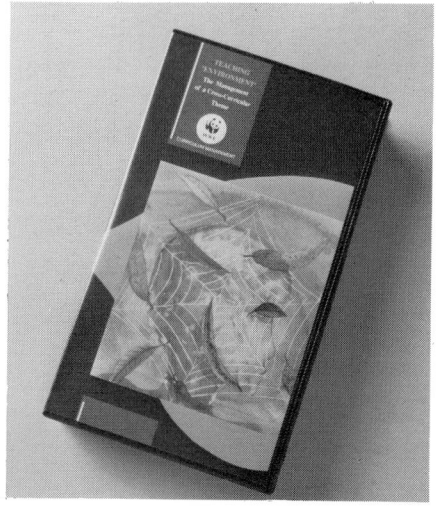

innovatory activities to allow teachers to reflect on environmental education in the widest sense. Every school taking environmental education seriously should have a copy of this pack and should build at least one staff development day around its contents.

Teaching Environment: The Management of A Cross-Curricular Theme argues for a whole-school approach to the topic and shows, through case studies from the Weald School in Billingshurst, snapshots of how environmental education can be developed as an integral part of learning in subjects as diverse as Technology, PE and Religious Education.

There are other videos available from WWF UK, and it is certainly worth writing for a copy of their resources catalogue.

> *Greening the Staffroom* (WWF UK/BBC Education, 1990)
> *Teaching Environment: The Management of A Cross-Curricular Theme* (WWF UK, 1991)

RESOURCES FOR ADULTS

Two resources in this category cater for adults with widely differing needs. First is *The Environment*, a basic skills pack aimed at those involved in developing adult literacy. The sheets in the pack detail a variety of clear and simple activities on major environmental topics like pollution, recycling and energy. Most sheets are designed to be photocopied by tutors and 'filled in'. The pack is selective in its coverage, but this is a strength rather than a weakness: many teachers will be put off by the size and scope of some of the other materials designed for use in the ordinary school classroom.

For students interested in studying the environment at degree level, the *Looking into the Environment* pack is one attempt to provide a home-learning package. With a three-hour video, well written text and activities booklet, a great deal of resource material is provided for would-be environmentalists.

The Environment (ALBSU, 1991)
Looking into the Environment (WWF UK/Open University, 1992)

CONCLUSION

The sheer quantity of available resources – across a variety of topics and for the whole age range – provides teachers with an unenviable job in selecting which, if any, to use. Considerations of how the topic or resource materials link to existing classroom work, how much teaching time will be needed (and can be afforded) to justify the acquisition of a particular teaching resource and how the work on the environment can be integrated into the curriculum must all come into play. A broad range of multi-media resources currently available have been included in this section: most are excellent in their intentions and packed with material. They certainly cannot be faulted on grounds of value for money. However, my major criticism is that many of them do make unrealistic demands on time in an already crowded curriculum. While environmental education can be regarded as an 'integrating' theme, which may help save time, this is not always easy when the material provided by publishers is so voluminous, and the responsibility falls on teachers to exercise their professional judgement about how to use the resources. Perhaps the best are those materials which act as a stimulus or springboard for further work and can be used in a variety of ways.

> *Vincent J Bunce is currently acting as Education Officer for Worldaware, an independent educational organisation concerned with world development education. Prior to this, he was a teacher of Geography to GCE A level in a South East London comprehensive school for ten years, an experienced Geography GCSE examiner and the author of a number of textbooks and articles. He now acts as consultant on the production of a variety of curriculum materials and is the examiner (University of Cambridge Examinations Syndicate) for the GCSE Syllabus in Natural Economy, which combines environment and development studies.*

Photographs for developing environmental education

THE ENVIRONMENTAL EDUCATION WORKING GROUP OF THE GEOGRAPHICAL ASSOCIATION

ASSESSMENT CRITERIA

A large number of locality-based photographs have been published by aid agencies, professional associations and other commercial publishers. These have proliferated since the introduction of the Geography National Curriculum at Key Stages 1, 2 and 3 in September 1991. Given the number of packs available, and the pressure on teacher time, teachers need to be able to select those photographs which will be of use to them. To do this, they need to ask the following questions:

- What values are implicit in the photographs?
- What sort of activities are encouraged by the teachers'/pupils' notes?
- What is the curricular context of the photographs?
- What themes are being developed?
- What is the nature of the teachers' notes?
- Are other resources/stimulus materials used or referred to?
- What is the quality of the photographs? How are they organised?

RESOURCES

The Geographical Association and Worldaware have produced *Focus on Castries – St Lucia*, a pack which is well targeted at Key Stages 1 and 2 Geography. Twenty-eight colour photographs are included, categorised into three sections. Teachers' notes outline an enquiry approach, which is appropriate to Geography, and include relevant black and white maps of different scales, as well as relevant statistical information. The notes then proceed to give each photograph an individual commentary. Additional activities are provided to

PHOTOGRAPHS FOR DEVELOPING ENVIRONMENTAL EDUCATION

develop further enquiries. The story of Castries is presented through a family – a technique which works effectively to keep the Geography people-centred, relevant and accessible to young learners. The photos are of high quality and represent a good mix of landscapes and close-ups of people.

Additional resources available to support this pack include: 1:50 000 OS map of St Lucia and 'Primary Geographer', No. 9, Spring 1992.

ACTIONAID's *Pampagrande* follows their highly successful pack, *Chembakolli*, and comprises 30 colour photos from this locality in Peru. The pack is organised into a series of booklets which provide background information about the locality and about Peru, some tasks based on the maps included, teachers' notes giving the curricular context (Key Stage 2 Geography), and some quotations from people using Bambamarca market (in the locality). The photos are of high quality and are organised into broad categories: landscape, family life, education, Bambamarca market and development. Photocopiable maps, diagrams and other resources are provided which, together with the teachers' guidance, give the backbone of

investigative tasks for learners. Such learning activities are not prescribed, encouraging teachers to 'customise' the resources for their own learning activities. Lists of further information sources are helpfully provided, and ACTIONAID are always careful to indicate what position these sources take on a given subject.

The Development Education Centre network has pioneered much effective work in visual literacy. *New Journeys* focuses on Kenya and Tanzania and adopts a cross-curricular approach for Key Stage 2. The approach adopted is to examine children's understanding of their own locality, suggesting ways to build on children's skills and firsthand experiences. Supporting materials are contained in a single booklet, which emphasises planning and stresses the importance of perceptions – Kenyans' perception of us in Britain – and includes a section on the problems of stereotypes. The pack is strong on staff development advice, highlighting approaches to teaching development issues. Its contribution to environmental education and to citizenship is very strong, and as such – perhaps more than many other photo-packs – it requires teachers to develop their own learning activities. The 24 photographs have been chosen to show a range of diverse lifestyles, which:

- children will be able to relate to;
- are issue-centred and not purely illustrative;
- can be used to illustrate several issues.

All resources have potential as agents of staff and curriculum development. These are typical of those produced by the Development Education Centre: they challenge assumptions, are provocative and seek to help clarify teachers' attitudes as well as to develop understanding.

Resources referred to in this review

Focus on Castries – St Lucia, V Bunce, J Foley, W Morgan, S Scoble, The Geographical Association and Worldaware, 1 Catton Street, London WC1R 4AB

Pampagrande, a Peruvian Village, ACTIONAID, 3 Church Street, Frome, Somerset EA11 1PW

New Journeys, Development Education Centre, Gillett Centre, 998 Bristol Road, Birmingham B29 6LE

Television, radio and video

MALCOLM WHITEHEAD

INTRODUCTION

Television is omnipresent. Over 90% of British, European, North American and Japanese households own or rent a television set. Even in communist China, the magic box is found in over one third of households.

The small screen is all things to all people. It is reactive, pro-active (witness the Live Aid and Comic Relief phenomena), an opinion-former, art form and a debilitating narcotic. We watch it, and ignore it, at our peril.

For millions of people, television provides their main source of information, awareness and entertainment. This review considers one area of television – natural history and environment programmes. It shows how these programmes can be incorporated into cross-curricular teaching on environmental education in primary and secondary schools by reviewing the educational resources associated with them. The review further describes the video resources available from three major conservation organisations.

Britain has always excelled in wildlife films. Celluloid ecology is a young genre, starting with the studio-based programmes of the 1950s and 60s (e.g. Granada's *Zoo Time* with Desmond Morris) and culminating with David Attenborough's superlative 'Life' trilogy (*Life on Earth*, *The Living Planet* and

Trials of Life). In addition to these landmark programmes, there has been a wealth of material from ITV (e.g. Anglia TV's award-winning *Survival*, Central TV's *Naturewatch*), Channel 4 (e.g. *Fragile Earth*) and the much-lauded BBC Natural History Unit. Wildlife and conservation programmes are also produced by BBC Education (Schools TV and Radio).

There is no shortage of material – quite the reverse – and most of it is superbly filmed and of the highest quality. The first challenge for any would-be explorer of the broadcasting jungle is to find out what is available.

FINDING OUT WHAT IS AVAILABLE

Monthly listings of natural history TV and radio programmes are published in the *BBC Wildlife* magazine which also features supporting articles about such programmes. You can video the programmes yourself or buy copies of the most popular ones (e.g. the 'Life' trilogy, various *Survival* programmes and National Geographics, etc.) from relevant department stores.

For a wider choice of environment and development films, consult the *Moving Pictures Bulletin* of the Television Trust for the Environment (TVE). TVE is a non-profit organisation established in 1984 by the United Nations Environment Programme (UNEP) and Central Television (UK) to promote environment, development, health and human rights issues through broadcast television around the world. It acts as a catalyst for new environmental productions and places particular emphasis on working with film makers from the economic south. TVE has co-produced over 10 programmes and has scooped all major broadcast awards at one time or another. It produces a catalogue of films available for distribution in developing countries.

BOOKLETS ACCOMPANYING TELEVISION PROGRAMMES

Many natural history programmes are augmented with booklets and/or full-scale books. Normally such literature is advertised after the credits of particular films. Booklets may be free or cost between one and three pounds. They provide good source material for teachers and secondary school pupils and are particularly useful for gleaning addresses of conservation organisations. Examples of recent booklets include: *Creature Comforts, Troubled Waters* and *Naturewatch – a way of life*.

Creature Comforts accompanies the 1992 series of *Fragile Earth* films which included 'Animal

Squad' (about the undercover activities of the RSPCA) and 'Listen to the Whales'. It details aspects of people's relationships with animals through myth, legend, conservation, exploration and science. The booklet is erudite, but might complement Humanities projects at Key Stages 3 and 4 of the National Curriculum. *Troubled Waters* is based on a 1991 series of *Fragile Earth* films about marine conservation. *Naturewatch – a way of life* accompanies Central TV's *Naturewatch*. It contains an extensive directory of conservation organisations.

EDUCATIONAL PACKAGES

One step beyond the film plus booklet is the educational package. Central Television produces a series of videos based on science, environmental and geography issues. *All Year Round* is a primary school programme supporting Attainment Levels 1–3 of National Curriculum Science. It comprises two video cassettes (thirteen and fifteen minutes respectively) dealing with the processes of life, life cycles, health education, Earth, atmosphere, space and sound.

Geography – Start Here and *Going Places* are Central TV's support material for Geography at Key Stages 1 and 2. Both explore the local environment and compare it with other places in the UK, France, Trinidad and India. *Geography – Start Here* is a single cassette of fourteen 15-minute programmes divided into three themes (about me, me and others, me and the world). *Going Places* develops the idea of similarities through differences and the uniqueness of local and remote places.

Many other videos and computer software packages for schools are available from Central TV, together with a range of documentary video programmes for school pupils and further, higher and adult education students. These include *Dead On Arrival* (world parrot trade), *Living after the Famine* (famine and aid issues in Ethiopia), *Pushed to the Edge* (wild plant conservation) and *We're All Green Now* (governments and the environment).

BBC Education provides extensive science, wildlife and environmental coverage for all levels of the pre-school, primary and secondary phases. Radio programmes like *Infant Science: See for Yourself* are linked to National Curriculum Science at Key Stage 1 and often tackle topics like animals, pets and mini-beasts. TV programmes like *Watch* (for ages 6–7) and *Zig-Zag* (for ages 8–10) regularly feature natural history topics like water, mini-beasts, flight and dinosaurs. *The Global Environment* (ages 11–14) and *Landmarks* (ages 10–12) cover programmes of study for National Curriculum Geography, History, Science and English.

All BBC Education programmes come with teachers' notes, booklets, and videos. Examples include: *Seashore*, a 45-minute video featuring three *Watch* programmes (rock pools, collecting things and sea birds). These programmes take a scientific approach, encouraging observation and the recording of results. Lots of ideas are provided for cross-curricular work.

An exciting new development from BBC Education is the video-plus series, based on *Zig-Zag* and *Landmark* programmes. Each video-plus package contains a video, teachers' notes, BBC fact-finder book and wall chart. Titles include *Water* (which contains six *Zig-Zag* programmes) and *Rainforest* (which contains four *Landmark* programmes).

The Global Environment is a new BBC video for primary and middle schools. With a running time of 200 minutes, the cassette contains ten programmes and documents key environ-

mental issues, including supercities (Asia), farming (Nepal, Kenya, USA), pollution (Canada, Mexico City), waste (New York), fossil fuels (France, Sweden) and rainforests (Peru).

The BBC recognises the vital role of environmental education within the whole curriculum. Accordingly, it has produced a teacher education video pack in collaboration with the World Wide Fund for Nature (WWF UK). The 30-minute *Greening the Classroom* video contains diverse imagery of environmental beauty and destruction. The video features talking heads and examples of innovative primary and secondary classroom practice, and it is accompanied by a staff development file.

VIDEOS FROM ENVIRONMENTAL ORGANISATIONS

Outside televisual services, a profusion of films and videos are available from many environmental organisations. The best source for videos about curricular management and

 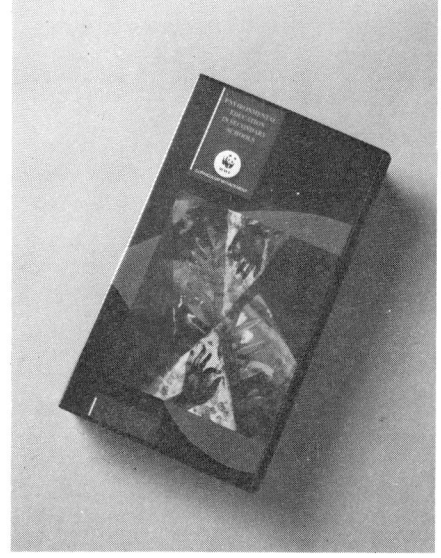

teacher education is WWF UK. They produce two 30-minute videos entitled *Environmental Education in Primary Schools* and *Environmental Education in Secondary Schools*. Both give practical guidelines and ideas for environmental education which are linked closely to National Curriculum attainment targets. Other relevant videos from WWF UK include *Environmental Education – Why Bother?* and *Teaching 'Environment' – The Management of a Cross-Curricular Theme*.

For secondary schools, WWF UK produce an innovative *Stimulus Video Pack* using silent clips to explore environmental issues. Sections focus on Amazonian rainforest, Britain's motorways, Californian irrigation, pesticides and acid rain in Europe. The 35-minute video contains three five-minute clips from Central TV and TVE. It is suitable for Key Stages 3, 4 and GCSE and comes with extensive support material focusing on National Curriculum Science, English and Geography and the cross-curricular themes of economic and industrial understanding and environmental education.

WWF UK and Central TV produce a video pack entitled *The Decade of Destruction*. Suitable for Key Stage 3, it features a 60-minute overview video of Amazonian rainforest issues in the 1980s. Four booklets – Media Studies, English, Science and Geography – contain teachers' notes and photocopiable pupil materials.

The International Centre for Conservation Education (ICCE) produces an extensive range of slide packs (some with optional audio cassettes) about environmental issues. These are suitable for Key Stages 3 and 4 and include titles about pollution, marine conservation, farming and conservation, renewable energy, acid rain and tropical forests.

ICCE has three flexible teaching packages for primary schools: *Wildlife in Danger*, *It's Your World – Don't Waste It* and *British Wildlife in Danger*. Each consists of 20–40 excellent colour slides, work cards, and teacher booklets geared to Science and Geography programmes of study at Key Stages 1 and 2.

One of the most established sources of wildlife films and videos for sale and hire is the Royal Society for the Protection of Birds (RSPB). Among their vast array of titles are a number of educational releases, each featuring three 10- to 15-minute films (for example, *All About Nests*, *Plumes to Peregrines* and *High Life of the Rook*). A training video for primary teachers (*Wake up to Birds*) shows how birds can be used to teach Science, English and Mathematics.

Television and video resources from the main television companies and environmental organisations are extremely professional in film-making skills, links made to curricula and support materials. We are spoilt for choice. The main areas of omission are programmes that teach pupils to examine critically the programmes themselves and the cultural

LIVING EARTH: A RESOURCE FOR LEARNING

Work cards from *It's Your World – Don't Waste It*

Slide from *Wildlife in Danger*

imperialism of television and that show how individuals and communities can make their own impact on the medium.

Resources referred to in this article

Magazines and booklets

BBC Wildlife magazine (from newsagents)

Moving Pictures Bulletin from:
Television Trust for the Environment (TVE)
46 Charlotte Street
London W1P 1LX
Tel: 071 637 4602
(The videos in the catalogue cost £15 in 1992, but there may be concessions if you write an explanatory letter confirming that you have access to a video recorder and stating your intended use of the tapes.)

Creature Comforts and *Troubled Waters* (both £3.00 – cheques payable to Channel 4 Television) are available from:
Creature Comforts/Troubled Waters
PO Box 4000
London W3 6XJ
Information on both booklets is available from:
Broadcasting Support Services
Channel 4 Television
60 Charlotte Street
London W1P 2AX

Naturewatch – a way of life is available free of charge from:
The External Affairs Department

68

Central Broadcasting Ltd
Broad Street
Birmingham B1 2JP

Central Television materials
All Year Round (two cassettes, each £40 plus £2 postage and packing + VAT, or the two together for £70 plus £2 postage and packing + VAT – teachers' notes, £2.95)
Geography – Start Here (£50 plus £2 postage and packing + VAT – teachers' booklet, £3.95)
Going Places (two cassettes, £50 plus £2 postage and packing + VAT – teachers' notes, £3)
Dead On Arrival, Living after the Famine, Pushed to the Edge and *We're All Green Now* (between £20–£25 plus £2 postage and packing +VAT)
Science, Environmental Issues and Geography catalogue
All available from:
Central Video Resources Unit
Central TV plc
Central House
Broad Street
Birmingham B1 2JP
Tel: 021 643 9898

BBC materials
Seashore (45-minute video, £29.99 incl. VAT)
Water (120-minute video containing six *Zig-Zag* programmes, £34.99 incl. VAT) and *Rainforest* (80-minute video containing four *Landmarks* programmes, £34.99 incl. VAT)
The Global Environment (200-minute video, teachers' booklet, £51 incl. VAT)
BBC Education resource catalogues and annual programmes listings
All available from:
BBC Education Information Unit
White City
London W12 7TS
Tel: 081 746 1111 (24-hour answering service)

World Wide Fund for Nature materials
Greening the Classroom (£28.99 incl. VAT and postage and packing – cheques payable to WWF UK) available from:
World Wide Fund for Nature
PO Box 963
Slough
Berkshire
SL2 3RS
Tel: 0753 643104

Environmental Education in Primary Schools and *Environmental Education in Secondary Schools* (videos, £6.95, synopsis videos, £6.25 and BBC-produced supporting booklets, £1.50)
Environmental Education – Why Bother? (ten minutes, £6.25)
Teaching 'Environment' – The Management of a Cross-Curricular Theme (20 minutes, £6.95)
Stimulus Video Pack (£19.95)
The Decade of Destruction (£24.99)
All available from:
WWF UK
Publishing Unit
Panda House
Weyside Park
Godalming
Surrey GU7 1XR
Tel: 0483 426444

The International Centre for Conservation Education (ICCE) materials
Slide packs for Key Stages 3 and 4 (available on VHS video at £16.95)
Wildlife in Danger (20–40 colour slides, work cards and teacher booklets, £14.95)
It's Your World – Don't Waste It (20–40 colour slides, work cards and teacher booklets, £15.95)
British Wildlife in Danger (20–40 colour slides, work cards and teacher booklets, £17.95)
All available from:
Department LEC 9
The International Centre for Conservation Education (ICCE)
Greenfields House
Guiting Power
Cheltenham
Gloucestershire GL54 5TZ

Royal Society for the Protection of Birds (RSPB) materials
All About Nests, Plumes to Peregrines and *High Life of the Rook* (all £10.25)
Wake up to Birds (22 minutes, £5.25)
All available from:
RSPB Film and Video Unit
The Lodge
Sandy
Bedfordshire SG19 2DL
Tel: 0767 680551

NB: New materials are being produced all the time, and most of the booklets accompanying programmes are subject to availability (many are never reprinted). However, most television companies will retain copies of past booklets, which they will be prepared to make available even if in photocopied form.

Malcolm Whitehead was Director of Education at Twycross Zoo, Leicestershire and is currently Training Director (Programmes) with the International Centre for Conservation Education. He is a zoologist and a member of the British Zoo Federation Education Committee. He is the author of the Naturewatch *booklet mentioned in this article.*

The answer is in the mix

JOHN D ROGERS

INTRODUCTION

When it was first launched, video appeared to be the ultimate teaching tool, the answer to every teacher's prayers. Years later, this initial enthusiasm has become dulled. There are clear reasons for this: the sheer abundance of video material has led to everyone becoming satiated with the form, and its impact has been dulled; video programmes that do not deal with the subject rigorously are switched off as readily as television programmes; the length of the average programme does not always dovetail into the slots available in the school day; the price is high; the machines needed were expensive initially, and they were temperamental; videos do not stand maltreatment and soon become tired, both literally and in terms of content; few educational establishments have the sophistication of a video cassette recorder which allows perusal of specified sections of a particular programme with ease. The fundamental problem with all audio-visual material is that of applicability.

I have found the most effective way to use audio-visual material at any level to be the skilful manipulation of available media. It is not necessarily the individual materials used in the mix – whether these are audio tapes, slides, segments of videos, numerous props (birds' nests, Perrier bottles, soup cans, holiday brochures, breathtaking pictures of the High Andes, soya plants), sympathetic blown-up pictures, or a useful selection of books – it is the way in which they are combined. The success of an audio-visual presentation ultimately depends on the individual's skill in manipulating the strands effectively – it is amazing what can be done with 36 slides and the contents of a junior school's playground bins!

If the school grounds can be used, so much the better, especially if the school has built up an in-house video library of its own environmental activities. Such use of in-house products and productions cannot be overvalued. Increasingly, schools have sophisticated video cameras and editing possibilities which make imaginative project work possible and which reinforce the idea of 'thinking globally, acting locally': it is all too easy with the all-glossy video productions to forget the harsh, unsanitary realities just outside the gates (or even within).

An invaluable visual resource to be used to emphasise and highlight screen productions is a good and comprehensive set of newspaper/press clippings from local and national papers. Parents will often contribute, and a willing school librarian (if available) can help to organise such resources efficiently. Often these extracts provide good up-to-the-minute supplements to other material. This is one way of avoiding the problem of audio-visual resources becoming quickly out of date, a problem which can otherwise only be resolved by specifically selecting resources with an eye to their shelf life.

RADIO AND TV

Programmes specifically made for schools and colleges are useful basics. Most schools use such broadcasts and are well aware of the material available. A good tape and video library in a secure store is of great use (don't forget to keep duplicate copies). Great emphasis needs to be placed on ease of retrieval from the outset – so many schools I have visited have a mountain of half-recorded video tapes, and no idea of their contents. As the programme details are available well in advance, recording or 'live' use in the classroom can be planned. The broadcasters' listings give guidance for 'age', 'ability', 'attainment target range', but a key point with all audio-visual material is that it can be made to be relatively universal by skilful use of specific sections, or a mixing of themes – which also helps dilute high costs of playback and production. (Schools will need to check whether they need permission to record off-air broadcasts, if they do not have already have an agreement.) Do not forget the fact that relatively few young people listen to speech radio – the novelty factor is useful.

Many one-off programmes or special weeks (such as One World Week) are worth recording for the many pearls they may provide for later editing and use. Well-known series (such as the David Attenborough 'Life' series), while undoubtedly of value – and, frequently, available for separate purchase – will have been seen by a significant minority of children beforehand. Increasingly, there are spin-off pre-recorded videos from all TV production companies (and other sources). Before introducing such programmes into the classroom, however, it is important to consider carefully the real use such programmes will present, especially given the inevitable repeat showings on terrestrial/cable/satellite channels.

SLIDE PACKS

Slide packs were the audio-visual tool of the 1960s and 70s and are becoming popular again, as teachers realise their considerable flexibility. It is easy to use a selection of frames from half a dozen sets and achieve precisely the result sought. Slides tend to have a longer shelf life and are suitably robust, as well as easily copied (again, check copyright, however). Local libraries, LEA school services, church groups, and local/national environmental organisations often have slide sets for hire or loan. Additionally, sets may be researched from the catalogues of production companies like the excellent International Centre for Conservation Education, Oxfam, RSPB, or the World Wide Fund for Nature. A general catalogue

LIVING EARTH: A RESOURCE FOR LEARNING

from *Acid Rain: The Silent Crisis*

from *No Trees ... No Life*

such as that issued by Concord Films Council is particularly useful for fairly definitive listings of audio-visual material.

Among the noteworthy slide sets is *Acid Rain: The Silent Crisis*. Though produced in 1985, the images and overview are good as introductory material. So often, children know the environmental phrases, but do not really understand what they mean. This type of no-nonsense presentation fills in the blanks. Similarly, educational audio visuals such as *Heating Up The Earth: The Greenhouse Effect* by Walters and Barrett is an extremely useful and accessible pack.

Another very stimulating production of the 1980s which is still sought out is the World Wide Fund and International Union for the Conservation of Nature's (WWF/IUCN) *A Green Earth ... or a Dry Desert*. Available from the International Centre for Conservation Education (ICCE) (with or without a commentary on cassette), its 80 frames present vivid images of tropical deforestation on a global scale. An updated (1992) schools version, *No Trees ... No Life*, is also available. *Making Peace with the Planet* is a meditative approach to the environment produced by the Methodist Church (Division of Social Responsibility) and ICCE. Its 40 frames trigger a deep response, especially from older secondary pupils. Mary Glasgow's *Ways of Life* offers an exploratory journey from the Equator to the Poles, investigating the idea of habitat linked to global climate and allied environment. ICCE's *Wildlife in Danger* is a very general approach in 40 frames, which may easily be adapted for use with younger children and provides a good starting point for relatively unsophisticated appreciation.

All these slide sets may be easily adapted, with a certain amount of skill and imagination, to suit the 9–18 age range and would prove to have a long shelf life. I have also used these items with groups younger and older than this range and have still found them a good basic introduction to a useful series of sessions. The cassettes are of much more limited use: in general, they are merely guides to the series as a whole and rely on each frame in consecutive order.

With about 30 good slide sets, plus sensible back-up and presentation, it is easy to cover all the key environmental themes – while providing links to others along the way – and to vary the approach from basic to intensive study.

SOME NOTEWORTHY VIDEOS

Threshold of Change is a 56-minute video which features Jonathan Porritt outlining his ecological philosophy: it is useful for older groups or for 'green awareness days' and is best used in its entirety. *The Water Connection* is a 20-minute Overseas Development

Administration (ODA) production. Used in its entirety, it is a graphic illustration of the problems of developing countries, particularly emphasising the importance of clean water supply – it uses Kenya and Sudan as examples. It is amazingly effective, even with 11 year olds, but it does require good back-up for maximum effect. *When The Bough Breaks* is a Central TV documentary, first shown on late-night television, of global conflicts between the environment and human society. The documentary was not widely seen when first broadcast and is a stimulating centrepiece for workshop/day activities at the older end of the spectrum; it is also good with adult groups. *Grounds for Change* is an excellent production from Hampshire County Council outlining the potential for using school grounds in environmental education: it is ideal for use with teachers, governors and parents as evidence of the possibilities and will convert even the most sceptical. *Greening the Staffroom* is a WWF production in the same vein as *Grounds for Change*, although possibly appealing to a more committed audience. It presents a complete programme for staff development – and can be off-putting – but it is easy to adapt to every school's needs and repays perseverance. *Stimulus Video Project* is another WWF offering by Ken Webster. It covers a wide range of issues from motorways to rainforests, using short TV documentary extracts and good pupil back-up resources. The pack is effective even with jaundiced 15 year olds, as the pace forces interest, but it requires skilful and breezy presentation if it is to be used to maximum effect.

CONCLUSION

However useful audio-visual material is, it is almost impossible to find a good tailor-made programme for practically any eventuality or theme. Mixed presentations are extremely successful but require an amount of experiment and imagination. It is difficult to define which material is suitable for which age group, because the same material can be used with several ability or age groups: it is the presenter who defines the boundaries. Well-structured presentations are the trigger for successful project work, and mixed-media presentations can certainly raise the consciousness of the jaundiced and quell the unruly – provided you are sure of your own ground first. In turn, in-house projects can enhance the next presentation and help to swell a school's stock of resources. Externally produced materials are good – any of the products mentioned in this review are worthy of consideration – but it is the in-house input which makes them truly special.

Resources referred to in this article

TV programmes (recommended, but not specifically mentioned above)
BBC: *Thinkabout Science, The Geography Programme, Search Out Science, Global Environment, Scene, Tomorrow's World, Horizon, Animal Country* and *Country File*

Channel Four: *Junior Geography, Science – Start Here, Science in Focus, IT Across the Curriculum*

Radio programmes (recommended, but not specifically mentioned above)
BBC Radio: *Topic Resources 5–7, English 9–11* and *Something to Think*

About, The Natural History Programme, Costing the Earth, Science Now and *The Living World*

Slide sets

Acid Rain: The Silent Crisis (40 frames, plus 19-minute cassette), Nigel Dudley, ICCE, 1985

Heating Up The Earth: The Greenhouse Effect, Bob Walters and Neil Barrett, EAV, 1985 (60 frames, plus cassette)

A Green Earth . . . Or A Dry Desert, WWF/IUCN AVP (80 frames, plus cassette)

Making Peace With The Planet, DSR/ICCE, 1988 (40 frames)

Ways of Life, Mary Glasgow (84 frames, plus 17-minute cassette)

Wildlife in Danger, ICCE/British Airways, 1989 (40 frames)

Video materials

Threshold of Change, Jonathan Porritt, Iota Pictures, 1987 (56-minute video cassette)

The Water Connection, ODA, VISCOM, 1988 (20-minute video cassette)

When The Bough Breaks, The Observer/Central TV, 1990 (55-minute video cassette)

Grounds for Change, Jane Young, Hampshire County Council/Portsmouth Productions, 1991

Greening the Staffroom, Graham Pike and David Selby, WWF/CGE/BBC Education, 1990 (30-minute video cassette included)

Stimulus Video Project, Ken Webster, WWF, 1991

John Rogers was until June 1991 the Librarian of The Conservation Trust in Reading, where he was responsible for maintaining the vast Resource Bank of information, as well as producing the summaries of material for inclusion in the Guide To Resources in Environmental Education. *Additionally, he advised many teachers, industrialists, and group leaders on environmental teaching material, courses and information provision, as well as initiating events along the lines of environmental empowerment. He is now an independent author and advisor.*

Wall charts and posters

JANE INGLIS

Children in school spend so much time surrounded by four walls that we do well to use that space to communicate. Posters and wall charts do this very effectively and offer enormous scope for educational use. Their value depends largely on how they are used. Posters that are on display for too long tend to be ignored. Commercial posters advertising past events are a real turn-off, and materials in school should not be left up to become dog-eared and out of date.

Posters and wall charts do, however, pose certain problems. For example, some publishers, eager to use every inch to full advantage, print on both sides of wall charts. If you have a glass door, this may not pose a problem; if you don't, the best solution is to photocopy one side of the chart and display it next to the other.

The World Wide Fund for Nature has been producing wall charts for many years. One of the first series, still available, was on *Resources* (see over). There are five well-designed charts (*Soil*, *Pollution*, *Wild Plants and Animals*, *Waste* and *Energy*), each with a great deal of information presented in blocks of text interspersed with coloured pictures, maps and diagrams. Each poster has copious black and white 'additional notes' on the reverse side which can be photocopied before the poster is put up. Users still have the problem of what to do with this material: is it aimed at pupils or teachers, and how should it be displayed? Sometimes publishers anticipate this problem and produce the notes in the form of a separate teacher booklet. WWF's later series, *Natural Regions of the World* (see over), has adopted this solution. The most important information, and the big questions looming over the future of our natural regions, are presented by means of colourful pictures, photographs and maps supported by text. A 37-page book of teachers' notes goes into much greater detail and provides suggestions for project work. The six topics covered are *Jungles*, *Wetlands*, *Deserts*, *Oceans*, *Mountains* and *Plains*.

WWF's most recent series is entitled *Environmental Impact 2000*. Ten colourful wall charts cover a range of themes including *The Energy Crisis*, *Water Resources* and *The Atmosphere at Risk*. There is a 31-page teacher guide. It is interesting that there is slightly less text on these charts than in the series on natural regions. I suspect that the education department at WWF has come to the conclusion, after years of experience, that it is counterproductive to load one chart with too many words, or to pack the column inches too densely: text must be rigorously edited and every word must pay its way if the medium is to be used to the best advantage.

In the *Environmental Impact 2000* series there is nothing on the reverse side. Colour, photographs, diagrams, cartoons, maps, charts, and graphs are all used to illustrate the text. This is designed for interactive use, with questions for debate based on the information on each chart. Visually these charts are stunning: they attract the eye from the other side of a room and draw the reader towards them. Clare Shorter's teacher guide is the best presentation I have seen of how this medium can be used with a class. It explains how secondary pupils of different ages could use the charts and suggests a dozen or more class activities associated with each poster. Most stimulating is a diagram showing 'educational objectives of wall charts'. Subject areas, key concepts, attitudes and skills are set out: there are far more on each list than I would have anticipated, especially the skills list, which has 20 items from 'analyse data' to 'suggest solutions'. Each stands up to detailed examination.

A poster in WWF's *Environmental Impact 2000* series

LIVING EARTH: A RESOURCE FOR LEARNING

So wall charts are not for just covering blotches and eyesores around the classroom. Initial impact contributes crucially to the success of a poster. Vying with the might of the advertising industry, educational posters have had to reflect current style and design. This means that they are more conspicuously quick to date than book jackets, and presentation has to be up to the minute, intelligent and professional if the wall space is to grab passers-by. The British Gas series on *Key Environmental Issues* seems curiously blind to this need. Uniformly designed, they present each issue in a long and wordy headline, under which is a black and white photograph surrounded by five columns of text which give the views of an independent expert on such topics as traffic in cities, secrecy over discharge into rivers, and how governments should go about safeguarding the environment. The series makes interesting reading, but it completely fails to justify presentation in poster form. I cannot imagine any school giving wall space to such a visual catastrophe; the material would be much more useful in book form.

But some charts succeed in presenting a huge amount of information. Shell Education Service's *Learning from Fossils* is an excellent example of the medium at its best. Anyone studying fossils needs a chart showing the geological ages, and a large flat surface lends itself to this better than one page of a book. In this wall chart, a huge central pillar rises from the pre-Cambrian age, 4550 million years ago, through the ages up to the tiny slice occupied by mankind. Pictures, photos and explanatory text surround the time scale. A colleague who teaches Geography commented that the material would be useful at sixth form and university level. The same applies to two posters by John Gribbin published by the New Scientist: *The Hole in the Ozone Screen* and *The Greenhouse Effect*. Both use a great deal of text and a restrained visual style, while still catching the eye. The poster is a good vehicle for pictures such as a south polar plot using 'false colour' images built up of data from weather satellites and showing the area of worst ozone depletion as a dark hole the size of the USA and Mexico. This needs to be studied at length, but it also has instant impact. Another

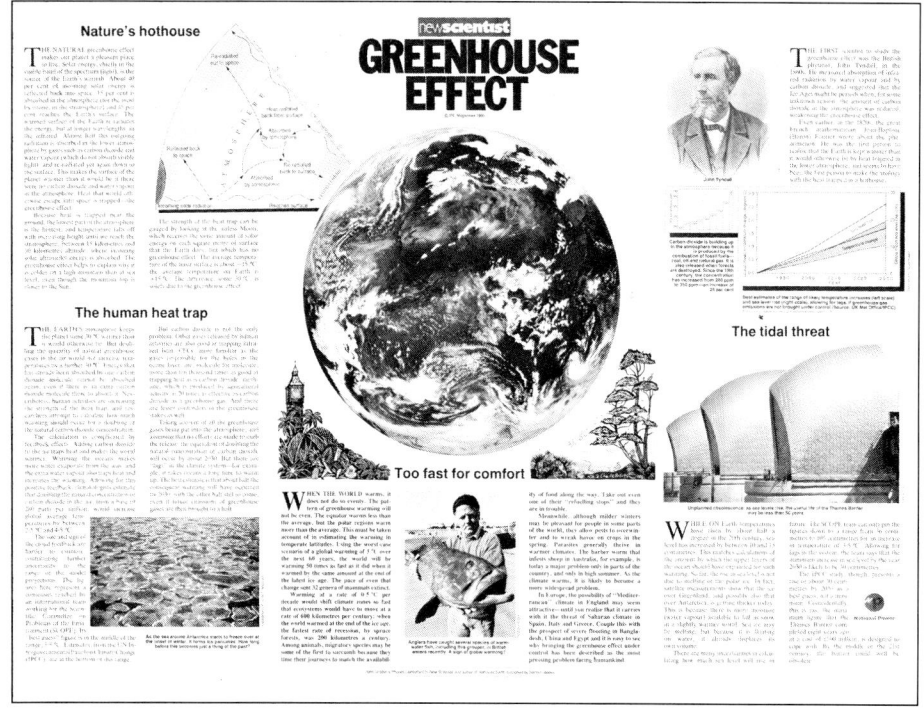

striking success for the poster format is WWF's *Earth at Night*. White blotches on a black background reveal the outlines of the continents, transport features such as the trans-Siberian railway, and controlled fires clearing forest or grassland. A brief but concise explanatory text in one corner lists the main sources of this 'light leakage' and describes how the data was assembled by different kinds of photography from space.

Similar themes get a very different treatment for a different age group in a series produced by Friends of the Earth for primary schools. Titles include *The Ozone Layer*, *Hidden Hazards in the Home*, *Global Warming*, *The Cycle of Water Pollution* and a jolly one on *How to Make a Robot Recycler* (for storing paper, etc.) out of a cardboard box. These posters are all in cartoon style, colourful and printed on 100% recycled paper. *The Ozone Layer* uses a particularly neat idea to communicate the links between our homes and space: a kind of 'tunnel in the sky' rises from one metre above the ground (showing a family at home among their foam-filled cushions, their fridges and freezers), up through the ozone layer and successive spheres into outer space. Some themes actually benefit from presentation in poster rather than book form, especially at a simple level. Cycles like that of water are complex but unified, and a large flat surface enables an artist to represent the whole concept while a writer can annotate it appropriately.

The same can be said of another New Scientist poster, *The Tree*. This too is drawn in cartoon style. The drawing of the tree fills most of the space; scattered on it are rectangles of text with smaller pictures and text about the tree's natural history and main uses, while a delightful border contains dozens of smaller boxes with drawings depicting the myriad tree products. This manages to say something from a considerable distance and to add more the closer you get to it. Children will probably spend long periods studying the border in detail, and the poster communicates a large part of its message in pictures rather than words.

LIVING EARTH: A RESOURCE FOR LEARNING

The amount of information presented varies from the poster with a brief message (the fewer words, the more it depends on visual impact) to complex charts with hundreds, even thousands, of words of text. Some effective brief messages include a poster advertising the Prince Michael Road Safety Awards (*You Can't Be Recycled: Stay Green, Use The X* – a green cross – *Code*) and a devastating combination of photography and (brief) text in the Athene Trust's poster, *Modern Farming – Factory or Free Range?*: this contains two sets of images, juxtaposing animal Belsens with contented stock in fields.

Material may sometimes be presented in a series of posters which need to be used together. Shell Education Service produces an excellent series of eight posters on *The Oil Story*. These use a limited range of colours, short text and a rather crude and dated visual style, but they convey a great deal of information in assimilable form for upper primary and lower secondary pupils. They begin with the formation of oil and work through the worldwide distribution of oil fields, drilling methods and oil-based products. Perhaps it is asking too much, but nowhere are the drawbacks of oil exploration and transport examined and discussed.

Posters may well be used in conjunction with other resources. This approach has also been pioneered by WWF, who produce a series of resource packs for primary schools. *Oceans*, *Weather* and *Antarctica* are presented by means of photocopiable worksheets, teachers' notes and, in each case, a colourful poster which draws children's attention to the theme. The *Antarctica* poster could work on its own: it uses a brief text, one main colour photograph of striking beauty and a few smaller ones to present some carefully selected facts and questions about the last great wilderness.

Most of my teaching colleagues thought that wall charts had very limited usefulness because of the pressure on time and space. They also doubted that pupils would absorb information presented to them in this form. We agreed that an ideal use of posters could result from advance liaison between a well-resourced and well-staffed school library and a subject department. If a teacher is about to focus on a particular topic, the library would display posters and wall charts featuring additional material, and pupils would be referred to the library. In this situation, a poster on a wall would be similar in function to a reference book. Given a really well-designed poster (like the best of those mentioned in this review), an interesting lesson (in which the teacher refers to material on the poster) and the opportunity to study it and make notes (in the classroom or library), I am sure that many pupils would find this a really useful extra resource. Environmental themes, which cross traditional boundaries between subjects such as Science and Geography, lend themselves particularly to the library's cross-curricular approach. However, one problem for the librarian is dissemination of information about the library's collection of posters and wall charts since, when they are not on display, they are probably hidden away in a poster chest. At least one can browse along a shelf of books! Open display racks are obviously an improvement on chests, though they are more vulnerable. But an alert librarian will keep teaching staff up to date on what the walls have to offer their teaching programme.

We in schools have learned a lot recently from the world of commerce, not all of it willingly. Here is a medium which advertisers use to great effect and which is often undervalued in schools. Our messages may be more complex and subtle than those of commercial advertising, but we can perhaps take a tip or two on communication and display. Finally, we should not forget that we can also, at many different levels throughout the school age range, encourage children to make their own posters and put up the result.

Resources referred to in this article

From the WWF UK (for address, see pages 69 and 70)
Resources: Soil, Pollution, Wild Plants and Animals, Waste and *Energy*
Natural Regions of the World: Jungles, Wetlands, Deserts, Oceans, Mountains and *Plains*
Environmental Impact 2000: The Energy Crisis, Water Resources, The Atmosphere at Risk, Ocean Resources, Plant Resources, Soil Conservation, Land Use Systems, Towards a Sustainable Future, Population and Urbanisation and *Industry and Pollution*
Oceans, Weather and *Antarctica*
Earth at Night

From the Shell Education Service
Learning from Fossils
The Oil Story

From the New Scientist
The Hole in the Ozone Screen and *The Greenhouse Effect,* John Gribbin
The Tree

From other organisations
Key Environmental Issues, British Gas
The Ozone Layer, Hidden Hazards in the Home, Global Warming, The Cycle of Water Pollution and *How to Make a Robot Recycler,* Friends of the Earth
You Can't Be Recycled: Stay Green, Use The X Code, Prince Michael Road Safety Awards
Modern Farming – Factory or Free Range? Athene Trust

*Jane Inglis is librarian at Hillside School, Borehamwood, where her part-time commitment enables her to undertake a range of other activities. These include running 'Reading for Pleasure' groups in a suburban library and a psychiatric hospital, writing, publishing, reviewing and teaching (French and environmental awareness). Her publications include a children's book about vegetarianism (*Some People Don't Eat Meat, *Oakroyd Press, 1987) and two books on food for Wayland (*Fibre *and* Proteins, 1992).*

The Pictorial Charts Education Trust

THE ENVIRONMENTAL EDUCATION WORKING GROUP OF THE GEOGRAPHICAL ASSOCIATION

The Pictorial Charts Education Trust (PCET) claims to be 'visual education at its best'. While only teachers can judge the accuracy of that description, if the popularity of its environmental charts is the chief criterion for making such a claim, then it may well be justified.

PCET was established about 50 years ago. At that time, it produced a variety of statistical diagrams and visual images designed to help people learn about global issues: these became the educational wall charts, a medium in which PCET still excels,

and which have proved some of the most popular of the Trust's range. The environmental wall charts follow a common approach: each measures 70 × 100 cm and deals with one environmental issue or topic, presented through a number of very strong images which include illustrations, photographs and diagrams linked by short passages of explanatory text. The text is well researched and carefully written, and no words are wasted. The images and the text are large enough to read from a few feet away and so could be used by a small group doing research on the topic. The language is generally straightforward and easily understandable by pupils aged 11+. Accompanying each chart is a set of notes for the teacher. These have four pages of A4 size and include more detailed information on the topic and ideas on how the topic can be presented to a class group.

The charts do not take a campaigning approach and avoid being over-sensational. The aim is to present the issue as one which requires attention. The charts also show what is being done to try and resolve the problems they highlight. They usually contain suggestions about what the individual can do and stress the importance of personal responsibility. Overall, they present a balanced view of serious problems.

The following is a list of titles of most relevance to environmental education: all are currently priced at £6.65 + VAT.

Most appropriate for children in the last two years of junior school or the first two years of secondary (Key Stages 2 and 3)
T82 British Wildlife in Danger
Most appropriate for children in the last two years of junior school or the first two years of secondary (Key Stages 2 and 3)
T83 Farming and the environment
Aimed at nine to 14 year olds.
T69 Tropical Rainforests
Aimed at eight to 13 year olds.
T68 The Ozone Layer
Secondary

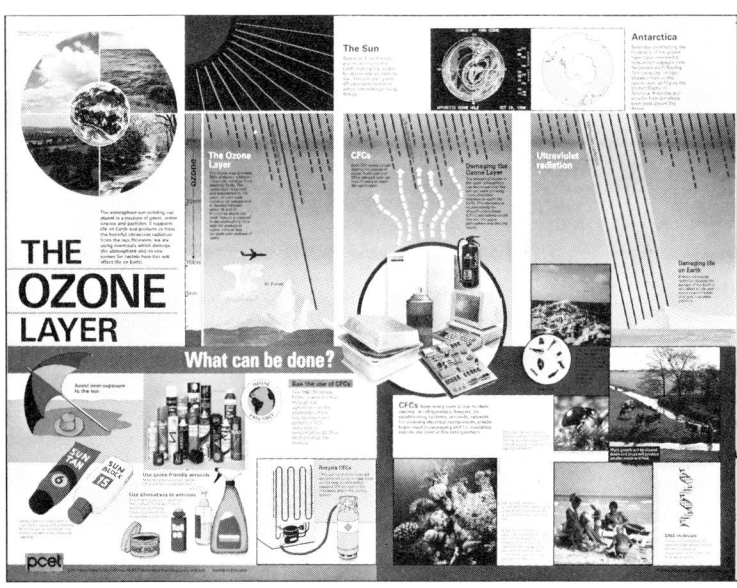

T59 The Greenhouse Effect
Secondary
T58 Acid Rain
Mainly secondary
T85 Conserving Energy
Key Stages 2 and 3
T56 Global Energy
Most appropriate for pupils in the last two years of junior school or the first two years of secondary (Key Stages 2 and 3)
T57 Recycling
The potential audience is wide, ranging from children of junior age through to adults – the subject matter is of undeniable universal relevance.

THE PICTORIAL CHARTS EDUCATION TRUST

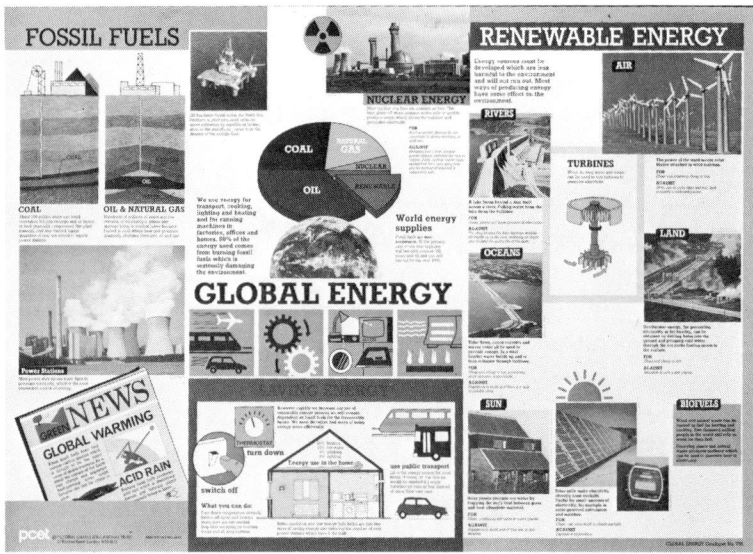

T60 Air Pollution
13–18 year olds, especially at GCSE Science and Environmental Studies courses
T61 Sea Pollution
13–18 year olds, especially at GCSE Science and Environmental Studies courses
T62 River Pollution
13–18 year olds, especially at GCSE Science and Environmental Studies courses
T63 Land Pollution
13–18 year olds, especially at GCSE Science and Environmental Studies courses

Catalogue available on request from:
Pictorial Charts Education Trust
27 Kirchen Road
London
W13 0UD
Tel : 081 567 9206

LIVING EARTH: A RESOURCE FOR LEARNING

FIELDWORK RESOURCES

The English Heritage Education Service

THE ENVIRONMENTAL EDUCATION WORKING GROUP OF THE GEOGRAPHICAL ASSOCIATION

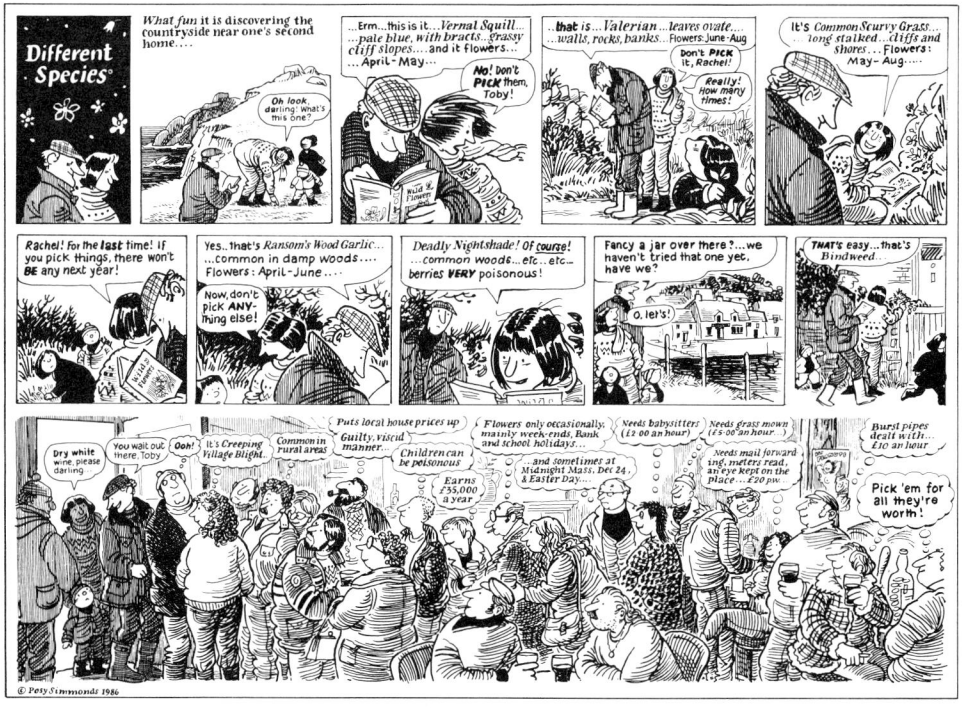

English Heritage is the main national body responsible for heritage conservation. It secures the preservation of the country's architectural and archaeological heritage and promotes knowledge about, and enjoyment of, the 350 sites in its care. English Heritage advises the Government on matters of conservation, listing and scheduling and is the major source of public funds for historic buildings, historic towns, ancient monuments and rescue archaeology.

The English Heritage Education Service aims to provide teachers with support in the form of courses, advice and resources. It also produces publications and videos which support fieldwork and demonstrate how visits to historic sites may support geographical and environmental education.

Information for Teachers, Teaching on Sites is a booklet which gives general advice about the education service and about making a site visit, offering a guide to English Heritage sites. The publication also provides booking advice to teachers of pupils of all ages.

The advice given on making a site visit is some of the best available and what makes this booklet really worthwhile. The advice is clear, and the guide does not hold back from telling teachers what to do and what not to do. For example, the first question it asks teachers to answer is to analyse their reasons for wanting to make a site visit in the first place.

The sections include: preparatory work teachers, pupils and helpers should do before the visit; the actual work they should do on site (this section has lots of ideas for activities beyond the worksheet); and follow-up work which avoids the mere account of the day of the 'who-I-sat-next-to-on-the-coach' variety. The booklet has a comprehensive list of all the sites in England, with a key which will help teachers with the period and nature of the site, region by region.

There are sure to be several sites near you. Use them: they are free, provided you book your visit in advance.

Teachers may not immediately turn to *A Teacher's Guide to Using Abbeys*, because they will not see it as fitting into Geography or environmental education. However, historic sites can make an interesting focus for geographical or environmental enquiry. Historic sites are places, left over from the past, which exist in the present. This means that when change – in the form of development – takes place in the area, the value and location of the historic site have to be given special consideration. The local authorities have a responsibility to plan for and control development; as part of their role, they work with English Heritage to manage the historic environment in the present and future. From an educational point of view, the starting point for an enquiry into an historic site may be to make an environmental assessment of the value it contributes to the community, a geographical analysis of the factors behind the site's location in the past and its relevance today, or an investigation into the impact of visitors on the locality of the site.

A Teacher's Guide to Using Abbeys is invaluable for interpreting abbey sites, which can vary from an outline plan in the foundations to a building still actively in use as an abbey. The booklet contains sections on the historical background and on understanding the site which include how to use source materials that might be available and information on the people who used the abbey. There is an excellent section on 'Preparing for the Visit', including activities for on-site work in the form of problems for pupils – such as how to design a café for visitors, or how to route a road to by-pass the site. There is also a section on relating the use of abbeys to the National Curriculum. Finally, there is an excellent bibliography and a guide to other resources.

The guide, written in an excellent, readable style, is informative rather than academic, and the approach taken is consistent with English Heritage's attitude to enquiry-based and investigative learning.

A Teacher's Guide to Using Listed Buildings is an excellent guide to undertaking geographical and environmental investigations with listed buildings as the focus. The introduction explains that local listed buildings link the present with the past and the future and fall within the first-hand experience of pupils. The investigation is rooted in the pupils' own environment, involving them in the history of their own area and in decisions which affect their own futures.

The booklet first explains the historical background to listed buildings and the process and controls that are involved in a building being 'listed'. The next section looks at the issues and asks the questions: What is conservation? Should conservation be enforced? What are the criteria for conservation? Who is interested? Who should decide? Where should the money come from? The following section involves pupils in the issues. As this section says, an issue-based approach to listed buildings will generate the need for further research, sharpen the focus and stimulate the involvement of pupils.

The material is, once again, linked to National Curriculum subjects, and there is a comprehensive bibliography and a guide to further resources.

Teaching On Site: History and Geography (see over) is a video for use in in-service and initial teacher-training for teachers of Key Stages 2 and 3 pupils. It shows teachers preparing ideas and materials and sorting out the practicalities for a visit with two classes to investigate Orford Castle and its surrounding landscape.

The video takes very much the same approach as *Information for Teachers, Teaching on Sites*, but offers a visual approach to the issues surrounding a site visit. One school, using the video in conjunction with the guidebook, devised an in-service activity that resulted in designing a policy statement and producing practical guidelines for the school on visits and fieldwork, to support History, Geography and environmental education.

As with the other publications mentioned, the philosophy is sound, focusing on an initial

examination of reasons for making the visit, the preparation for site work and the follow-up required to make the visit a worthwhile learning experience for pupils.

For further ideas on using historic towns and sites as the focus for an investigation into an environmental issue, see the article, 'Examining the future development of an historic town', in Section 2 of this book.

Resources referred to in this review

Information for Teachers, Teaching on Sites
A Teacher's Guide to Using Abbeys
A Teacher's Guide to Using Listed Buildings
Teaching On Site: History and Geography (video)

The English Heritage Education Service
Keysign House
429 Oxford Street
London W1R 2HD

Using zoos for educational purposes

MALCOLM WHITEHEAD

INTRODUCTION

Nature is a mosaic of species, habitats and situations which has always been affected to a greater or lesser extent by people. As we approach the twenty-first century, the 'nature' and 'wildlife' that previous generations took for granted are increasingly under threat from human behaviour; and yet it is human intervention – people acting individually and collectively – upon which the conservation of nature depends.

There are few pristine wild places left, and what 'wilderness' there is constitutes a broad spectrum, from protected areas to intensively managed populations of captive animals. Modern zoological gardens fall somewhere towards the latter end of the spectrum, although their functions and potential remain misunderstood or opposed by some. All sensitive, thinking people would campaign for the closure of bad zoos. Good ones, however, are getting steadily better and perceive their role as conservationists through captive breeding, education, scientific study and leisure. This is ex-situ conservation undertaken away from the wild, although it involves a growing number of projects linked to the field (there are, for example, over 100 animal re-introduction programmes currently in progress).

This article:

- describes the educational function of zoological gardens;
- examines the niche, aims and objectives of zoo education;
- details target audiences and subjects that might be taught/learned in zoos;
- explores the educational provision of member collections of the British Zoo Federation;
- offers hints to teachers planning a zoo visit.

USING ZOOS FOR EDUCATIONAL PURPOSES

WHY VISIT ZOOS?

Zoos are the only institutions to keep collections of living animals (often) from all over the world. In this sense, they are unique. Visitors can explore the fauna of Amazonia, Africa or Antarctica in a single day. 'You'd have to travel over 31,000 miles to see this in the wild,' proclaims an advertising brochure from New York's Bronx Zoo. Few people have the resources to do that, but most are able to visit a zoo. Worldwide, about one billion people – a fifth of humanity – do so each year.

Critics maintain that the experience is not educational, because zoos distort animal behaviour, present species in isolation (out of ecological context) and reflect the hegemony of mankind over other sentient beings. Advocates dispute this and, as evidence of the value of zoos, cite growing trends towards naturalistic enclosures, zoo geographical and habitat immersion displays, environmental enrichment (i.e. occupational therapy), improved husbandry, welfare and breeding results in progressive collections. They also value zoos as sources of real, first-hand experiences. The elephants *are* enormous. The gibbons defend their territories with ear-splitting whoops. Parrots preen, boas bask, meerkats forage and penguins really *do* smell of fish.

In Britain, over ten million people a year visit the 50 or so member collections of the British Zoo Federation. Such zoos aim to provide educational opportunities for all sectors of society. The provision may be informal (through guidebooks, graphics and events for the public) and/or formal (through structured programmes for primary and secondary school pupils, tertiary students, special needs classes, youth and adult groups). Almost one million school pupils receive structured education in Federation zoos each year.

ZOO EDUCATION DEPARTMENTS

Teachers wishing to avail themselves of such services should contact the education department of their local zoo. Depending on the size and resources of the collection, this department will be anything from a literature-only facility, one person probably doing a variety of jobs (e.g. keeper, marketing, education) to a full-blooded teacher's centre/school in the zoo. An education department should contain staff qualified and/or experienced in teaching biology and related subjects (e.g. psychology, art, etc.) and may offer teachers a free preliminary visit for planning purposes. Some zoos mount periodic or regular INSET courses, but generally it is best to check first with the individual zoo what it has to offer.

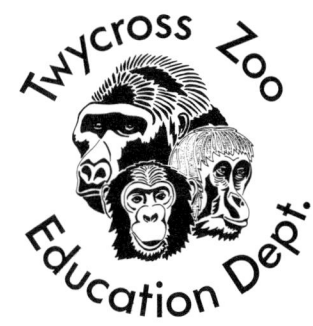

With imagination and skill, any subject, from art to zoology, can be taught in a zoological garden. Biology is the obvious choice, and a zoo visit introduces a dynamic extra dimension into the 'Life and Living Process' section of National Curriculum Science. This is true for Key Stages 1–4, GCSE and A level.

Take taxonomy, for example. At Key Stage 1, pupils might compare types of body covering (fur, feather or scale) by observing real animals and, in some collections, touching living or preserved specimens. Older groups might use this hands-on approach to examine vertebrate characteristics and construct keys to classify zoo animals. At the upper end of the secondary school, classification is shown to play a major role in elucidating evolutionary relationships and cataloguing biodiversity.

Life processes like feeding, locomotion, growth and reproduction come alive when, for example, children observe tigers and then handle tiger skulls – or when they note the sequence of limb movement in a galloping giraffe, the adaptation to heat gain and loss in reptiles and the parental care of scorpions, sea-lions or swans.

OTHER CURRICULAR POSSIBILITIES

If Biology is the bedrock of zoo education, there are many cross-curricular strata to be explored. How about Physics or Maths? School pupils could practise the skills of counting (how many legs/spots/animals, etc?), measuring (size of animals and enclosures), estimating (how heavy is an elephant?), tallying (counting the frequency of animal behaviours or measuring the popularity of different animal enclosures) and map reading in the zoo.

Some zoo study visits may combine a scientific approach (or eschew it) with other ways of looking at the world. Younger children could undertake 'Animal Olympics' sessions where they perform animal movements and adaptations in front of relevant enclosures (can your pupils knuckle-walk like gorillas or arm-swing like gibbons?). This not only reinforces the concepts of adaptation and ecological niche, but also uses physical education to develop co-

ordination and motor skills simultaneously. It is a short step from this to exploring the natural world through dance, drama, music, mime and role-play.

Zoological gardens offer a profusion of stimuli for aesthetic and creative work. Local art college foundation students and school pupils can draw or illustrate animals and familiarise themselves with problems of size, shape, symmetry, pattern and movement. Reference sketches might form the basis of graphics, models, collages, fine art or jewellery. Similarly, linguistic and social skills are enhanced by observing orangutans or ostriches. This will be the first time some pupils have ever seen such creatures, or even undertaken a peer group journey outside the school. The possibilities for language development, vocabulary enlargement, speaking, listening, creative writing and poetry are endless.

Researching animal habitats, ecology and behaviour could lead to work linked to the National Curriculum in Technology and Geography. Pupils might collect zoo data and design environments for animals and zoos. Where animals come from might provide a focus for Geography at Key Stages 1 and 2. Even History could be tackled – particularly areas associated with discovery, exploration, use of animals in different cultures and the architecture of older zoological gardens.

A zoo study visit may integrate several curriculum areas into one programme of study like rainforests or young animals, which may also include the cross-curricular themes of economic and environmental awareness. Economic awareness studies might be built around a financial analysis of the zoo operation and/or its role in the tourist industry. For older pupils, the economic value of wildlife and its use as a sustainable resource are applicable. Environmental awareness pervades all good zoo education programmes. Endangered species, global and local conservation, habitat destruction, animal rights and the role of the zoo in conservation are appropriate topics of study through zoo visits.

PLANNING THE VISIT

Having decided what to study, the teacher can plan a zoo education strategy with the local zoo. It is best to build into the visit plans for work to be done before and after the visit; education departments can advise teachers about how to organise this. Most collections produce a catalogue or list of literature that may be teacher- and/or pupil-based. This provides information, ideas for activities at school and in the zoo, pupil-based worksheets and references, contacts and glossary.

Some zoos provide self-help or total teaching packages. A number offer direct teaching sessions which vary from 30 minutes to two hours in length. Such sessions are adapted to suit a group's specific requirements in terms of age, ability and curriculum needs. They may take place in customised classrooms and/or outside in the zoo. This kind of zoo education often uses a multi-faceted approach, which may include some of the following elements, singly or in combination: lectures, slides/videos, question and answer sessions, hands-on specimens (live and/or museum), animal games and drama, art and craft workshops, zoo observations and so on. Done well, such sessions catalyse enthusiasm and motivate pupils by providing a series of biofacts and artefacts that will not be encountered at school or elsewhere.

Like a field trip, a zoo visit warrants data collection. What, how and when to record it depends on the age, ability and study programme of the pupils. For younger children, 'being an animal', talking about it, colouring and drawing might be appropriate. Pupils at Key Stages 2–4 can be given opportunities to collate, organise, analyse and interpret data. Worksheets with open questions or sketch pads may be used. Perhaps behavioural check sheets could be employed, or video, cameras, cassettes and computers. Some zoo education departments even produce computer databases.

At its best, zoo education satisfies all learning areas (aesthetic, linguistic, moral, scientific, technological, human and social, mathematical, physical and spiritual) and has the potential to convert awareness into action. It can be relevant, pro-active and affect attitudes about human impact on, and human responsibilities to, the planet. Good zoo education offers lasting, experiential and cost-effective ways of delivering the National Curriculum. It is *not* about treasure trails and disgruntled children slumping into coach seats with the plaintive cry of 'Oh no, do we *have* to write about it now?'

A list of zoos is obtainable from:

The Federation of Zoological Gardens of Great Britain and Ireland
Zoological Gardens
Regent's Park
London NW1 4RY
Tel: 071 586 0230

Malcolm Whitehead is Director of Education at Twycross Zoo, Leicestershire, a zoologist and a member of the British Zoo Federation Education Committee. He is the author of the Naturewatch *booklet mentioned in his article on 'TV, radio and video'.*

Tools and equipment

STEWART ANTHONY

INTRODUCTION

This article will consider the range and types of equipment which are most useful for fieldwork and identify equipment which represents good value for money and is durable. My aim is not so much to name and review specific pieces of equipment as to explore some of the criteria that you should bear in mind when selecting such equipment.

The range of equipment available for fieldwork is vast, and it is extremely difficult to select the equipment which will best suit your purposes. By and large, however, the two principles I have learned from bitter experience are:

- buy the best quality equipment you can afford (the best is not always the most expensive);
- buy metal and wooden products rather than plastic.

Before you buy any equipment it is important to consider the use to which it will be put. Some items (such as measuring tapes) can be shared with other departments in the school if they are only likely to be used two or three times a year. Alternatively, if measuring tapes are not going to be used more often than that, you might consider using rope and metre rules instead. As a general principle, there are cheap and effective home-made alternatives to nearly all pieces of equipment. Do your pupils *need* expensive and accurate equipment, or will they learn just as much from using cruder equipment? The answer is probably that simple equipment is often very acceptable – except that pupils may not respect it as much as they would a piece of 'proper', bought, purpose-made equipment.

ESSENTIAL ITEMS

Rubber gloves
These should be available to children during pond studies because of the risk of Weil's Disease – at Capel Manor, we use disposable 'surgeon's' gloves, but kitchen gloves would do very adequately – although rules of basic hygiene should be observed (i.e. always wash hands carefully after all pond work; make sure that children do not ingest pond water and that children with open cuts, etc. do not come into direct contact with such water).

First Aid kit
Even if you are just going to the far end of the school field, it is advisable to have one of these to hand.

SOME ESSENTIAL FIELDWORK EQUIPMENT

Pond nets
There is a wide range of pond nets, with interchangeable nets of different mesh sizes. Prices vary widely too, from about £10 to £40. For school use, the very fine mesh is a waste of money. Choose nets with a simple construction and a good strong net frame fixed securely to the handle. The best buys at present are nets by Griffin and George which have interchangeable handles and easy-to-change net bags. A good tip is to buy two or three spare net bags at a time and to encourage children to carry them upright with the 'net up' – otherwise it drags along the ground and tears the net.

Metre rules
There are advantages and disadvantages to both plastic or wood rules. On balance, plastic ones are preferable – but check that the markings don't fade, and encourage children not to use them as walking sticks.

Ground spikes
These are metal spikes about one foot long and are very useful for checking soil depths and fixing the ends of tapes.

Tapes
'Fibron' type tapes are good and very durable, but if they get wet or damp, make sure to dry them off thoroughly (on a radiator).

Quadrats
Personally, I prefer home-made quadrats made from 'netlon' wall support for climbing plants. These are available from garden centres, come in brown or white and are very inexpensive; they can be cut into pieces of about half a metre square (each half metre is about 10 squares by 10 squares). 'Netlon' wall support is very useful and long lasting.

Pond trays
Go to the local photographic shop and buy white 'developing trays' of different sizes – they are very suitable for pond work and studying leaf litter in woodlands.

TOOLS AND EQUIPMENT

Pooters
The small plastic ones made by Osmiroid are preferable.

Beating sheets
You can use old white sheets cut up into squares (about 1m x 1m) which can then be laid on the ground underneath trees.

Hand lenses
Plastic lenses scratch easily, but good glass ones are expensive and easily lost. At Capel Manor, if groups need this detailed study, we tend to bring samples into the centre and use a large stand magnifier or microscopes – the effect is much more impressive for younger children. We reserve good hand lenses for use by older students.

SOME LESS ESSENTIAL ITEMS

Light meters
These are often combined with moisture meters, and whilst we have found that these are good, they don't last long.

Electronic equipment
Electronic equipment is available for measuring oxygen, temperature, nitrogen, pH and various other physical features, and it can now be linked up to computer displays. My estimate for the minimum cost of such equipment is £100, and the cost can be much higher than this. The equipment undoubtedly has its place in work with older students, but you need to be clear of its overall value to your work. There is also the danger that overuse and over-reliance on such equipment (which produces easily obtained and detailed results) may obscure consideration of other ecological relationships which may be more important and relevant.

Plastic spoons
These are generally free and are very useful for pond studies and for getting animals on to the spoon for a closer look.

Petri dishes
These dishes are invaluable for a wide range of field studies.

Soil augers
The cork-screw type of soil auger is the most useful, but you will need to buy a broom handle to turn it. For most soil studies I prefer to use a small spade to dig a soil profile.

pH papers and distilled water
Both are very useful.

Thermometers
These are useful, but they keep breaking. At present there does not seem to be an obvious solution to this problem, although protected thermometers (e.g. soil thermometers) are available.

Suppliers

Where should you get equipment? There are two large suppliers of school scientific equipment (Griffin and George and Philip Harris). However, while their products are generally good, they are, I think, over-expensive: I would suggest that you look in their catalogues and then see if you can get or make the equipment at a cheaper price. Listed below are a few addresses, but very often a local supplier will provide equipment and service more suited to your needs.

Osmiroid Ltd
Fareham Road
Gosport
Hampshire
PO13 0AL
Tel: 0329 232345

Griffin and George
Bishop Meadow Road
Loughborough
Leicestershire
LE11 0RG
Tel: 0509 233344

Philip Harris
Lynn Lane
Shepstone
Lichfield
Staffordshire
NS14 0EE
Tel: 0543 480068

Stewart Anthony is the head of Environmental Education and Training at Capel Manor Horticultural and Environmental Centre, where he is responsible for environmental education work involving over 25,000 children each year. He has previously worked as a school teacher and as a lecturer at the Peak National Park Study Centre. During the 1980s, he was Regional Co-ordinator for The Institute for Earth Education. He has worked with residential, day visit and school and general public groups and has taught people of all ages from infants to undergraduates.

HUMAN RESOURCES

Using the local authority in environmental education

JULIAN AGYEMAN

INTRODUCTION

This article looks at the range of expertise gathered in the local authority. Until recently, many schools may have looked to their local education authority to provide guidance on the subject of environmental education. As in most curriculum areas, this would have been delivered through the involvement of an advisor or, more likely, an advisory teacher. With the 'reform' of local education authorities, however, such positions are in decline where they have not already died out completely. This might appear to increase the isolation of schools and force them to evolve their own position on environmental education without reference to any outside body; in fact, there are many aspects of a local authority which schools can still use to great effect in order to expand the frame of reference of its programme of environmental education. Before we consider these, however, we need to remind ourselves why it is a valuable exercise to move the issue of environmental education outside the school in the first place.

The local environment, and the communities who live in it, represent an extremely rich resource for environmental education at all key stages. It is a great advantage to focus on local issues – such as the closure of a popular bus route, pollution from a factory chimney or a community campaign to save a piece of ecologically valuable land – because these are intrinsically interesting and relevant to pupils in a way which classroom-based projects can seldom hope to be. Projects of this kind also move the subject of enquiry outside the classroom and involve pupils in the people and places of their immediate environment. The advantages of this approach are that such projects:

- offer pupils real opportunities for experiential learning;
- allow them to develop a local 'environmental literacy';
- engender an awareness of their environment and of their place and responsibilities within it.

In addition to these points, if pupils are further asked to follow the development of a local issue through press cuttings, committee reports, interviews and statements from interest groups, they will come to see the part the local authority plays in making decisions regarding most aspects of the quality of the environment. This gives them an important insight into the subject of local politics, while playing an important part in that area of their education which equips them for 'citizenship'.

WHAT RESOURCES DO LOCAL AUTHORITIES POSSESS?

Local authorities are perhaps the greatest local source of information about the local environment. It is they who are responsible, through an 'environment committee', for implementing most environmental policy, including the 1990 Environmental Protection Act. Not only do they contain *physical resources*, in the form of records, maps, plans, committee reports and other data related to local environmental management; they also house *human resources*, people with environmental skills who are often underused by educational establishments. The list of people who manage our local environments varies from authority to authority, but, typically, a county council, city council or London borough will have some of the following:

Officer	Role
Environmental health officer	pollution control, housing, restaurants, licensing, animals, health and safety
Planner	land use, development control, development planning, census, statistics, geographical information systems (GIS), conservation areas
Architect	design of buildings, contracts
Landscape designer	design of parks, open spaces, wildlife areas
Civil engineer	maintenance of structures, e.g. bridges
Arborist	maintenance of trees
Horticulturalist/parks officer	management of parks, floral displays
Ecologist/conservationist	promotion of the value of wildlife and nature conservation
Waste management/ recycling officer	promotion of sound methods of disposing of and reducing waste
Trading standards officer	promotion of sound (including 'green') consumer practice

These people tend to be very busy, but increasingly they see school work as being an important addition to their 'enforcement' or day-to-day activities. The theory is that, if you 'catch them young,' the population will develop a greater 'environmental literacy' and be more sympathetic to the role of the local authority as environmental manager and there will therefore be less need for enforcement.

Many fruitful, interesting and rewarding projects have taken place as a result of collaborations between teachers and the local authority and its officers: architects have worked with children to design houses for people with disabilities and the elderly; conservationists have created school nature areas and estate and community green spaces; recycling officers have developed school poster competitions; planners have helped children to replan their areas with children's needs in mind.

The list of possibilities is endless, constrained only by time and imagination. An added bonus of having a councillor or committee chair on your side is that you gain publicity in the local media.

CONTACTING YOUR LOCAL AUTHORITY

In order not to waste both your, and the council's, time – and as a way of developing mutually beneficial links with officers and/or their departments – the following code of practice may be useful:

1. Decide what skills are needed to help you in your project.
2. Decide which officer best fits this need (there may be more than one; use the list above).
3. Write to the chief officer/director, stating the day/time when you would want to see the officer, what you require of the person, any equipment you would like to see, the pupils' age and the topic area under study. Copy the letter to the school governors.
4. If there is no reply to your letter, follow it up with a phone call.
5. Once you have a named contact, arrange a meeting.
6. Be clear about what you need from the meeting and think about what information they require from you: what age are the pupils? how many are involved? are you wanting to visit a site? how many adults will supervise? are there any health and safety requirements related to your project/visit?
7. Prepare your pupils; both they and the officer must know what to expect.
8. Make sure that, on the visit, you do not leave the officer alone – she or he is unlikely to be a teacher, and a large group may appear daunting!
9. Thank the officer on behalf of the school and the pupils.
10. Ask the pupils to write a thank-you letter to the chief officer/director.

Some local authorities now have 'environmental co-ordinators', people who are responsible for developing and co-ordinating environmental matters (charters, policies, strategies) across departments. Their corporate role makes them useful contacts in terms of environmental projects, and they often have an educational/promotional remit in their job descriptions. Find out from your town hall if the local authority has an environmental co-ordinator. Alternatively, you can ask the environmental advisor at the Local Government Management Board (tel: 0582 451166). Remember, local authorities are the agencies which protect our local environment. Use them wisely, and you and your pupils will benefit from the co-operation.

Julian Agyeman is now a freelance environmental education advisor, having previously worked for many years as an advisor in two London boroughs.

Interview with Alan George, Unilever Plc

LIVING EARTH

The following piece is an edited extract of a much longer interview between Living Earth and the Education Liaison Manager at Unilever plc, Alan George. Given that this project itself has been an example of a company's involvement in the world of education (for a description of Unilever's sponsorship of *The Living Earth – a resource for learning*, see pages 2–3), it seemed logical to ask Unilever about the importance it attached to its links with schools.

LIVING EARTH: Could you briefly describe your role within Unilever?

ALAN GEORGE: I am Education Liaison Manager for Unilever, and I have a national brief which has two main strands. The first one is to help operating companies strengthen their links with schools and colleges locally within a broad policy framework. There are 25 companies in Unilever, with 40 sites between them, so there are 40 operations which relate to local communities and local schools – in addition to the company head offices – some of which produce materials for schools nationally. The second strand is to represent Unilever to national bodies concerned with educational policy. So I sit on a variety of education committees: the CBI (Confederation of British Industry), Employment Department, Engineering Council and so on, representing Unilever's interests in their discussions. I also have good contacts with the government departments concerned with education.

LIVING EARTH: Are you also involved with organisations like the NCC (the National Curriculum Council) and SEAC (the School Examinations and Assessment Council)?

ALAN GEORGE: Not directly. When it comes to representation to government, we prefer to work through the CBI. I'm on the CBI education policy panel, and it's a good channel through which to discuss and develop policy decisions. And I think it's better for the CBI to be the spokesperson rather than to have hundreds of companies trying to chip in.

LIVING EARTH: And what is the broad remit of your department, as far as schools and colleges are concerned?

ALAN GEORGE: Our method of working – we're a small department – is mainly to initiate national projects in association with appropriate partners. The partners may be publishers, they may be professional associations and so on, and these projects have to meet two requirements. The first is to meet Unilever's priorities for educational involvement. The second is to involve our companies wherever possible; indeed, many projects originate with companies themselves. In this programme, our first priority is to work with teachers. It's been our first priority for as long as I can remember. In terms of curriculum development, our main areas of interest are Economic and Industrial Awareness, Science and Technology.

LIVING EARTH: Why the focus on teachers, rather than on the pupils?

ALAN GEORGE: We're concerned with winning the hearts and minds of teachers, both in terms of persuading them to accept the values of business and wealth creation and also to help them to use industry as a teaching resource to help prepare young people for adult and working life.

LIVING EARTH: But there must be a spin-off that you're anticipating? Is that in terms of the way in which teachers then present themselves and their work to pupils or the way in which they then think about their own role within society?

ALAN GEORGE: There are short-term and long-term reasons. Let me start with the long term. You've heard the phrase 'Licence to operate'? As a business, we have no absolute right to operate. We operate with the co-operation of society, the consumers, government and so on. We have to earn their respect. So that's a long-term requirement, we would like teachers to look favourably on business – as members of society, a vital element of society. And we need to propagate that view both locally and nationally. Locally through community involvement, because we need to be effective as important members of communities; in fact, it's quite relevant to the whole issue of the environment, because that's an area where a company's operations have a direct impact on communities, and you can do a lot of harm both to your community and to your reputation. It also applies nationally: on the national level, we're concerned about the sort of society in which we will do business in the future. Another reason for becoming involved in education is that there is more and more evidence that the state alone cannot provide a sound education system. They know that, although they don't always behave as if they do. And as you've seen recently, they're trying to put more of the onus on business. Although we are concerned about some of these demands, we accept that we should be involved in a partnership with education. Those are the long-term priorities. The short-term priorities are all about educational standards, skill levels, recruitment needs.

LIVING EARTH: How much of your activity will have been initiated by your company and how much of it will have arisen in response to overtures from schools?

ALAN GEORGE: There's a fair balance between schools and companies. Sometimes we're approached by schools, sometimes companies themselves say, 'This is what we want to do. Let's go and talk to some schools.' But you'll find across our 25 companies that there are different policies: one company may say 'We'll pick, say, two or three primary and two or three secondary and work with them'; others will say 'We'll take on all-comers if the requests are reasonable.' It depends on their policies for community involvement, as well as their resources.

LIVING EARTH: A related question – have your companies also found that the incidence of requests from schools has increased dramatically in the last five, ten years?

ALAN GEORGE: I would say, yes, the demands have increased, but, again, because we've thought through our priorities, we should be in a position to establish our own programmes and do enough to be able to say to some schools 'Sorry, but we're doing our bit. You can be involved in one of these programmes, but we don't want to hear any suggestions for major new initiatives, given that we're doing so much already.'

LIVING EARTH: Is it Unilever's experience that schools are making more and more requests for an involvement in environmental education?

ALAN GEORGE: I would certainly confirm that the enquiries we get represent a growing interest in this area. But it's not a problem for us.

LIVING EARTH: I think maybe what I meant by that goes back to the old suspicion of teachers and schools about industry. There is inevitably, as far as the environment is concerned, a sense among a lot of teachers, and a lot of young people, that industry is antithetically opposed to the environment, that it is leading to the destruction of the environment rather than to the sustaining of it.

ALAN GEORGE: Well, obviously there are pros and cons, and I think that we have to explain to young people's teachers that there is an economical element to all this, there are choices to be made. These are choices which, if they think about it seriously, they may not want to make!

I think the crux of the matter is whether you should take the environment as a subject in its own right or whether you should treat it as part of other subject areas. As you know, the National Curriculum regards environmental education as a cross-curricular theme and, as such, it should permeate everything else. I think in general that is how we would like to see it because, no matter what we do in the educational area, it will touch on the environment in some way. Any pupil or teacher who has contact with one of our companies will be confronted with environmental questions, no matter where they are. A successful business has to be concerned about the environment: it wouldn't survive unless it did. The question is 'How?', 'How fast?' and whether what we do meets the expectations of certainly some of our critics.

I'm not one of these people who believes that it's a five-day wonder; I don't think schools are going to tire of it. I think there are genuine concerns, I think there are serious problems in Science and the chemical industry, and we have to face up to those. We must obviously give a balanced approach, but also to show that we care about the environment in all that we do. I'll come on to one or two examples of what our companies are doing. Lever Brothers at Port Sunlight had a project with local schools on the recycling of plastic containers. Now that may not be earth-shattering, but it's an issue – how you handle plastics in the environment. A second example is the research laboratory up in Port Sunlight – the major centre for environmental control in Unilever – it has a whole department which advises our companies throughout the world on environmental control, and they've worked with local schools involved in TVEI (Technical and Vocational Educational Initiative) on an effluent treatment project, obviously Science-based. The third example in fact comes from a company called Crosfield Chemicals in Warrington who, despite initial reluctance, did agree to allow a team of schoolchildren in to do an environmental audit of the company. It was quite brave, because the company themselves hadn't done it – it was breaking new ground – and they were quite worried about the outcome. But apparently it was done responsibly and there were some very good discussions about it.

LIVING EARTH: And that was in response to a request from students?

ALAN GEORGE: It was, yes. It was a project they were involved in, and they asked if they could come in and audit the company.

LIVING EARTH: That's very interesting. And presumably the company then responded to the students' audit or met the students afterwards?

ALAN GEORGE: Oh yes, they had a very long discussion about what they had found and some of the issues that were raised, and apparently it was a very constructive engagement and it worked out much better than the company had expected. They were afraid of the students discovering some problems and alerting the Press or whatever. So those are three examples. Another example is the use of CFCs as aerosol propellants, and I know that Elida Gibbs have worked with their trade association to produce a pack for primary schools on ozone depletion. It's an example of how an industry has reacted to criticism which they see as a direct threat to their products. Quite different from, say, a research laboratory making its know-how available to young people in an unthreatening sort of sense on both sides. There are a variety of reasons for the responses.

LIVING EARTH: What benefits do you get from these links, thinking mainly about the environment for the time being?

ALAN GEORGE: Well, one outcome is people's understanding of the balance of the arguments. We know that the environmental movement is quite effective in propagating certain points of view, mainly in an emotive sense, but obviously children have to understand, for instance, the economic motives for doing something. I think also we would like to have them believe that companies do behave responsibly; we're not here to destroy the environment or to harm individuals. We're here to create wealth by making products people want, but in a responsible way. There's also the point, which I'm sure will come out in your project, that we're continually breaking new ground in terms of our understanding of what's happening in the environment. We've yet to face some of the issues that will come with the use of bio-technology, which raises all sorts of environmental questions. We won't go into those for the moment, but you can imagine there's a whole new field to be explored there. So it is a question of understanding the balance of the issues.

LIVING EARTH: Going back now to the whole issue of school/industry links, in what way do schools benefit from these links? I mean, presumably you do research which assesses how successful they have found these programmes?

ALAN GEORGE: Believe it or not, we don't! I think that assessment in this area is fraught with difficulties. I think the reason why in my view you can't apply true evaluation methods is we're talking about *partnership*. Now if you accept the spirit of partnership, it means two sides, it can be more, coming together and discussing their common interests and deciding how they can work together. The partnership concept implies a sharing of objectives. It's not a case of Unilever doing its thing, schools doing their thing, and somewhere in the middle there's an interaction. And if you accept that as a principle, then I don't think you have to apply a scientific method of evaluation. There will be some adjustments obviously, but partnership is the concept that binds the two together. If you compare the way that we in the UK operate with, say, the Germans or the Japanese, it's totally different. In Germany, industry plays a major part in the educational service, they almost dictate what the nation needs, or used to – it's changing now. Whereas we've had a very much hands-off policy, and I think we have resisted becoming too far involved.

If you look at what industry wants from education, it's pretty basic. There is a CBI document which says 'We want all children to have a broad and balanced education, we want literacy, we want numeracy'. But providing those building blocks are in place, children should be free to develop their own interests. I don't think we should be interfering too much beyond insisting that the basics are in place.

LIVING EARTH: Is there some kind of clash between what you are required to show as a department for your involvement with schools and what you would want to show to schools as the benefits of that involvement?

ALAN GEORGE: No, we're pretty open about what we do, both within the business and with schools, but there are one or two examples amongst our companies where they've done things wrongly. One example is where a certain company decided to donate something like £30k of computers to one school and have the department labelled the so-and-so computing centre. Then they realised what a horrendous mistake they'd made, because all the other schools in the vicinity said, 'What the hell? Don't we matter?' and they realised that it was a mistake and that they should have spread that resource more evenly among them.

If you want to be seen as a responsible member of the community, and the community can be quite large, you've got to be seen as such by everyone in the community, not just one school.

Industry and the environment – friend or foe?

MARY BARRY

INTRODUCTION

Nobody disputes the need for environmental education. Ozone depletion, acid rain, CFCs, endangered species, waste pollutants and deforestation are high on the agenda of people in schools, businesses and governments across the world. To address the universal concern about environmental damage, sustainable economic growth and the threat to human survival requires informed action, but there is no real agreement as to how this should be done and who should be responsible for doing it. Inevitably, environmental education involves dealing with fundamental economic, scientific, moral and political controversies.

These environmental concerns have a direct bearing on the world of business, from global issues of sustainable development to local issues of process pollutants and waste deposition. But where does responsibility for the environment lie?

INDUSTRY AND THE ENVIRONMENT

Responsibility for 'clean' industrialisation is divided between governments who have the power to regulate policy, environmentalists who have knowledge and expertise about the impact of industrialisation on the Earth's resources and surrounding communities, and industry which has the technical 'know-how'. Industry has a responsibility to use this technical knowledge to advance industrial output in ways that ensure the development of new markets in new and established communities without damaging the social or natural fabric of the community. This means that industry should adopt practices that ensure concern for the Earth's resources by monitoring the impact of industrial activity on the community and the surrounding environment – as well as by introducing procedures that minimise the use of raw materials and energy, reduce waste and prevent pollution.

Companies have realised that caring for the environment is not a matter of choice: it is vital for success in business. Consumer choice, market share, recruitment and staff retention increasingly depend upon environmental practices. Many businesses are now adopting the ethic for sustainable operating practices which minimise negative effects upon ecosystems as an integral part of corporate policy. This means that environmental education is a necessity for all those who are involved in business. However, much can be done by beginning the educative process in schools.

SCHOOLS AND THE ENVIRONMENT

Young people often have a genuine concern for problems in the environment, especially where natural or human consequences are potentially catastrophic unless something is done. In preparation for the challenges and responsibilities of adult life, schools are helping pupils acquire the knowledge, values, attitudes, commitment and the skills needed to analyse controversies and take action to protect and improve the environment.

There are important opportunities for learning about environmental issues in the National Curriculum subject orders for Science, Geography, History and Technology. There is also the cross-curricular theme of 'environmental education', which finds its way into other cross-curricular themes such as health education, careers education and guidance, economic and industrial awareness and education for citizenship.

It is easy to assume that decisions and the impact of people's actions about the environment are made by other people and are therefore someone else's responsibility. As consumers and possible future producers, young people should be encouraged to consider their role as decision-makers within their local community, the world of work and the wider community. The question is, how can awareness and understanding be developed in a way that enables young people to see how business, government and environmental agencies are striving for the development of sustainable societies?

PARTNERSHIP IN ACTION

Members of the business and wider community can play an important part in school-based curriculum activities which address environmental concerns. They offer a sense of realism for the students and provide information from a range of perspectives.

Active learning approaches, such as those encouraged in *Industry and the Environment – Friend or Foe?* (a recent publication for schools and colleges), enable young people to confront environmental issues. Business partners and external agencies can act as consultants in the classroom, the workplace and the local community by providing information, considering solutions and offering an overview of how organisations are tackling environmental issues.

Activities can be developed which consider issues such as:

- company policy and how organisations attempt to ensure the implementation of policy development from the board room to the shop floor;
- eco-labelling and the environmental impact of products at different stages of their manufacture, distribution, consumption and disposal;
- the role of the trade unions in ensuring safe working environments;
- the siting of waste treatment plants and their impact on local communities;
- the role of government at national and international level, and the impact of their decisions on communities across the world.

Ultimately, whatever processes are used to raise the consciousness of young people and other members of our community, it is essential that young people are equipped with the skills needed to analyse controversies which enable them to take on an active role in the decision-making processes which will impact on them as global citizens.

Recommended resources

Caring for the Earth – a Strategy for Sustainable Living, Earthscan Publications (available through the World Wide Fund for Nature)

Industry and the Environment – Friend or Foe? edited by Mary Barry, Julia Fiehn and Andrew Miller, SCIP/MESP Publications, University of Warwick, 1992

Young Eyes: Children's Views of the Future Environment, report commissioned by BT, prepared by the Henley Centre for Forecasting

Your Business in the Environment – a DIY Review for Companies, Coopers and Lybrand Deloitte, Business in the Environment, 8 Stratton Street, London W1X 5FD

Mary Barry is currently the Regional Manager, London, of SCIP (School Curriculum Industry Partnership), in which role she works in partnership with the worlds of education and business to develop curriculum activities for young people. Prior to this, she worked as a History teacher and a Careers Education and Guidance co-ordinator in Kent and Merton, and as an advisory teacher for Curriculum Development in Merton.

How school links with business can help

JAN HUSSEY

If young people are to be well prepared for working life, inside or outside of industry and commerce, it is vital that industry and education should work together. To achieve understanding of each other's role, there can be no substitute for up-to-date, first-hand experience. Making links with the business world can be a simple process and one from which a school or college can derive considerable benefit. It may also give teachers the satisfaction of being able to make a positive contribution to a company. There are a number of national and local organisations which work to enhance the links between schools and business. Similarly, there are numerous facilities available to help individuals, groups and institutions, and a list of some of the organisations which provide them is given at the end of this review. Their work is complementary, and each has a part to play in ensuring that young people may become more aware of the vital role and functions of industry and commerce in creating the nation's wealth and resources.

School/business links may involve the following activities:
- teacher placements; business placements within education; management training and development with an industrial perspective;
- student work experience; compacts; simulations; enterprise schemes for students;
- conferences; resources (including publications).

This review focuses principally on the Teacher Placement Service, with a brief introductory look at teaching resources produced by companies.

RESOURCES PUBLISHED BY COMPANIES

The *UBI Directory of Teaching Materials from Industry and Commerce*, published annually by Understanding British Industry (UBI), gives brief details of the resources published by 237 organisations. Many of the resources are free of charge. The directory is fully indexed by topics and also by curriculum subjects. An example of an entry follows:

004
Aluminium Can Recycling Association
1 Mex House
52 Blucher Street
Birmingham
West Midlands
B1 1QU
021 633 4656 or 0800 444222
(Teacher's file)

Free teacher's file including how to set up a schools-based aluminium can recycling programme, teacher's notes, wall posters and a directory of centres buying aluminium cans for cash. Free magnets and leaflet for pupils. Video (aluminium production, recycling) available on loan.

Suitable for Primary, TVEI, Secondary, CPVE, GCSE/Standard Grade

Single copies of this directory are available, free, from the Information Officer at UBI. A large stamped addressed envelope should be enclosed with your order please.

THE TEACHER PLACEMENT SERVICE

A placement in industry as part of a teacher's continuous professional development can meet a wide range of curriculum and management objectives. A placement can also help to meet needs which are identified within the institutional development plan.

The Teacher Placement Service was established in 1989 and operates in England, Scotland and Wales. In England it operates as an activity of local education/business partnerships and is funded by the Employment Department; in Wales, funding is through the Welsh Office. In Scotland, funding is from Scottish Enterprise and Highlands and Islands Enterprise. UBI provides a central and regional management team. UBI is a project of the CBI Education Foundation, which is a registered charity.

There are 150 teacher placement organisers, and they are able to give individual attention to placement needs. They arrange placements, prepare company people and teachers for placement, supply briefing materials, support schools which are delivering their own placement programme and advise on follow-up strategies.

Both pupils and schools benefit from teacher placement: pupils benefit by being presented with real examples to enhance their classroom resources. Managers in education have found that placements add a valuable perspective from industry. A wide range of issues can be addressed which may include financial control, staff appraisal and development and marketing.

Placements are central to school/industry activity. They enable the teacher to experience today's business world at first hand. They may also involve other types of school/industry activity: for example, a placement could be linked to a management workshop (available through the UBI National Education Programmes Unit), and the placement might also involve establishing or reviewing student work experience.

Placements are very flexible and may be arranged as a block of time spent in the company and/or a number of days spread over some weeks. This is one of the things to negotiate, with the help of your teacher placement organiser (TPO). To make contact with your TPO, contact the Teacher Placement Service centrally at the address given at the end of this section.

Teacher placement schemes can also lead to important local publications, an example of which – with a specifically environmental theme – is the Northamptonshire publication, *We Have a Road* (extract shown opposite). This marked the culmination of a placement programme involving teachers from all phases of education and brought life to 11 national curriculum subjects and five cross-curricular themes. Teacher placements were with a variety of companies concerned with construction and transport, as well as with farms and the Northamptonshire Wildlife Trust. For this project, teachers and pupils examined, first hand, habitats that were lost and damaged and considered new habitats that were created. The movements of small mammals, birds of prey and invertebrates gave rise to fascinating projects.

The following are ways in which teachers benefit from school/business links:

- widening of perspectives from direct experience of business;
- stimulus for curriculum development;
- better understanding of career needs;
- updating and developing of specific skills: discovery of hidden skills;
- improved opportunities for relevance within the curriculum and development of cross-curricular themes;
- raising awareness among employers of current developments in education;
- stronger partnership with business based on personal contact;
- stimulation and enhancement of economic awareness;
- positive effect on the image of the school in the community.

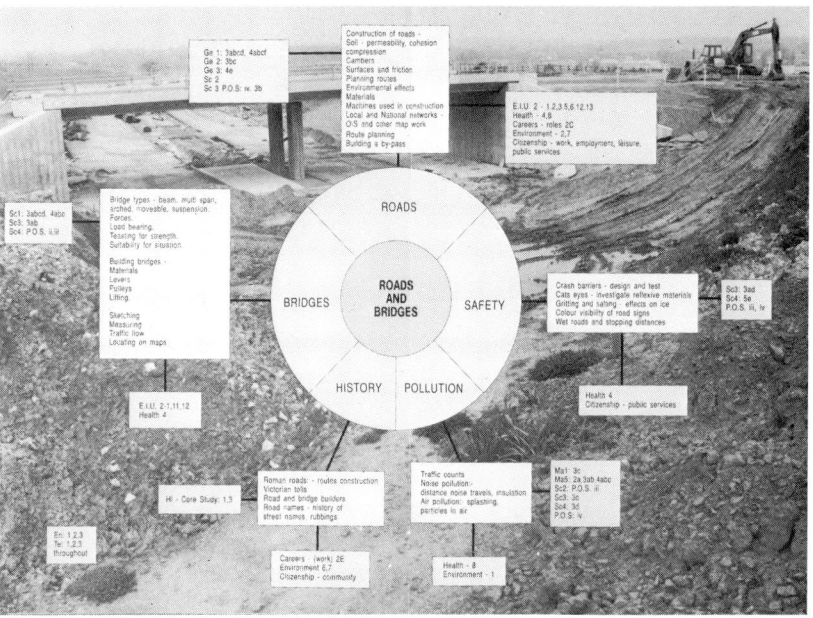

HOW SCHOOL LINKS WITH INDUSTRY CAN HELP BUSINESSES

For business, it is important that young people have a positive attitude to the role of industry and business in society. The improvement of the image of business is vital, because companies are competing with each other and with other employers to recruit a workforce with the right education and training. For both these reasons, it is important that businesses work with schools, since teachers' perceptions of industry affect the workforce of the future.

The following are ways in which a company benefits from school/business links:

- the development of a more positive attitude about the role of business in society;
- an enhanced image of the company (and of business, generally) within the community;
- the chance to make a real contribution to education;
- communication with the future workforce;
- a widening of staff and management development opportunities;
- the provision, through teacher placement, of someone external to the company to bring a new perspective to a task or problem;
- further knowledge and experience of the education system;
- an opportunity to clarify skill needs;
- a chance to influence the curriculum.

There is now a greater awareness then ever before of the interdependence of education and the economy. The benefits to both industry and education of better understanding can be most effectively realised through both sides developing a productive partnership – which means spending time together.

COMMENTS MADE BY EMPLOYERS

'The teacher comes to you to find out about business, so why don't you go to the teacher to find out about education? I accepted the challenge and spent five days, spread over two terms, in my local comprehensive school. I shadowed the Head, I shadowed a teacher, I spent a day shadowing a fifth-form pupil and that indeed was a fascinating experience. I saw how the school functioned – *from the inside* – and, at the time, I believed it to be the best course I had ever attended.'

'It is always refreshing for well-informed outsiders (i.e. teachers) to make constructive comments and relay their considered impressions of us and of our operators.'

'As a college governor and human resource manager for my company, I am convinced that teacher placements are a better way to link industry with education than any way we've tried before.'

'People who spend too much time focusing on daily tasks become bored, boring and ineffective ... We became involved because we wished to influence young people, but we quickly discovered what a marvellous renovating experience it was for supervisors and managers.'

'Education is changing. Education is the business of the whole community. Education and business are working together in a true partnership with gains for both partners. Carefully planned partnership activities with realistic objectives are benefiting business, teachers, children and young people.'

National organisations involved with school/industry links

Understanding British Industry (UBI)
Sun Alliance House
New Inn Hall Street
Oxford
OX1 2QE
Tel: 0865 72258
Fax: 0865 790014

Teacher Placement Service
Understanding British Industry
(Address, telephone and fax numbers as above)

Young Enterprise
Ewert Place
Summertown
Oxford
OX2 7BZ
Tel: 0865 311180

Business in the Community
227A City Road
London
EC1V 1LZ
Tel: 071 253 3716

Engineering Council and Neighbourhood Engineers
10 Maltravers Street
London WC2R 3ER
Tel: 071 240 7891

Association of British Insurers
51 Gresham Street
London EC2V 7HQ
Tel: 071 600 3333

Banking Information Services
10 Lombard Street
London EC3V 9AT
Tel: 071 626 9386

Building Societies Association
3 Savile Row
London
Tel: 071 437 0655

CRAC Education and Training Programmes
Sheraton House
Castle Park
Cambridge
CB3 0AX
Tel: 0223 460277

Industrial Society
Quadrant Court
49 Calthorpe Road
Edgbaston
Birmingham
West Midlands
B15 1TH
Tel: 021 454 6769

ORT Trust
ORT Resource Centre
Kipling House
43 Villiers Street
London WC2N 6NE
Tel: 071 839 6800

School Curriculum Industry Partnership/Mini Enterprise in School Project (SCIP/MESP)
SCIP National Headquarters
Centre for Education-Industry
Westwood
University of Warwick
Coventry
West Midlands
CV4 7AL
Tel: 0203 52950/1

Standing Conference on Schools' Science and Technology (SCSST)
The Science and Technology Regional Organisation (SATRO)
76 Portland Place
London W1N 4AA
Tel: 071 278 2468

Trident Trust
91 Brick Lane
London E1 6QN
Tel: 071 375 0245

Understanding Industry
91 Waterloo Road
London SE1 8XP
Tel: 071 620 0735

Jan Hussey is Senior Information Officer at Understanding British Industry (UBI), where she has worked for over six years, providing information, publicity and internal and external communications with reference to school/industry activity and UBI programmes. UBI has been in operation for 15 years and is a project of the CBI Education Foundation, a registered charity.

Links with local industry

PHIL COOPER

The development of school/industry links involves the establishment of a firm partnership, which ensures that links are never one-sided and that both parties work together for mutual benefit. Hillcrest School has had a variety of links with local industry for a number of years. These have included: work experience programmes for pupils in both Years 10 and 11, visits to companies as 'An introduction to the world of work' programme which is linked to the careers course in Years 7 and 8, company involvement in the development of 'mini company' and 'mini enterprise' education in Year 10, and a series of projects linked into curriculum work.

Over the past two years, the school has developed links with the Hulbert Group of Companies, and with Precision Steel in particular, largely as a result of a one-year headteacher's secondment into industry which the Principal of Hillcrest School, John Bateson, completed in 1990. Following this secondment, the company committed itself to further links with education and covered expenses to allow me to be directly involved in the company for one afternoon per week for a one-year period.

The Black Country Green Award, initiated by the Groundwork Trust and sponsored by the Express and Star News Group and Central Television, provided further opportunities for the school to involve itself in local industry. One of the criteria for the award was the involvement and support of local industry in restoring an area of derelict land. The Hall Lane Pool Restoration Project, as it became known, is ideally situated between the perimeter of the school campus and that of Precision Steel. In addition to the involvement of Precision Steel, the project also required the school to contact and develop links with other community groups: the West Midlands Police Force (whose representative, PC Friday, has recently been appointed the first West Midlands Conservation Officer), staff at the Saltwells Nature Reserve and local youth clubs. The project was submitted for the Black Country Green Award as a collective enterprise and, despite strong competition from other schools

LINKS WITH LOCAL INDUSTRY

in Dudley, Wolverhampton, Sandwell and Walsall, Hillcrest School won the award. All parties gained considerable publicity from the project, particularly Precision Steel.

The area of derelict land to be restored by the Hall Lane Pool Restoration Project

David Bellamy with Melanie Harold from Hillcrest School and at the back, from left, Jamila Begum from the Frank F. Harrison Community School, Samantha Swain from Pennfields School and Julie Fereday from Shireland School

Bellamy rewards top 'green' pupils

PRECISION STEEL'S LINKS WITH HILLCREST SCHOOL

1. Hall Lane Pool Restoration Project
There was total commitment to restoring the site on the part of the company. Precision Steel made time and machinery available in the early stages. A Precision Steel employee who was interested and qualified in photography produced photographic documentation of the site as it was and in the course of the project.

For this task, the employee linked with pupils from the school who showed a similar interest in photography.

2. Map and logo
School pupils produced a prototype of a map and logo which was to be sent by Precision to customers, giving the location of the site.

3. Visits (Years 7 and 8 pupils, ongoing)
As part of the careers programme, 'An introduction to the world of work', Years 7 and 8 pupils visit the company and follow up these visits with safety posters which are then displayed at Precision Steel. Prizes for these posters are awarded to pupils by Precision Steel.

4. Visits (Year 9 pupils, ongoing)
Year 9 pupils are involved in interviews with Precision Steel employees as part of an English project.

5. Work experience
Six pupils were involved in a work experience programme during July 1992. Precision Steel considered this programme, the first it had held, highly successful.

6. TEC Toyota Award
Submission for £1,000 award sponsored by Toyota. The award was to be used to research the effect of corrosion on steel, as part of the Science programme.

7. Using Precision Steel as an 'Industry Mentor' with the school
A September '92 initiative – pilot scheme for Dudley Authority.

8. The school is investigating the possibility of Precision dividing the responsibilities of a Youth Training employee between acting as the warden of the Hall Lane Pool – when it is restored – and standard Precision duties.

Phil Cooper has taught Science at Hillcrest Community College, Netherton, for 22 years. In addition to his Science duties, he is also responsible for co-ordinating work experience and has been centrally involved in forming links with industry. He has recently been appointed marketing officer at the school.

National and local environmental groups

SOPHIE YANGOPOULOS

The following organisations offer valuable education services which provide teachers with teaching strategies and resources for delivering environmental education in schools. It is almost impossible to separate the organisations completely, since most are in some way linked to others: many have, for example, co-ordinated joint projects and networks of resources and ideas.

Friends of the Earth – School Friends

Subjects: Cross-curricular
Age: Primary and secondary

Friends of the Earth, one of the leading environmental pressure groups in the UK, have collected and researched data on environmental issues for over 20 years on which they rely to present strong cases in campaigns. It is this expertise and information which is being offered to schools through the School Friends scheme.

Through its education programme, Friends of the Earth aim to encourage young people to participate actively in protecting and improving the environment. The School Friends scheme provides accessible, accurate, reliable information and additional activity materials on environmental issues for schools. It is often difficult to find basic, succinct background information – facts and figures to back up the exploration and discussion of environmental issues. The *Towards Tomorrow* leaflets are excellent in their clear, factual content and their outlining of key topics (e.g. recycling and ozone depletion). They have concise explanations of the problems and the action needed to reverse the damage done. Project idea sheets accompany each leaflet.

The development of resources by the School Friends team has resulted in the *Green Your School* pack (also in the starter pack for new members). The approach here is to use the school buildings and grounds to develop environmental awareness, understanding and action in a local-to-global context. The pack is an excellent cross-curricular resource with information, action sheets and teachers' notes based around a school environmental survey. It is an extremely flexible resource. The survey explores key environmental issues relating to the school, looks at possible adverse effects of the school on the environment and highlights ways in which the school can improve its environmental record.

Friends of the Earth have also produced an 'Air Pollution and Transport' wall chart for primary schools and 'Investigating Air Pollution' for secondary schools. These are cross-curricular and investigate the issues of air pollution through a series of imaginative exercises.

School Friends (i.e. members of the School Friends scheme) receive an annual mailing of educational materials and the quarterly Friends of the Earth magazine, *Earth Matters*. There is also a 20% discount on all Friends of the Earth publications.

Council for Environmental Education

Subjects: Cross-curricular
Age: Primary, Secondary, Tertiary, Youth service

The Council for Environmental Education (CEE) is a registered charity representing and working with the 80 national organisations which make up its membership.

CEE operates through the formation of partnerships with its members, central and local government, business and industry and other organisations and individuals.

CEE carries out research and produces a range of publications in line with CEE's three main objectives:

- to influence and develop policy at all levels as it relates to environmental education;
- to influence, develop and disseminate good practice in environmental education;
- to increase the effectiveness and coherence of the environmental education movement.

Publications include *Newsheet* (10 issues per year) which provides details of new environmental education resources, services, events and courses. The *Environmental Education Resources Sheet Series* gives details of teaching resources on a wide variety of topics. INSET training materials for environmental education as a cross-curricular theme for use in schools are currently being developed: the Introductory Module and Science are now available and English and Geography modules are due for publication in 1993. *EARTHworks*, a pack of practical ideas for environmental youth work, provides a framework for policy and training, together with resources for action. *EARTHlines* is a newsletter for youth workers involved in environmental education.

Research is currently being carried out into the information needs of teachers and youth workers with the aim of improving the provision and use of information and resources. Occasional briefing papers interpret the results of research projects or the significance of important developments or documents.

As an organisation which researches and assesses the possibilities for environmental education within all sectors of education and which develops resources in association with many other environmental and educational organisations, the up-to-date services provided by CEE are invaluable in keeping abreast of developments in environmental education.

Worldaware

Subjects: Cross-curricular
Age: Primary and secondary

Worldaware provides a selection of resources about economically developing countries, development issues and development education. Many of its publications explore the links between environment and development education. Although Worldaware is primarily an educational agency, promoting education about development issues, the very nature of certain approaches to development makes the environment a key focus of its work and an integral part of appropriate strategies for sustainable development.

Worldaware has a wide range of resources, involving teaching strategies for both primary and secondary education which closely integrate environment and development issues. Resources include handbooks for teachers as well as activity packs, wall charts, simulations and computer software. The Worldaware catalogue is a superb compilation of resources, including those specifically combining environment and development issues. The resources address environmental concerns in localities in economically developing countries and show how these relate to our own concerns. The resources are drawn together from a number of development and environmental organisations, including charities, NGOs (non-government organisations) and commercial publishers. Some examples follow:

Earthrights – ideas and activities to help young people (primary and secondary) to understand complex environment and development issues;
Renewing the Earth – activities based on CAFOD's campaign on the connection between development and the environment;
The Atlas of the Environment – WWF atlas containing over 200 maps and diagrams which is supported by up-to-date facts about key environmental issues. The atlas shows what action is being taken and what still needs to be done.
Women and the Environment – this is a booklet of case studies which examines issues relating to women and the environment.
Tourism, Environment and Development Perspectives – this presents a thoughtful overview of the field, giving a range of interesting case studies which examine tourism's impact on the economy, society, culture and the environment.
Cartoon Discussion Sheet on the Environment – this contains a six-sided A4 cartoon and information, illustrated by photographs, on the topic, listing points for discussion.
The DIY Earth summit Pack – this provides briefing materials and activity sheets for teachers and youth leaders wanting to organise a conference on the key issues which formed the agenda at the Rio Earth Summit in 1992.

Worldaware has a resource centre whose staff will help with ideas and will direct enquirers to appropriate resources: these can be viewed on the premises. For those wanting to bridge the gap between the local environment of pupils and the local environmental concerns in places that are unfamiliar (primarily in economically developing countries) and, by exploring the relationship between these concerns, to develop a global awareness, Worldaware is an important resource.

WWF UK (World Wide Fund for Nature) – Teacher Representative Scheme

Subjects: Cross-curricular
Age: Primary, secondary, tertiary

WWF exerts a far-reaching influence on environmental education which extends to schools, higher education, professional associations, television and international education projects.

WWF has published over 200 educational resources, including books, multi-media packs, videos and posters. These resources are developed and written by professionals – practising teachers, educationists, experienced authors and environmental experts. They cover a wide range of subjects and all educational levels from primary, through secondary to tertiary. To support this wealth of material, WWF has put together a comprehensive range of resources specifically on the management and evaluation of cross-curricular inputs (for details of these, see the article on 'Multi-media packs' by Vincent J Bunce and, particularly, pages 57–58) and is developing and trialling INSET courses and packages for environmental education.

In addition, there are resources to facilitate community action and an array of materials to inform the general public. All these materials are informed, challenged and enriched by their work in a variety of continents that include Asia, Eastern Europe, Africa and South America.

The Teacher Representative Scheme, which opened to all secondary schools in October 1992, was extended to primary schools in October 1993. Teacher Representatives receive, on behalf of the school, the annual WWF Education Catalogue, listing all WWF's resources, and, termly, new resources leaflets. These resources may be purchased by anyone in the school at a discount of 25%. The school also receives *Lifelines*, the termly teacher's newsletter. A 24-hour answerphone hotline is open to enable teachers to call out of working hours with queries or requests for information. This new service is free of charge to the school and the teacher.

WWF has been, and continues to be, at the forefront of the promotion of environmental awareness and education, nationally and internationally. Membership of the Teacher Representative Scheme gives schools easy and cheaper access to WWF's resources and services and to one of the largest education departments of any environmental group.

Learning through Landscapes

Subjects: Cross-curricular
Age: Primary and secondary

The Learning through Landscapes Trust is an informative and consultative body for schools embarking on long-term cross-curricular projects to use their grounds as an educational resource. The Trust developed out of a research project to assess the relationship between the school environment and the learning, play and development of the children in that environment. The research project found that a few schools had already developed their grounds as learning resources. A recommendation was made to set up a trust to collate and develop an information network which would encourage more schools to build on and improve existing ideas and practices. The Trust has a database of projects all over the country which can be drawn on to help plan and implement initiatives and provide support and ideas for overcoming hurdles. It produces two videos and a range of books which show what transforming school grounds into a rich educational resource can achieve.

Learning through Landscapes will provide information on other local initiatives and organisations which could be of use, such as the Countryside Commission, Groundwork and the RSPB. Many projects are carried out within regional groups of support teams and often with local education authority support.

Two new areas of research are being opened. One is a joint project with WWF about play and the informal curriculum – how play is crucial and can be improved through school grounds design. The other is an assessment of the state of school grounds across the country called 'School Watch'. Schools are encouraged to carry out a site audit – a valuable cross-curricular learning experience in itself – and will add to the Learning Through Landscapes database on the state of school grounds developments.

Membership of the Trust entitles schools to newsletters, activity sheets (which suggest improvements to school sites), publications developed from examples of good practice, access to the databases and information about sources of funding. Membership may also be arranged through the local authority (there are currently 33 affiliated authorities): this membership offers a flexible consultancy service which may include, for example, organisation of INSET and site advice.

With much emphasis on the idea of 'thinking globally, acting locally', using the school grounds is a step towards encouraging pupils to look at their own immediate environment, assessing how it is used and how it could be improved and actively taking part in the development of their ideas for changes. For schools embarking on the long-term development of their grounds as an educational resource, Learning through Landscapes provides a valuable service, primarily as an information network of ideas and help.

Centre for Alternative Technology

Subjects: Cross-curricular
Age: Primary to post-graduate

The Centre for Alternative Technology (CAT) is a living and working community which develops and promotes sustainable technologies for green living. It has a display and education centre offering practical ideas on environmentally sound practices, where it displays organic growing, low-energy building and wind, water and solar power, there being no mains connections to the site.

The Centre is an invaluable resource for promoting environmental awareness and understanding and demonstrating how this can be put into practice. Visits to the Centre can cover all the relevant National Curriculum requirements for the core and foundation subjects, as well as specifically addressing the cross-curricular nature of environmental education. It is possible to organise day visits and residential work for pupils, with courses designed for the particular requirements of the group. A better idea, however, is for the teacher to undertake a preliminary visit and to use the Visitors' guidebook and introductory booklets with pupils before their visit. The Centre also provides residential courses specifically for teachers, with practical information on how to incorporate green issues and environmental awareness effectively into school teaching.

Green Teacher is produced by one of CAT's education officers: it is an informative resource, which allows subscribers to contribute themselves to the publication (see the article on 'Journals and magazines', page 35). CAT's *Buy Green By Mail* catalogue provides an impressive array of books and products to promote sustainable environments and green living. Resource lists for school teachers are also available.

CAT offers a 'real' experience of a wide range of alternative technologies which is relevant to all ages and interest groups. To many teachers outside the area, mid-Wales may seem like a long way to go, but, for any environmentally aware teacher, the benefits of such a practical model of environmental sustainability should not be overlooked. In instances where it is impossible to give pupils the experience, teacher courses and *Green Teacher* should play an important role in developing environmental education in schools across the country.

Civic Trust

Subjects: Cross-curricular
Age: Primary and secondary

The Civic Trust works to improve the urban environment. It is concerned with the 'best' features of the past, good new developments and more effective participation in the planning process, especially by local communities.

The Civic Trust promotes the use of local places in education. It is a useful resource for schools through its focus on the quality of the built environment and change (in the past, an area of the curriculum often not used to its full potential). It is particularly relevant at the local level, which is an emphasis of National Curriculum Geography.

Since most schools are based in urban areas, many of the Civic Trust's ideas are widely applicable: these include looking at brickwork, assessing street furniture and examining the planning process involved in changes to the local environment. In relation to the latter, project officers in the Urban Regeneration Unit of the Civic Trust involve schools and colleges in the process of urban regeneration in their particular project areas.

Although based in London, the Civic Trust encourages links between schools and local amenity societies across the country. These are local groups concerned with the changes being made to their own local area or town. They vary in size and degree of knowledge and participation in the planning process, but they can provide useful information about local issues.

A publication, *About the Urban Environment* (for lower secondary schools), provides ideas and activities for appreciating the complexity of the urban environment, identifying the causes and issues surrounding environmental change and investigating how individuals can influence change.

The importance of the Civic Trust for teachers is more in the information and the contacts it can provide to enable schools to develop further projects rather than in the provision of curriculum materials. The Trust provides an opportunity to integrate schools more fully into the community and it also promotes the cross-curricular theme of citizenship which is an integral part of environmental education.

Details of organisations referred to in this review

Friends of the Earth – School Friends
26–28 Underwood Street
London
N1 7JQ

Council for Environmental Education
School of Education
University of Reading
London Road
Reading
Berkshire
RG1 5AQ

Worldaware
1 Catton Street
London WC1R 4AB

World Wide Fund for Nature – Teacher Membership
Panda House
Weyside Park
Godalming
Surrey
GU7 1XR

Learning Through Landscapes
Third Floor
Southside Offices
The Law Courts
Winchester
Hampshire
SO23 9DL

Centre for Alternative Technology
Machynlleth
Powys
SY20 2AZ

Civic Trust
17 Carlton House Terrace
London
SW1Y 5AW

Sophie Yangopoulos teaches Geography at Grey Coat Hospital School, Westminster, London, where she is also the teacher responsible for promoting environmental education. The author of Cities, a Better Life? *(CWDE, 1992) – a Key Stage 3 Geography resource on urban environments in London, Mexico and Brazil – she is currently completing an MPhil in environment and development education at the Institute of Education, the University of London.*

Interview with the Young People's Trust for the Environment and Nature Conservation

LIVING EARTH

The following is an edited version of an interview with Sally Webster, the Assistant Director of the Young People's Trust for the Environment and Nature Conservation (YPTENC).

LIVING EARTH: Tell me a little bit about your charity.

SALLY WEBSTER: The Young People's Trust for the Environment and Nature Conservation was founded in 1981 by its director, Cyril Littlewood, under a different name, The Young People's Trust for Endangered Species. We offer education within the environment and aim to provide environmental material for young people to learn about, take an interest in and, we hope, as a result, to wish to protect the environment in the future. We are an education service for schools, pupils, teachers,  young people in general, and we are basically an information service. We receive hundreds of letters every week and we send out free information in the form of factsheets on any environmental topic. We do ask for stamped addressed envelopes, of course, but we never turn any requests down, and most of our information is free. Membership to the trust is free too, to schools and individuals. (People may buy badges, etc., if they wish to, but in general all our services are free.) We also operate a schools lecture service to infant, junior and secondary schools mostly, but also to youth clubs, Guides, Brownies. On that basis we send out lecture invitations to schools, mainly in the home counties, because only two people in the Trust actually provide the lectures – the director, Cyril Littlewood and myself, the assistant director.

LIVING EARTH: Probably an obvious point, but you are a charity, aren't you?

SALLY WEBSTER: Yes, we are an independent registered charity.

LIVING EARTH: Funded by ?

SALLY WEBSTER: Funded mainly by companies. We have a company sponsorship scheme. We're not a fund-raising charity – some schools are a little frightened that there are going to be some fund-raising strings and that we're going to ask for donations, but we don't. Sometimes the children will send you some money off their own bat or try to raise some money from a cake sale or whatever, and, of course, we're grateful for any donations, but we never press it at all. We have 16 major companies who provide a donation every year. In return for that donation we run The Young Environmentalist of the Year Award scheme, YEYA for short. It's a competition for the children of the employees. They can submit a project to do with the environment. Sometimes in the past, we have specified particular projects they can choose. Last year they could choose any topic they wished to write on. We have it at two levels: junior and senior. A junior winner and a senior winner are selected, plus runners-up, depending on the company. Then we get together at a big celebrity lunch at the Dorchester Hotel in November. Celebrities, giving freely of their time, are invited to present 'Otter Oscar' Awards. Company representatives and the winners' families also attend. The companies receive something worthwhile for their donation, and their generosity allows the Young People's Trust to offer most of its services free of charge.

LIVING EARTH: How many lectures do you expect to perform in one year?

SALLY WEBSTER: We do on average about 300 lectures a year. We also publish some newsletters: *Conservation Education* and *Whale Tail News* in which we write about environmental topics which are hopefully of use to teachers and pupils alike. We send these out to all schools on our mailing list – we have about 3000 who are registered with us. Once the schools get to know us, some of them will book us on a termly basis or an annual basis. If one particular teacher is interested in environmental topics they will bring you in every year or term for a particular topic for a class.

LIVING EARTH: So the topic is selected according to the school's curriculum interest rather than by what you want to do yourselves?

SALLY WEBSTER: Yes, or sometimes the school teacher or headteacher is particularly interested in the environment and so they say, 'Can you come and talk about it, in general?' So we just talk about all sorts of thing like disappearing habitats, endangered species – anything – covering all the major topics and then follow it up with slides or a film about a particular animal or habitat that will interest that particular age level. Or the school might say 'We're doing a topic on rivers, rainforests or pollution. Can you do something on that?' and so we'll specialise on that and talk about that in detail and then show slides or a film appropriate to that subject.

LIVING EARTH: And how big are the groups you talk to?

SALLY WEBSTER: They vary. Sometimes it's just a class, up to about 30, sometimes it's a year group, like 60 or 70, or it's the whole school. If it's primary, then they like to divide it into infants and juniors, because obviously it's easier to speak to two different levels, and the visual material is not always suitable for the very tiny ones. If it's a junior school, it may be the whole school; if it's secondary, it might be a GCSE group, a year group or whatever.

LIVING EARTH: I imagine these sessions are not like lectures – there's a lot of interaction? But presumably the smaller the group, the easier this is to happen?

SALLY WEBSTER: Yes, that kind of thing works quite well at primary level particularly, where you can't really shut them up because they're all telling you stories about the hedgehog that they saw and so on. It's more difficult to encourage secondary pupils to respond verbally, especially in a large group. With junior schools it makes for more variety; you can get them more involved, and it's easier with a small group, because you can get them to join in and get a discussion going at the end of the film. I normally try to include a question-and-answer period at the end. Lectures usually last about one hour for secondary and junior groups, including a half-hour film or slide presentation. The length of the session is, of course, considerably reduced for infant groups.

LIVING EARTH: Going back to how schools approach you in the first place. Say I was a teacher who was wanting to use your services and I apply for a lecture. How do you organise that, if you haven't worked at my school before?

SALLY WEBSTER: On receiving the application, I try to phone within a day or two and ask if a particular topic is being undertaken. Sometimes the answer is 'No,' but sometimes they can be very specific. Sometimes they will write a detailed letter of exactly what the year group is doing and what they'd like to cover. Others leave it entirely up to the speaker. That's usually the only contact before. Sometimes they book up to a term ahead. Sometimes they want it pretty quickly, like 'Can you come next week?' or whatever. Usually it's a few weeks in advance, but they expect you to be fully booked up, so they are always surprised if you can make it next week.

LIVING EARTH: These multi-media presentations, do they involve slide, films, tapes?

SALLY WEBSTER: Yes. Slides, films, videos. With large groups, you know, whole schools of several hundred, it's usually difficult to show a video – because it's such a small screen – so normally we show films or slides. The only equipment we ask schools to provide is a screen or a blank wall, some black-out – which isn't always very effective! – and a table. We have our own projectors and so on. A lot of schools just don't have that sort of equipment these days.

LIVING EARTH: Do you see any pattern emerging in the topics schools are asking for? Are they all rainforests or are they more local?

SALLY WEBSTER: The most popular ones are pollution, rainforests, general habitat studies, but rainforests is a very popular topic. Quite a lot are keen to know about the local environment and British wildlife and British habitats as well as more global issues, because a lot of the children don't realise that even in their own locality there are problems. They are very keen to know what to do, if they can help. And sometimes it results in them getting involved in something practical in the school – so many of them have wildlife gardens and ponds, we will assist with practical projects, such as pond dipping, tree studies, etc. It just depends on the school and how keen they are to get involved.

LIVING EARTH: Do you organise any kind of follow-up work to assess the success of your talks, or do you just rely on seeing whether people continue to keep in touch?

SALLY WEBSTER: Some of the teachers ask for advice on some follow-up work. Most of them don't wish to worry us about it. We provide factsheets when they ask. If we have been studying heathland habitats and reptiles, for example, then we can supply the appropriate factsheets for follow-up work. Occasionally they'll send some of the children's work, but in general we're not in too much contact with the follow-up work.

LIVING EARTH: Do you find the interest in the environment has continued to increase on the part of the teachers and the pupils . . . or is it showing signs of tailing off?

SALLY WEBSTER: No, it's not tailing off; it is increasing. I think mostly because it is part of the National Curriculum, and teachers are so geared to the National Curriculum now that they have to study the environmental topics, so it's an on-going thing. Also, the general interest that the media have in the environment is reflected in the schools' programmes. Many more schools now are forming these environmental areas; practically every one has a little wildlife area, or an environmental area within the school grounds, and so they are involved on a practical basis.

LIVING EARTH: The service is available to all places of education – infant, junior and secondary – although from what you are saying, it is used much more by infant to junior?

SALLY WEBSTER: It is, yes. It's the primary schools, mainly.

LIVING EARTH: Because secondary schools are tied up with the National Curriculum?

SALLY WEBSTER: Yes, they have a more strict regime, less leeway.

LIVING EARTH: Say I was a History teacher or a Modern Languages teacher in a secondary school and wanted to focus on an environmental issue within my subject, would you be able to focus on something as specific as that?

SALLY WEBSTER: Yes, we would try to, yes. Sometimes it's hard to get hold of the visual material. Up until now, anyway, we've been able to cater for all requests.

LIVING EARTH: As long as they're spelt out in advance?

SALLY WEBSTER: Yes, that's right.

LIVING EARTH: You say you're geographically limited to one or two hours' travel from your home base. Does that mean that you have to leave out schools above, say, Hertfordshire?

SALLY WEBSTER: Yes. But sometimes if we have enough requests for a particular area we can then afford to stay there for a week, say, and do a lot of schools in that area. But generally we're based here and are geographically limited. I might add that as more funds, hopefully, become available in the future, we intend to employ regional field officers to enable schools in other areas to take advantage of our lecture service.

LIVING EARTH: So, say schools in Tyneside or Lincoln were to pool together and have six days of visits lined up?

SALLY WEBSTER: Yes, if they were to organise themselves to give us a week's work, we would be able to do that. I ought to mention also here that we run a residential course which is open to children from all over the country. We don't have our own field centre, but we use a field centre down in Swanage in Dorset which caters for school parties. We run about nine or ten weeks of residential courses there between Easter and August, mainly for school groups, because during term time it is not possible for individuals to come. We cater for about 40 at a time and we do general habitat studies in the Swanage area, because it's an excellent area for heathland, rocky shores, woodlands and so on. We again try to gear that to the National Curriculum. Generally the same schools come every year and we have two or three extra requests each year, but we usually have to turn them down, unfortunately. At the moment we cannot cater for more than nine or ten weeks, because, while we are away running the field courses, no school lecture visits can take place. In the future we hope to employ somebody part-time to run our field courses and perhaps expand them, because we could fill in practically the whole year if we tried.

SHIRLEY BARLOW, HEADTEACHER AT MERIDEN PRIMARY SCHOOL, HERTFORDSHIRE, ADDS:

As head of a primary school with pupils from four to eleven years, it is not often that I announce a visitor who is greeted with unanimous enthusiasm! That, however, is the case when we put visits from Sally Webster, the speaker from the Young People's Trust for the Environment and Nature Conservation (YPTENC) into the diary.

The YPTENC's speaker service is offered free of charge and approaches environmental matters in a warm and inspiring manner. Each visit Sally makes is structured so that appropriate age groups are combined. The number of sessions in a day is open to negotiation, and she is prepared to attempt a marathon!

Each talk is accompanied by a film or slides, all of outstanding quality, which cover subjects as varied as the secrets of the hedgerow, the life cycles of reptiles, the endangered rainforests. The subject matter is discussed in advance and Sally will suggest topics, as well as respond to requests for specific curriculum components (whole school and/or very small group involvement is also possible, if these are considered the most appropriate approach).

Children of all ages write to thank Sally, often requesting further information about some animal or habitat. They always receive a reply, accompanied by factsheets on the subject requested. This friendly, personal and reliable channel of communication delights the children and enhances their English skills as well as their knowledge of the environment. The factsheets become a valuable resource both for the individual pupil and the school as a whole.

Many children become members of YPTENC: this is another free service, unless they wish to display their enthusiasm, in which case they have to pay for a badge. The Young People's Trust for the Environment runs as a free service and provides an excellent resource for children of all ages.

I am always delighted and privileged to welcome Sally Webster, and to have regular contact with the same team member enables a positive relationship to develop. I am sure all schools would find the YPTENC speaker service of great value and enjoyment.

> Young People's Trust for the Environment and Nature Conservation
> 95 Woodbridge Road
> Guildford
> Surrey
> GU1 4PY
> Tel: 0483 39600
> Fax: 0483 301992

Using an environmental education consultant

JULIAN AGYEMAN

INTRODUCTION

Until recently, most schools will not have had to 'buy in' expertise in a particular area: it will have been provided free of charge by an advisory teacher, or a member of a professional development or curriculum support service of the LEA. However, the 1988 Education Reform Act and subsequent legislation have changed the nature of advisory and support services. Schools now have to pay for these services, either through Service Level Agreements (SLAs) with the existing LEA advisory teams (or what is left of them), or by hiring someone from one of the growing band of educational consultancies. There are currently no guidelines for these arrangements, so how do you know whom to hire? Consultancy can be a minefield for schools. The following ideas may help you to clarify your thoughts and select the right person for the task.

WHY HIRE A CONSULTANT?

There is a first point to be made here which is so obvious that it is often overlooked: there is no sense in hiring a consultant, especially in financially constrained times, if the skills and services for which you are hiring them are already available in school. Before going any further, check that there is no teacher, ancillary member of staff or parent who is not only equipped to perform the task you have in mind, but indeed keen to do so. Only when you are sure that you do not have the human resources within school should you think of approaching people outside school.

You first need to think about *why* you need a consultant. You may want to involve her or him in a long-term piece of work such as planning and managing an 'environment week', devising, raising funds for and building a school nature garden, or developing a school environmental policy and carrying out an audit. Alternatively, you may want someone on a shorter-term basis (perhaps for one day only) to carry out a specific training task, INSET or the like.

There are many good reasons for hiring an environmental education consultant. An external consultant:
- can be objective;
- provides fresh ideas and approaches;
- is often free from institutional and/or procedural constraints;
- may provide you with new contacts and sources of information/resources;
- may be able to 'customise' work for you;
- may be a specialist and have an excellent track record and broad experience.

If consultants can provide most of the qualities listed above, it will be well worth your while making friends with them!

THE CONSULTANT'S BRIEF

When you are sure that you need to hire a consultant, the next step is to draw up a consultant's brief. Even if you have a particular person in mind, this can be a good way of clarifying your objectives. The brief *must* be precise: it is, in effect, your contract with the consultant.

Obviously, the brief for a consultant depends on the nature and duration of the work that you want completed. Whatever your requirements, however, any good brief should contain:
- background information about your project;
- a description of the work you want done;
- an indication of the budget;
- an indication of the timescale;
- full details of key stages/programmes of study and attainment targets (if relevant).

It may be that for short-term (say, one-day) projects, you do not need to go into as much depth as this in the brief. However, for more lengthy projects, you should include all this and also ensure that the brief covers all details relating to job requirements and conditions and to contractual matters.

FINDING A CONSULTANT

Once you have decided that you want a consultant and have sketched out a brief, all you have to do is find a consultant. This poses another problem, because there are no 'official' ways of finding consultants . . . yet. For the foreseeable future, if you want to find out which consultants are available, what services they offer and who comes with a particularly high recommendation, the best thing to do is to ask around and, generally, to keep your ears

open. Failing such word-of-mouth information, you could approach the following for help:
- your LEA;
- the Council for Environmental Education (see page 122 for details);
- Friends of the Earth Education Department (see page 121 for details);
- WWF Education Department (see page 124 for details).

USING YOUR CONSULTANT

It is best to go through your brief with your consultant, spelling out the key areas of *what* you require, *when* you require it, and *how* much you are prepared to spend. Payment, the source of many problems, should be mutually agreed, either as a fixed price contract or as an agreed daily or hourly rate. Fixed price contracts tend to be used on longer-term projects, with the payment being made in stages; for shorter-term contracts, payment tends to be made at the end of the consultancy.

For longer-term projects, arrange for regular updates on the consultant's progress. This is essential: it shows the consultant that you are interested and also allows you to identify and act upon any potential problems before they become critical.

AT THE END OF THE CONSULTANCY

What you do after this kind of consultancy is also important. If you are pleased with the consultant, you are likely to want to use his or her services again. A little praise would, therefore, not go amiss, particularly since good consultants tend to be in demand. Always evaluate the project with the consultant, and another member of staff, where appropriate. Be honest and ask the consultant how she or he feels the school provided for her or his work.

Consultancies in school can add a new dimension to staff teams, bringing fresh ideas and different insights with them. However, for the uninitiated they can also be a nightmare. If you spend some time over it – going through the guidelines mentioned above and talking to other schools – the time you spend employing a consultant could be rewarding way beyond the end of the consultant's contract.

Julian Agyeman is now a freelance environmental education advisor, having previously worked for many years as an advisor in two London boroughs.

section two

THE CLASSROOM TOOLBOX

ART

We belong here

CHRIS THOMAS

From the readiness of pupils to display work they have done on environmental issues in the form of posters, advertisements, paintings, montages and sculptures; it would seem that, for them, visual representation possesses an immediacy and a power which can often only be matched by other non-verbal art forms like drama and music. Photographic and film images of environmental disaster and of the poverty and illness of developing countries may have lost the power to shock us into action, but other forms of visual representation – which depend crucially on the relationship between what is being represented and the person representing it – may still be able to do this.

An enduring aspect of artistic activity has been to explore and define the relationship between the human world and the natural world, and the article that follows borrows as much from prehistoric art as it does from the land art to which it also alludes. A reflective activity, it offers a useful reminder to pupils that the environment is all around them and is not just concerned with the Amazonian rainforest.

Aims

- to understand how we and others express our relationship with significant places through art
- to realise the value of an environment
- to relate pupils' experience to historical contexts
- to use an Art and Design activity to explore real and relevant group issues
- to extend pupils' concepts of the functions of art

Resources

- camera and colour print or slide film
- a step ladder to take pictures from (optional)
- pupils may like to consider appropriate clothing
- ad hoc props: be prepared for the group to want to use whatever comes to hand; the key thing is that each item is agreed by the whole group
- visual material on, for example, Stonehenge, prehistoric cave paintings and Peruvian ground drawings, Victorian follies, American land art of the 1970s (Smithson, Christo, DeMaria, Heizer), British artists (Richard Long, Andy Goldsworthy, Chris Drury, Anthony Gormley, Ian Hamilton Finlay)

Preparation required

You will need to appoint a teacher or some other adult to take a photographic record of the event, since much of the value of this activity lies in the discussions about the event and its appraisal through the photographs.

ACCOUNT OF THE ACTIVITY

Introduction

This is an open-ended group activity which uses the pupils themselves as the medium for the work and the school environment as the forum for that work (the only assumption that it makes is that a group of pupils *will* relate to some place in the school). It asks the pupils to consider themselves as a group or small community and to make a statement with their own bodies that expresses their relationship to a particular place, a statement that says: 'We belong here'.

This is an activity which has been used at primary and at secondary level; suitably adapted, it could easily work as a Dance or Drama activity, and it could even be used as a tutorial or PSE activity. By its very nature, the activity will be carried out in different places with different pupils, and the results will vary in the same way that the interactions of groups and environments vary. The results are often visually crisper if some thought is given to what the pupils wear (a common colour, for example), but this is not essential. The quality of the outcome will mostly depend on the preliminary work the pupils do before they are released to negotiate and improvise their response.

Stage One

This is a very open practical activity, and care needs to be taken to underpin it with an appreciation of how other people have related to their environment. This innately human quality can be easily understood by pupils if they are asked to think about the way in which they used to build dens (or still do) and about the other sorts of places where they like to play (Chris Drury often makes shelters as sculpture).

Show pupils some of the historical examples mentioned in the Resources above and ask them to consider the following questions in relation to these:

- To what extent are these examples an expression of their makers' feeling that 'We belong here'? To what extent are they not?
- Who were the works made for?
- What purpose did they serve?
- Why were they sited in these particular places?
- The works may have been interpreted differently at the time when they were made: can you think of examples or suggest reasons for this?
- What must it have been like to experience the making of these pieces?
- What sort of relationship must the makers have had to the place in which they made these examples?
- What else can these examples mean to us?

This discussion should last about 40 minutes, and you should prepare for the discussion by securing as much background information about as many of the examples as possible. Towards the end of the discussion, pupils should understand that the central question to which you are seeking answers is: 'What sort of relationship between people and environment produced this example?'

Stage Two

In order to increase pupils' empathetic understanding of these examples, you could invent a story about how one of these examples came to be made. A dramatic way to do this is to push away the furniture, seat pupils on the floor in a darkened room and tell them how the shaman went underground to make a rock drawing. To take the example of the prehistoric cave drawings in France: if you explain that the caves were rarely occupied, except by wild animals, that the works were, in some cases, made as far as three miles under the ground and that there were only primitive flaming torches and home-made materials with which to do the drawings, they will come to understand some of the practical difficulties involved. They might also understand that there was some sort of communal sociological need for the drawings to be made at all and that they should not, therefore, see Lascaux as an example of how the average cave family decorated its front room. This storytelling should take about 40 minutes.

Stage Three

Organise the pupils into manageable group sizes: there should be between eight and 16 pupils in each group – sometimes larger groups work better than small groups. You now present them with the brief, which is:

- to decide amongst themselves where they relate to in the school (inside or outside);
- to go there and to improvise some sort of arrangement of themselves in their place;
- to photograph a number of improvisations within the timescale allowed.

It is important that pupils are made responsible for clearing permissions, where necessary, and for warning others who may be affected by the activities.

Stage Four

In order to maintain the pupils' motivation and interest, it is important to have the photographs processed in time for the next lesson, in which the activities are 'debriefed'. An appraisal of the various activities featured in these photographs will address many of the same questions suggested in Stage One of this activity. Additionally, pupils could relate their experience back to the historical examples discussed at the outset and discuss any similarities that occur to them.

It would be time-consuming to discuss the issues raised by each group's performance and the nature of their relationship to the place they chose, and it might destroy some of the enthusiasm that the activity is likely to have generated. You will need to exercise discretion here, but the debriefing session provides an opportunity for you and your pupils to learn some valuable lessons.

Some groups may feel that they could improve significantly on the appearance or presentation of their work and might ask to repeat the session. This can often be productive, and the second chance should be seen as a second draft which reinforces what they have learned from the debriefing. Alternatively, the photographs of the activities may prove to be the stimulus to further creative work, at the discretion of the teacher.

ASSESSMENT OF THE ACTIVITY

Any assessment of the activities should take account of the aims listed above. It may or may not be appropriate to assess individual pupils' achievements here, since the whole activity is designed as a group experience, and some pupils will find it hard to talk about their individual experience of it or contribution to it. If possible, record the debriefing on audio or video tape: this provides ample evidence of the group's achievement in relation to the aims. Individual pupils' understanding and contributions might be appropriately assessed through questionnaires or taped interviews which could include such questions as:

- What was your part in your group's activity?
- Did your presentation have anything in common with the examples shown at the beginning? If so, what?
- Which of the examples shown at the beginning did you like, and why?
- What did you like about *your* group's ideas?
- Is the place that your group chose a place you go to very often?
- If you had the chance to perform your activity again, would you change it in any way, and, if so, how?

Chris Thomas is currently Head of Art at Cranbrook School.

DRAMA

Drama has an immense contribution to make to environmental education. It enables pupils to role-play situations in which one person or a group of people is in conflict with another, to examine the consequences of particular courses of action on a community or individual and to gain some insight into attitudes or ways of thinking which might otherwise remain alien to them.

The two articles that follow examine threats to the global environment, but in each case the focus is on the individual, local and human reaction to the threats. While the two projects will not necessarily increase pupils' factual knowledge of the issues, they will certainly enhance their understanding of the human implications of certain patterns of behaviour.

Neptune and the sea people

KATE CLARKE, SARAH KEMP, MALCOLM GREEN AND DOMINIC ACKLAND

Aims

- to introduce participants to the flora and fauna of the seashore
- to highlight some of the problems of dumping waste into the sea
- to give people the feeling they have the power to bring about change

Resources

Neptune will need: a trident; a gown; a crown. The sea people will need: blue/green clothes; gowns; gold headbands.

The teacher will need: a spare gold headband; task cards; thermometers, compass, etc. as required; plastic bags; two cloths for ritual and a box or block on which to place the items; a large conch shell or something similar (part of this equipment enables the teacher to assume the role of a sea person, if necessary).

ACCOUNT OF ACTIVITY

Introduction

This drama was first performed as a training session for workers in the field of environmental education at The Rising Sun Country Park and Countryside Centre in North Tyneside. Thereafter, the same drama was used with groups of primary schoolchildren between seven and ten years old. It has also been used, again at The Rising Sun Country Park and Countryside Centre, as an event on a guided walks programme.

There are two stages, or two possible strands, to this activity. It is up to the teacher and the group to decide in which order they will tackle these or, indeed, whether they will concentrate on one strand alone. For the first stage or strand, the structure of the story is clearly established in advance and participants have a firm framework within which they may work. For the second, the structure is much looser and more susceptible to personal interpretation, and the participants have to contribute to the content of the drama as much as to the enacting of it. For this reason, if both stages are to be attempted, it may be a good idea to start with the more organised framework of the first stage. The aims are, however, the same in both cases, as are the methods by which these aims are to be realised: both take the perspective of Neptune, Lord of the Seas, and the Sea People, whose lifestyle has been disrupted by pollution.

Stage One

The first stage involves telling the story of a human diving into the sea and being shown the impact of human activity on the marine world. It is up to the teacher to decide whether she or he tells this story or gives it to the group for them to construct into their own drama.

The story starts with the human, Kelp (who, for the sake of this exercise, is a woman), diving on an old wreck to try to find its treasures which people have often sought but never discovered. She has a 'feeling' that something special will happen today. Kelp finds a peacock hidden in weeds – a ruby eye falls out, which she pushes under her glove. With this 'booty', Kelp makes for the surface, but is intercepted by sharks, who surround Kelp and nudge her, firmly but gently, towards the cave.

Kelp hits her head on a rock in an attempt to escape and blacks out. On coming to, she is in a cave lit by coral, full of laughing voices – there are mermaids and mermen beckoning her further inside. There, Neptune is enthroned in a big cavern; he asks what Kelp is doing there.

Kelp replies, 'I was exploring.'

Neptune rejoins, '*Exploiting*, not exploring – let the dead rest in peace and the living live in peace.'

Neptune takes Kelp on a journey around the sea in his sea-horse chariot, in order to show Kelp evidence of human destruction. On their return, Kelp tries to remove the peacock from the arm of the throne on which Neptune is sleeping. Waking, Neptune counters, 'Have the lot.' He pulls a rope, and treasures fall on Kelp's head.

Kelp wakes up on board the boat; she is being fanned by concerned fellow divers. They question her about things she has been muttering: 'The seas will die; we must stop before it's too late.'

'I'll explain someday,' Kelp says.

'Did you find the treasure?' they ask.

Kelp feels the ruby in her diver's glove.

'No,' Kelp says, 'nothing at all.'

Stage Two

This stage again involves participants using the roles of Neptune and the sea people: it is based on a story which appears in the World Wide Fund for Nature's publication, *Stories of People and Nature*. When the drama was used at The Rising Sun, volunteer helpers and the teacher took the roles of the sea people and Neptune: however, although the storyteller and Neptune really need to be played by adults, there is no reason why older children could not be briefed to take on the role of the sea people.

The basis of the drama lies in Neptune's attempt to regain the trust of the sea people, a task in which the teacher (as storyteller) asks the participants (as themselves) to help. The task involves the elaboration of a ceremony or ritual, which is a vital part of the activity and gives meaning and credibility to the drama.

The following notes are suggested as an outline only of how this stage might evolve and they should not be stuck to rigidly. Depending on the nature of the group, the teacher should adapt and change this outline as appropriate.

Notes for the role of the sea people
- They are angry and tired of humans dumping their waste into the sea.
- They have lost their energy and their ability to dance and be joyful: as a result, they are losing power and ageing prematurely.
- They respect Neptune, but they have given up hope and do not believe her or his ideas for celebration and ritual.
- The sea people are suspicious of any overture of friendship or any approach made to them by humans, whom they do not trust (the people taking the role can feed in their own reasons for this).
- They are well versed in knowledge of sea flora and fauna.
- They *guide* the young people who approach them, they do not lead them and they should not influence the gifts the young people decide upon.

Notes for the role of Neptune
- Quiet and calm, projecting powerful presence.
- Communicative, respects, encourages, reassures the children.
- Maintains a powerful presence in the background, while the young people are engaged on the task.
- Directs all aspects of the ritual and celebration.
- Has a gentle, kind and trusting relationship with the sea people.

Sequence of the drama

1. The storyteller (e.g. the teacher) establishes the character of Neptune by telling a story about him.
2. Group organises a frozen tableau involving Neptune and the sea people (see opposite).
3. Neptune steps forward and speaks to pupils:

'I need your help. The sea people need your help. A lot of damage has been done, by humans to the sea people. They have become aged, subdued, angry and hurt. They have been good to humans and guarded the waters. Now, although they still have deep knowledge of the sea, they are losing their powers.

NEPTUNE AND THE SEA PEOPLE

You humans asked us to look after the sea and now you are destroying the sea and the sea people.

I have an idea, however, which may change this and bring joy back to my people. Will you help me with a task?'

4. Neptune explains the task to the pupils: they are to collect sea treasures to present to Neptune in a special ritual and celebration. They are to enlist the help of the sea people in the process. These treasures should represent special gifts, which have meaning and significance to givers and receivers.

5. Pupils find sea people to work with. (A good way to do this is to give each pupil a name on a card which corresponds to the name of a sea person: their first task is to find the sea person of that name and to enlist her or his help. Those pupils who are too shy to do this may stay and work with Neptune.)

6. They search for sea treasures; information is fed in by sea people. Together, they decide on their gifts and establish what they stand for.

7. Afterwards – in groups, pupils:

i) assign meaning to their gift;

ii) compose a dance, song or poem about it. (Sea people help their groups prepare this.)

8. There follows a ritual with Neptune, who makes an introductory speech (see tableau below).

Neptune asks each sea person to step forward and report on the pupils:
– Have they (the sea people) learned to trust the humans?
– Do the humans understand the sea?
– Are they committed to their task?

9. Groups present their special gifts and announce their significance (e.g. 'We bring this gift – a shell – it stands for strength and beauty as it is both strong and beautiful'). Neptune blesses each gift and repeats the significance loudly for the general gathering (e.g. 'Thank you for this gift – it will be a symbol of strength and beauty for my people'). Neptune then puts everything on a cloth on the block in the centre of the 'stage area'.

10. When Neptune has gathered sea treasures on the cloth on the block in the middle, he invites pupils to dance around this.

11. Sea people join in the dance. In the course of this ritualistic ceremony, they are rejuvenated.

12. Neptune thanks the pupils for their effort and exhorts them to go and tell others what they have learned. The ritual ends in whatever way seems appropriate for the group.

This activity was first undertaken as part of a programme of work at The Rising Sun Country Park and Countryside Centre in North Tyneside. The Centre features 400 acres of nature reserve which is open to all people; it specialises in cross-curricular countryside and environmental education, relating much of its work to the National Curriculum and working with pupils from all phases and abilities in group and individual short- and long-term projects.

The Rising Sun Country Park and Countryside Centre
Scaffold Hill
Whitley Road
Benton
Tyne and Wear
NE12 9SS
Tel: 091 266 7733 or 091 266 3524

The wise wet-woman (or wizard)
ROSEMARY LINNELL

Aims
- to introduce basic issues of land and water use, and the economics of farming
- to motivate further fact-finding and class work and to introduce simple map-making skills

Resources
- a large sheet of paper and felt-tip pens or fat wax crayons
- a well (a small fenced-off area of an otherwise bare room)
- a large supply of 'buckets' (containers that suggest carrying water, from washing-up bowls and beakers to bottle caps)
- follow-up material on water, nomads and deserts (WWF and Oxfam have good resources to use here, including wall charts and display posters)

The original lesson used a 'thunder sheet' – a sheet of tin (or thin card) which made a noise like thunder when shaken and served as a control factor; the 'wet-woman' also wore a ragged cloak covered with weeds and hung with plastic frogs, fish, turtles, etc. to add to the fun and the sense of drama. Neither is necessary. The wet-woman may be represented by the teacher, a student, a helper or another teacher.

ACCOUNT OF ACTIVITY

Introduction
The activity needs to take place in a classroom with tables stacked up or, ideally, in hall space. The lesson is described in the form of a concentrated Drama project taking half a morning, but it may be split into several lessons. It is appropriate for pupils in Years 2 or 3.

Stage One

Introduce the drama. The children may work alone or in 'family groups'. They make a map of 'Sandy Village' (they need to think about why the village is called 'Sandy Village'). First site the well and indicate its place in the room. It is the only source of water in the village and is looked after by the wise wet-woman. Mark N, S, E and W on the map. Each group draws in their house and a field or garden. The villagers live mainly on what they produce, so there should be a class discussion of what they might need, e.g. a cow or goat, pigs, chickens, vegetables, pulses or cereals, fruit, firewood, etc.

Stage Two

Avoid spending time on 'building a house' by getting the children to stand to the North or South (or wherever) in relation to the well and to each other. Each group has a varied collection of buckets. They then get to work to tend their land. Go about questioning each group on their work and emphasising potential problems such as 'Do you have to go far for firewood? What does the pig eat? You must be running short of potatoes. Is the soil very dry? Is the hot sun making the vegetables wilt?' In a large class unused to organising drama, the questioning could be done in the form of a village meeting chaired by the teacher.

Stage Three

Thunder! The wet-woman puts on her cloak. She announces that the villagers may now fetch water. She asks each group what the water is for and 'fills' the buckets for them, rather grudgingly, saying they will need to come back for lots more water for cooking, washing and to use on the land. Before the end of the queue, she announces that the well is getting low: she will only give each group half measures, so they must go back and get smaller buckets. As the measures continue to decrease, the villagers are compelled to collect their water in containers as small as bottle tops. Finally, the well is shut down altogether.

Stage Four

The wet-woman shakes with thunder and calls everyone together. The well is now dry. There is no more water in the village, no nearby rivers, no underground springs, no rain. The well may fill up again, but not to the same level. They have all used extravagant amounts of water. What is to be done? The villagers argue that they could have put washing water on the crops, etc. or they may want to move on to find somewhere else to live. Whatever decision they make, life in future will be a struggle. It is at this point that the Drama activity ends.

Stage Five

The children can research ways of cutting down or saving water. They can research or devise techniques of condensing moisture on the soil, mulching, re-using water, etc. If their decision was to move, then some reference material on nomadic life, depopulation and desert areas may be followed up.

Other possibilities

The map may be used for further drama. A government official suggests help with building wells and a road, to be paid for by an International Loan, which will in turn have to be repaid with crops. At first, harvests are good, but then the loan must be repaid with interest. First half, and then all, of every family's land will be taken for cash crops. The issues are complex, but the drama will certainly produce a strong response.

ASSESSMENT OF ACTIVITY

The lesson was originally devised to introduce World Wide Fund for Nature resource material on the above topics in an inner city school. It led to whole-school displays and assembly presentations. Special Hearing Unit children were deeply involved in all the activities. The children's ideas were used, even if they were not geographically consistent. Any discrepancies, such as potatoes and lentils being grown together, can be ironed out during the follow-up activity.

Rosemary Linnell has long experience of both theatre and teaching, working with a wide range of participants from the very young to adult Drama students. As part of the team at the ILEA's Curtain Theatre, she acted as an advisory teacher for many inner city schools, helping to plan and operate projects such as 'The wise-wet woman'. She is the author of several books on the uses of drama as a learning method.

ENGLISH

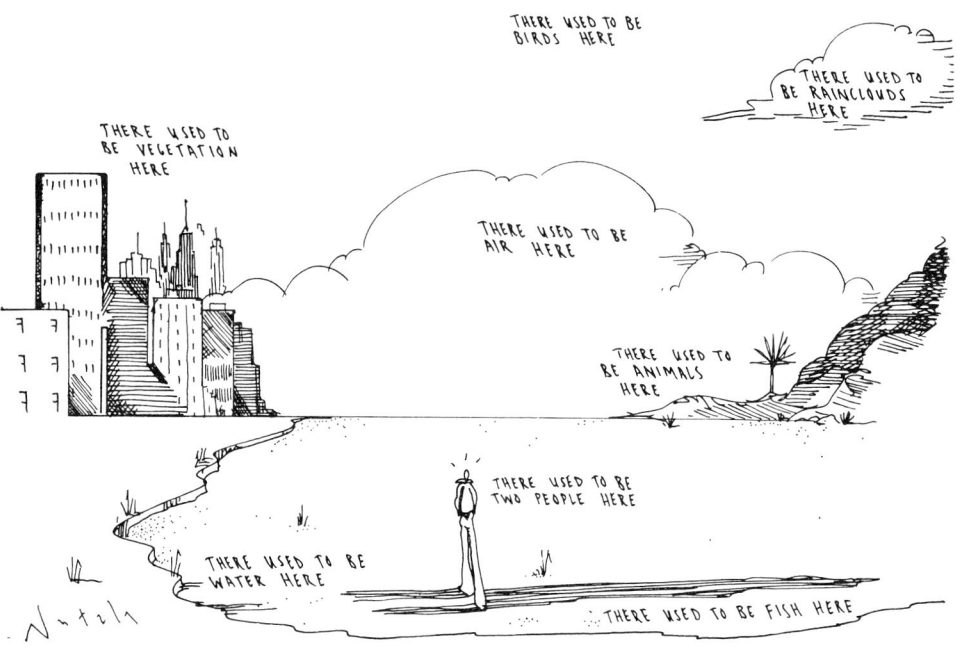

The twin aims of the English curriculum are to give all pupils the power to articulate their own experience of life and their own sense of identity and to initiate them in the language and literature of other peoples and cultures – past and present – so that their understanding of others may be enhanced.

The two articles that follow approach the subject of the environment in different ways. The first examines it as the chosen subject of writers over a period of time and shows how the late twentieth-century preoccupation with the human impact on the environment belongs to a centuries-old literary tradition. The second takes the subject of the environment as a means of honing the linguistic and presentational skills of pupils in an attempt to convey a message convincingly.

A level literature and the environment

NEIL MACRAE

Aims
- to promote understanding of the terms 'pastoral', 'industrial' and 'environmental' as they apply to literature
- to show students that the environment has been a subject of concern for writers for many centuries and to illustrate the different forms this concern has taken

Resources
- texts or photocopies of the texts discussed here (i.e. 'Hares at Play' by John Clare, extracts from *Tess of the D'Urbervilles* by Thomas Hardy and *Hard Times* by Charles Dickens, 'Auguries of Innocence' by William Blake and 'Windscale' by Norman Nicholson)
- other texts that students might be interested to research in the light of these activities
- supplementary material as required by the teacher

ACCOUNT OF ACTIVITY

Introduction

The activities described in this article have been developed for use with some texts typical of those studied on many A level English Literature syllabuses (Years 12–13). The same activities may, with some adjustment, be used with a wide range of other texts studied at this level, together with some less familiar texts which have an environmental theme (a short list of texts is given at the end of this article). This work has also tremendous cross-curricular potential – particularly in Art and History – and you may wish to develop this aspect further in consultation with colleagues in other subject areas.

The focus of the group of activities here is to develop student understanding of the contrasting concepts of the pastoral, the industrial and the environmental as they appear in some typical A level texts. Each activity, introduced by a poem or an extract from a novel, addresses some contemporary environmental issues in the context of texts with which students may be familiar. Students are encouraged to develop connections between the world of the novel and environmental issues, both old and new.

For the three linked activities presented here, students will need to be familiar with the novels, but the poetry stimuli are best approached as unfamiliar texts. You may, of course, wish to add your own materials as stimuli – literary texts, photographs, period illustrations and so on.

Stage One

Begin by asking students to consider the novels they have read so far in their A level course and to identify any which have passages of writing which look at the *rural* environment.

Ask students to work in pairs and to address the following questions:

- What can you remember of the descriptions in these novels? What do they tell you about the countryside?
- What feelings do you think the writer has about the world she or he is writing about?

Discuss any issues raised before moving on to the poem below. It's by the early nineteenth-century writer, John Clare, but students should approach it as an unknown text.

> *The birds are gone to bed the cows are still*
> *And sheep lie panting on each old mole hill*
> *And underneath the willows grey-green bough*
> *Like toil a-resting – lies the fallow plough*
> *The timid hares throw daylight fears away*
> *on the lanes road to dust and dance and play*
> *Then dabble in the grain by nought deterred*
> *To lick the dewfall from the barleys beard*
> *Then out they sturt again and round the hill*
> *Like happy thoughts dance squat and loiter still*
> *Till milking maidens in the early morn*
> *Gingle their yokes and start them in the corn*
> *Through well known beaten paths each nimbling hare*
> *Sturts quick as fear – and seeks its hidden lair*

(The spelling and punctuation here are reproduced as in the original text.)

Students, working collaboratively in pairs, could make notes on the following questions to help focus their developing understanding of the poem:

- What can you say about the writer of this poem and the world that is described?
- Imagine that you are standing where the poem is set. Describe the features of the landscape around you and the feelings of the poet towards them.

- Now try to read *between* the lines and build up a portrait of the poet, thinking of her or him as someone you might meet. You may find these questions helpful:
  - Where does she or he live?
  - What might she or he do for a living?
  - What do you think are some of the poet's concerns and interests?
  - What does the poem say about the world in which the poet lived?

Students should have now begun to build up a portrait of the poet and his world through their discussions. At this point you could introduce some biographical information, placing Clare in his contemporary context:

Clare (1793–1864) wrote about the natural world he knew well. A ploughman living in the flat Cambridgeshire countryside, he took part in one of the most profound changes to happen to the system. The introduction of the controversial Enclosures Act was to change the face of the English countryside and create a rural landscape which remained largely unchanged until the 1950s. This eroded the rights of the small farmer and removed many of the common rights held by country people for centuries. The open expanses of the Cambridgeshire countryside were covered with new, quickly growing hedges and the open expanses of agricultural land parcelled into smaller fields.

How we interpret apparent environmental progress and conservation depends very much on our historical viewpoint. Students will now be able to begin to place their twentieth-century understanding of John Clare's poem alongside a developing knowledge of eighteenth- and nineteenth-century environmental concerns. For example, they might now be able to make the connection between the major change brought about by the Enclosures Act and the current environmental battle to *save* the hedges which were considered such a blight in Clare's time. Since the end of the Second World War, England and Wales have lost over 20,000 miles of hedges, and there is now a sustained campaign to save those that remain.

Students can reflect on the apparently conflicting information here by addressing questions such as these:

- Is it possible for someone living in twentieth-century Britain to have the same response to the rural environment that Clare has here? If not, what has been lost? Has anything been gained in the same process?
- Are there other texts you are studying at A level which reveal changes in the way in which we view the countryside?
- Are there other texts you are studying which criticise a development which we now consider to have been for the good?

Stage Two

This activity introduces a writer studied by the vast majority of A level students. Thomas Hardy, writing some 50 years after Clare, also describes a changing country landscape – and, again, people are the cause of this change. The following extract, from *Tess of the D'Urbervilles*, could be introduced without acknowledgement:

> *The season developed and matured. Another year's instalment of flowers, leaves, nightingales, thrushes, finches, and such ephemeral creatures, took up their*

> *positions where only a year ago others had stood in their place when these were nothing more than germs and inorganic particles. Rays from the sunrise drew forth the buds and stretched them into long stalks, lifted up sap in noiseless streams, opened petals, and sucked out scents in invisible jets and breathings.*

Ask students to work again in pairs and to address the following questions:

- What can you say about the natural world as it is described in this passage?
- What views do you think the writer has about the world he describes?

Clearly, although Hardy and Clare are both writing about the countryside, the feelings presented in each passage are quite different from each other. In order to help them to clarify these differences, you could give students some biographical information about Thomas Hardy. You could develop this further, and complement it, with a passage like the following. This extract again comes from *Tess of the D'Urbervilles* and it illustrates the environmental changes recorded by Hardy as Victorian industrial society began to impose itself on the farming communities of Dorset – the Wessex of his novels:

> *The work sped on till breakfast-time, when the thresher was stopped for half an hour; and on starting again after the meal the whole supplementary strength of the farm was thrown into the labour of constructing the straw-rick, which began to grow beside the stack of corn. A hasty lunch was eaten as they stood, without leaving their positions, and then another couple of hours brought them near to dinner-time; the inexorable wheels continuing to spin, and the penetrating hum of the thresher to thrill to the very marrow all who were near the revolving wire cage.*

Using their developing knowledge, students could now begin to discuss Hardy's view of these changes.

Later on in this novel, Hardy is explicit about some of the long-term results of these changes:

> *Cottagers who were not directly employed on the land were looked upon with disfavour, and the banishment of some starved the trade of others, who were thus obliged to follow. These families, who had formed the backbone of the village life in the past, who were the depositaries of the village traditions, had to seek refuge in the large centres; the process, humorously designated by statisticians as 'the tendency of the rural population towards the large towns', being really the tendency of water to flow uphill when forced by machinery.*

This kind of passage clearly illustrates that the environment is not just a passive feature of the natural landscape, but something living and dynamic, actively interrelated with all that we do.

You can apply the scientific concept of 'Gaia' – the notion that the earth is a complete self-sustaining biosphere – usefully to literature. The space-scientists who first put forward this view were initially trying to develop experiments which would reveal whether life forms existed on other planets. Within Gaia, the living planet, every organism – from microbe to human – is linked in some way to every other organism. The winds and waves, animal migrations and patterns of reproduction are all interrelated in a complex global life-support system.

It's a concept that Thomas Hardy or Wordsworth would probably have been at home with. Teachers could develop these interests with reference to the theories of the social scientist, Alvin Tofler. Tofler suggests that human civilisation has been delineated by three major developments, or waves, of change. The first was the discovery of agriculture, the second the Industrial Revolution, and the third wave an acknowledgement of our environmental responsibilities centred on our imaginative use of information – about ourselves, each other and the world we inhabit. The technological resources possessed by western civilisation needs to be harnessed to the third wave rather than the second.

A changing understanding of that first agricultural revolution informed John Clare, and the inevitable conflict between this change and the pressures of industrialisation is one of Hardy's major concerns in *Tess of the D'Urbervilles*, as we have seen.

As we move into an increasingly urbanised twenty-first century, the problems caused by the success of the second wave become ever more apparent. By the year 2000, 50% of the world's population will be urbanised, compared with 14% in 1900. The next stage of this activity looks more closely at a writer much concerned with life at the height of the Industrial Revolution and the problems it presented for his characters.

Stage Three

By the time Thomas Hardy was voicing his criticisms in 1891, many had joined him in opposition to the 'progress' brought by unchecked late Victorian industrialisation. But at the start of the Industrial Revolution, over one hundred years earlier, writers had been more likely to celebrate what was happening around them. What happened in between was the realisation that the industrial dream was becoming ever more frightening, such that one writer could describe one of the new industrial towns with nightmarish horror:

> *It was a town of red brick, that would have been red if the smoke and ashes had allowed it; but, as matters stood, it was a town of unnatural red and black like the face of a savage. It was a town of machinery and tall chimneys, out of which interminable serpents of smoke trailed themselves for ever and ever, and never got uncoiled. It had a black canal in it, and a river that ran purple with ill-smelling dye, and vast piles of buildings full of windows where there was a rattling and a trembling all day long, and where the piston of the steam-engine worked monotonously up and down, like the head of an elephant in a state of melancholy madness.*

As before, teachers could show the passage to students without acknowledgement. Charles Dickens's *Hard Times* is widely read at A level, and the passage above is often anthologised.

Working once more in pairs, students could address the following:

- What does this writer think of the environment she or he describes?
- Try to build up a portrait of the writer imagining her or his interests and concerns from the evidence in the passage.

Students may now be given some biographical details about Charles Dickens, who is here describing northern Coketown in *Hard Times*. He is, of course, writing about pollution. Less than 20 years after *Hard Times* was written, Angus Smith in Manchester described the effects of what he called 'acid rain'. He had noted that the rain falling on the city contained sulphuric acid, caused by an atmospheric reaction between a mixture of pollutants and the oxygen in the atmosphere. Today, this form of air pollution has destroyed one third of the trees in the Black Forest, and around the world acidified water is damaging the ecosystem by leaching nutrients out of the water and activating dangerous heavy metals in the soil.

You could ask students how many of Dickens's concerns in the passage are ones which we still share today and use their answers to develop an approach to a second, equally important, issue.

Immediately after the passage above, Dickens goes on to describe how the lives of those who live and work in Coketown have been polluted in more subtle ways. People are 'equally like one another' and everything in the town is 'severely workful'.

Dickens's concern is how the society created by the Industrial Revolution has been ethically polluted too. Today, technological progress can create some striking anomalies: for example, a single nuclear submarine would typically cost as much as the annual education budgets of 23 developing countries around the world. Bombs or books? Simply *living* in the twentieth century can be hazardous.

And, as Norman Nicholson's poem below – often widely anthologised – illustrates, the nature-industry debate has received a new twist in the late twentieth century. Once more, the poem can be introduced to students without acknowledgement. You might, however, ask students to consider Blake's 'Auguries of Innocence' first:

Auguries of Innocence

> *To see the world in a grain of sand,*
> *And a heaven in a wild flower;*
> *Hold infinity in the palm of your hand,*
> *And eternity in an hour.*

William Blake

Windscale

> *The toadstool towers infest the shore:*
> *Stink-horns that propagate and spore*
> >   *Wherever the wind blows.*
> *Scafell looks down from the bracken band,*
> *And sees hell in a grain of sand,*
> >   *And feels the canker itch between his toes.*
>
> *This is a land where dirt is clean,*
> *And poison pasture, quick and green,*
> >   *And storm sky, bright and bare;*
> *Where sewers flow with milk, and meat*
> *Is carved up for the fire to eat,*
> >   *And children suffocate in God's fresh air.*

Norman Nicholson

Students could now discuss in pairs the issues raised by this poem and address the following questions:

- What is the poet's view of how the Windscale Atomic Power Station has changed the environment around it?
- What other environmental issues are referred to in this poem? How may these be addressed on a global level? Discuss this in relation to the following quotation from the influential Brandt Commission Report:

> *In the global context, true security cannot be achieved by a mounting build-up of weapons (defence in a narrow sense), but only by providing basic conditions for solving non-military problems which threaten them. Our survival depends not only on military balance, but on global co-operation to ensure a sustainable biological environment.*

Other possibilities

You could develop the links further between students' A level texts and the environmental issues in the world today. Although there are few contemporary novels which address specifically environmental issues on current examination syllabuses, a short list of novels both old and new which could develop this work is given below:

Bleak House Charles Dickens
Coming up for Air George Orwell
Cider With Rosie Laurie Lee
Dune Frank Herbert
Howards End E M Forster
Make Room! Make Room! Harry Harrison
Mansfield Park Jane Austen
Mary Barton Elizabeth Gaskell
Soft City Jonathan Raban
Stark Ben Elton
Wuthering Heights Emily Brontë

Neil MacRae was until recently an advisory teacher and is now head of English in a Hertfordshire secondary school. He has produced a number of professional materials for publication and is currently editing a media resource package for his local education authority.

Environmental collage

JOHN MCKELLAR

Aim

- to raise awareness of the environment and to invite pupils to reflect on the positive and negative aspects of their own environment

Preparation required

Seek out as many poems, articles, extracts, photographs and pamphlets as possible on the environment, both local and general. (I have found the Oxford University Press poetry anthologies very useful – A Third Poetry Book, Another Third Poetry Book, A Fourth Poetry Book and New Angles – as well as Heinemann's Axed Between the Ears which is edited by David Kitchen; I've also made extensive use of our own school anthology, Dew on a Cobweb Shines, which has some excellent poems and stories.)

Obtain a copy of Free Stuff for Kids (see p.162), which has numerous addresses for environmental posters, etc. at low cost.

ACCOUNT OF ACTIVITY

Introduction

This activity covers all attainment targets in National Curriculum English and the main statements of achievement, including (because writing is involved) attainment targets 4 and 5. The nature of the activity is such that it is able to accommodate a mixed-ability class through differentiation by task as well as differentiation by ability (on common tasks). A range of assessments is therefore possible within the National Curriculum criteria.

The collage represents the pupils' response to the idea of the environment in as wide a context as possible. There is a danger, however, that the context could be *too* wide and the concept too huge for the pupils to make meaningful or personal responses to, so a fruitful way into looking at the environment in its widest sense is to focus on what the environment means to the pupils in their own experience. This enables pupils to move from the specific to the general.

Stage One

Explain what is meant by a collage and what the finished display should seek to achieve in its visual impact. The class then begins by working in small groups of four or five, making lists of what they perceive to be the positive and the negative aspects of their own environment. These lists are displayed and discussed, and from the discussion one master list is agreed on which represents collective feelings about the immediate environment.

Stage Two

Ask pupils how they could inform people about their environment. Suggest, if the idea is not immediately forthcoming, that people would like to read a booklet about the area. Pupils agree that they should create their own booklets about their environment which would form part of their completed collage.

Begin work on the booklets; pupils focus on those aspects of their own environment which are of interest to them. While this work continues, time is made for pupils to read the relevant pages from *Free Stuff for Kids* and to choose an address for materials and information. In their own time, pupils draft and re-draft letters, address envelopes and post their requests for information. (This stage obviously involves some expenditure, and the simplest solution is for the teacher to make out personal cheques and to have these reimbursed by the school.) Letters are posted and pupils continue with their booklets.

As pupils work on their booklets, additional material (in the form of, for example, poems and articles to read and assimilate) can be offered as and when appropriate. These materials should be at hand for pupils to read and respond to as their booklets are completed. Photographs provide more stimulus for comment and writing. Pupils may request to write a poem or a story; encourage them to do so. The first large sheets for display material are made available and work is mounted.

Stage Three

Within a week the requested materials should begin to arrive at school, and pupils will have stimulus material which takes them beyond their local environment. Issues such as tree planting, wildlife, litter, woodlands, hedgehogs, birds and so forth open up a more general context. This transition from the specific to the general is easy to make, particularly because the pupils will be motivated to read the materials since they are addressed to them personally and they have ownership over them. Many of the materials will have their own activities (some to be coloured and written about) crossword puzzles, questionnaires. There is a wealth of visual material to be photocopied, cut and mounted.

The classroom activity consists of many individual or paired tasks with the ever-increasing display sheets providing a focal point for completed work to be proudly mounted. Pupils are engaged in various kinds of writing and reading and speaking and listening. When the display is complete, it will fill the wall in the main corridor and receive an instant audience of all the people involved in the school. One way to consolidate the awareness is to ask the pupils to write personal statements reflecting on what they have done and learned.

ASSESSMENT OF ACTIVITY

The activity is well suited to the conditions in a primary classroom, where it is possible to award more time than is usual in a secondary school. A lot of paper and materials are required, and some mess can be expected.

The activity works well with low-achieving or mixed-ability classes because of its open-ended nature. It is essential, however, that materials are at hand to challenge more able pupils; since the collage deals with personal responses, there are any number of possibilities open to such pupils. The open nature of the activity ensures that all pupils, whatever their ability, can make a contribution. The fact that the work starts with an examination of local environmental issues helps the less able to identify with the work. Some of the commercial materials contain difficult writing, however, and Special Needs pupils will require support in accessing the information.

Pupils enjoy the idea of completing a task and mounting it. The empty spaces on the large sugar paper slowly disappear, and progress is seen to be made. The evidence of the collage taking shape is a key motivation to further effort.

The activity is busy and demands a lot of energy from the teacher. The varied and constant input required of the teacher makes National Curriculum assessment (difficult at the best of times) even more demanding. However, there is a wide variety of writing available, and pupils and teacher need to sit down from time to time and read through materials: this in itself provides opportunities for assessment.

References

> *Free Stuff For Kids* (ISBN 1-85015-279-9) is published by Exley Publications Ltd. It costs £2.99 and is available from Exley Publications Ltd, Chalk Hill, Watford, Hertfordshire WD1 4BN.
> *A Third Poetry Book, Another Third Poetry Book, A Fourth Poetry Book, New Angles 1* and *New Angles 2*, J L Foster (ed.), Oxford University Press.
> *Axed Between the Ears*, D Kitchen (ed.), Heinemann.

> *John McKellar is currently head of English and Creative Arts at West Redcar School, County Cleveland. He started teaching in 1974 as a specialist teacher of Drama. He has since worked in a number of schools as a teacher of English, Head of Drama and Head of English. He is co-author of* Interactive English – Six Case Studies, *published by NATE (the National Association for the Teaching of English).*

GEOGRAPHY

Geography is in many ways the natural home for environmental education. It provides us with real places where real environmental issues have real impacts on people, and it offers pupils the opportunity to go beyond description and explanation to make predictions and to offer possible solutions. By allowing pupils to focus on an issue of local or global significance, it also teaches the important lesson that there are no simple answers and that solving an environmental problem in one place may create environmental problems in another.

The two articles that follow both choose the immediate local environment as the focus for their activity. Neither article offers pat solutions; the learning outcome in each case is an understanding of the complexity of the issues and of the plurality of the human positions taken on these issues.

The Mobil Greensight Pack
video project

MARTIN ROBERTS

Aims
- to produce a home-grown mini-documentary on a local building development issue as support for syllabus units on 'Work and Employment' and 'Urban Patterns and Processes'
- to allow pupils to participate in a group learning experience
- to enable pupils to submit a final version of their documentary to the GCSE board as part of validated coursework
- to produce a video resource for use in future GCSE lessons as a local case study

Resources
- access to VHS video-recording equipment, portable cameras and editing facilities
- blank video cassettes
- collaboration from colleagues in Media Studies, the Media Resources Officer and colleagues in Design/Technology
- *The Mobil Greensight Pack* (produced by Living Earth) – optional

Preparation required
See the introduction to the account of the activity below. Depending on how the project is organised, you will have to secure permission from the senior management team and from parents for the pupils to leave the school's premises.

You will also need to provide basic training in a variety of skills, for example: video recording, interviewing techniques, editing, letter writing, using the phone to make enquiries, using researching techniques, etc. The precise nature of these skills will depend on the project and the way of working chosen.

In a similar way, other preparation will be required as the project evolves. It is a good idea to have an idea of important local environmental issues, the people involved in the local planning departments, local environmentalist groups, any contact names or numbers that may prove useful.

ACCOUNT OF ACTIVITY

Introduction

This is an activity which originally formed part of the development work which led to the publication of Living Earth's *The Mobil Greensight Pack*: the pack demonstrates how to produce a video presentation (or some other form of audio-visual presentation) on an environmental matter of perceived local importance. While it would be worth referring to the pack for further information, the essence of the project is to organise a group of pupils into working independently towards the completion of this production. The subject of the investigation may either be given to the pupils or chosen by them. The work may take place within timetabled lessons, or it may be organised as an off-timetable project, as part of a club's activities, for example. The project places the teacher in the role of facilitator as much as in the role of instructor: her or his responsibility is more to guide pupils towards the best way of working and the most profitable areas of investigation than to tell them what to do. For this reason, it also means that a lot of a teacher's time is taken up in negotiating: with the pupils, with other members of staff and with people outside the school who are needed for the project.

This particular activity was undertaken by a small group of Year 10 Geography pupils as part of their GCSE work. The work lasted for four weeks and was organised into eight two-hour sessions. The work was specifically relevant to Geography (in particular, to AT2 and AT4, although virtually all the competences in AT1 could be related to the project), but drew also on the skill areas of Information Technology and Personal and Social Education. It also involved important careers work.

The 19 members of the group were divided into four working teams: a research team, design team, film crew and writing team. Each team had specific duties/tasks throughout the project, although sometimes the whole class would hold project discussion/progress meetings.

Organising the project

The project was introduced as part of the normal programme of study for the GCSE unit on 'Work and Employment'. The case study in this context was the extension to the Earls Court Exhibition Centre – already a hotly disputed local issue for the pupils and their families! The subject had been suggested by the local Environmental Health Officer, who turned out to be a useful partner early on in the project. The pupils knew about the development, but the full relevance and scope of the issues only impinged on them as the project developed.

Table 1 (below) presents a breakdown of the project's schedule and gives an account of what work was involved in each two-hour session. Table 2 (opposite) presents a breakdown of each of the four teams' responsibilities in the course of the project, and Table 3 (opposite) indicates the specifically geographical (or environmental educational) information that emerged from the project. These tables demonstrate the opportunities presented by project work of this kind: pupils learn to deploy a range of demanding life skills in pursuit of a target which they themselves have helped to define, and in the course of which they are able to make the connection between a local development and wider, even global environmental issues. The achievements of the pupils, as evidenced from these tables, are impressive: to have researched the opinion of so many different interest groups (the Environmental Health Officer mentioned above, representatives of the construction company responsible for the site development, local residents, the Green Alliance, planning officers in the local authority) is some achievement – to be able to collate all this information into a 15-minute programme presenting a clear position on the subject is more than even they imagined they were capable of at times!

```
"GREENSIGHT"   PILOT        SCHEDULE : ST. MARK'S SCHOOL

SESSION 1: INTRODUCTION                    SESSION 2: GETTING STARTED
Aims and objectives outlined               Identification of specific tasks within
Identification of work groups (see diag.2) the working groups
Allocation of groups                       Selection of location/case study
Role of the                                Initial "brainstorming" of group ideas
Class Teacher/Living Earth _ discussion
Establishment of "code of conduct"         Outline of Industrial Case Study chosen
Establishment of overall task (see diag.2) PLENARY TIME: PRODUCTION MEETING
Identification of group leaders               line-management responsibility/tasks
Identification of possible locations          "The next step"

SESSION 3: TRAINING WORKSHOPS              SESSION 4: QUESTION TIME
Training session with groups:              Questions to panel of "experts":
(W) Film Studies teacher/English teacher      Representatives from
(F) Film Studies teacher + M.R.O.             The Living Earth
(D) Art & Design teacher                      Green Alliance
(R) Geography/Humanities teacher              Industrial Management (Case Study)
                                              Film Company or MRO
plus compilation of questions for
Session 4                                  environment/industry issues and role of
                                           film investigation/critical awareness

SESSION 5: PREPARATION                     SESSION 6: ANALYSIS (1)
(R) and (F) off site to interview          PRODUCTION MEETING: progress report
EHO; Company Reps; Local residents;        analysis of data/preliminary editing/
Local Authority                            initial production
(D) preparation of captions/logo etc       (W) editing and soundtracking
(W) preparation of draft script/ideas      (F) filming captions etc
    for soundtrack/storyboarding           (D) package and display preparation
                                           (R) follow up and preparation of
                                               package exercises

SESSION 7: ANALYSIS (2)                    SESSION 8: FINAL PRODUCTION MEETING
(W)  editing and soundtracking             viewing of draft video
(F)  reshooting/backgrounds                review of soundtrack
(D)  package completion/display            comments and reactions
     production                            discussion of outcome
(R)  finalising programme notes            evaluation and self-assessment
                                           appraisal of package format
PRODUCTION MEETING: progress report        date and venue of final display

Key to working groups:  (W) writing team  (F) film crew  (D) design & presentation
                        (R) research team                                     team

PILOT SCHEDULE TIMING: Each session  approx. two hours
                      Total schedule = sixteen hours
                      School timing = four weeks class time
```

Table 1

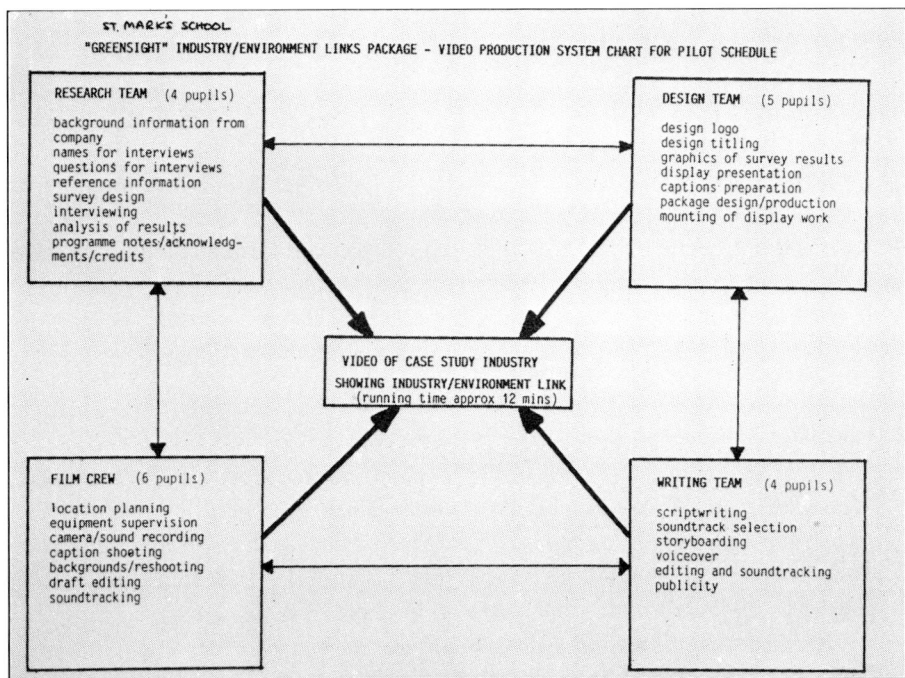

Table 2

Table 3

A lot of hard work goes into projects of this kind, however, and not just on the part of the pupils. Careful structuring and organisation of the eight sessions were essential so that each working group had a clearly defined set of tasks to complete. Pupils were also constantly reminded of their collective responsibility to produce the final video on time – and that this involved working to a tight deadline. The teacher's responsibility is to be aware of what each team is working on at any one time, what help or input they will be needing for that task, who will be able to provide this if the teacher is working with another team at that time – in other words, maintaining overall control of the project while appearing to be merely supervising procedures.

The outcome (a 15-minute mini-documentary with accompanying programme notes and display poster) was subsequently used both in Geography lessons and as a joint coursework submission. The benefits in terms of the pupils' motivation and interest were apparent to all, but the real bonus was the ability of the pupils confidently to discuss and recall a wide range of allied issues and to apply these to the detailed knowledge of a local case study which was effectively quoted in their GCSE examination responses. Later generations will also identify with the pupils' own resource and will undertake similar projects, gradually providing a bank of home-grown local visual aids. I have subsequently adapted the *Mobil Greensight Pack* approach for use as part of a seven-day residential fieldwork project with Year 11 pupils and with a Media Studies group studying a local urban issue of the provision of accommodation for homeless families.

ASSESSMENT OF ACTIVITY

Undoubtedly the success of the project depends on a high degree of staff commitment to the approach, which is the key to motivating the pupils. However, the sense of achievement at the end is most gratifying – on both sides! The involvement of colleagues from other departmental areas has led to further cross-curricular planning, and the school's relationship with local authority departments and other outside agencies has been enhanced through their active involvement and encouragement in real educational/curriculum development. We have all learned more about the relationship between industry and environmental issues as a result of this project than would have been possible in purely classroom-based work.

Martin Roberts has been an Inner London teacher since 1975, head of Humanities at Pimlico School, Westminster, since 1989 and a consultative moderator and assistant examiner for the 'Avery Hill' GCSE Geography syllabus since 1988. His special curriculum interests include residential fieldwork, environmental education and alternative approaches to learning through collaborative techniques, all of which were put to good effect when he acted as educational consultant to the Mobil Greensight Pack, *produced by Living Earth in 1992.*

Examining the future development of an historic town

THE ENVIRONMENTAL EDUCATION WORKING GROUP OF THE GEOGRAPHICAL ASSOCIATION

Aims

Geography is concerned with the study of places, the human and physical processes which shape them and the people who live in them. By developing pupils' sense of place and their understanding of environmental processes, Geography makes a significant contribution to environmental education. More specifically, this activity aims:

- to show how environmental education can be taught through enquiry into relevant and real issues to give purpose and structure to investigations;
- to explore planning constraints and issues in the urban environment;
- to show how the site and situation of a settlement are governed by historical and geographical factors;
- to show how other professionals and members of the community can work with pupils;
- to empower pupils to make informed decisions about their own lifestyles and the impact such decisions can have on the environment;
- to make pupils familiar with the decision-making processes that exist within society and to enable pupils to participate in them in order to play a part in managing change.

The activity enables teachers:

- to hold an INSET day planning an environmental enquiry and devising appropriate learning activities to explore the issues;
- to demonstrate the contribution of working with people other than classroom teachers, such as the advisory teacher for environmental education/humanities, the education

officer from English Heritage and an officer from the Design and Conservation Section of the County Planning Department;
- to design their own enquiries in their own area and to recognise the potential of historic sites as a basis for environmental geography educational work.

National Curriculum relevance

The activity is especially relevant to National Curriculum Geography (AT 5, Environmental Geography – the quality and vulnerability of different environments and the possibilities for protecting and managing environments; AT 4, Human Geography – settlements; AT 1, Skills, map work, fieldwork and enquiry; AT 2, Place, locality and home region) and National Curriculum History (AT 1, Knowledge and understanding of history; AT 3, The use of historical sources; Stuart and Tudor times (Key Stage 2); the making of the UK: Crown, Parliaments and peoples 1500–1750 (Key Stage 3)).

Resources and preparation

- Fieldwork at Bolsover Castle, in and around Bolsover Town, using the conservation area.
- Information gathered from the Bolsover District Council, Bolsover Civic Society, the Design and Conservation Section of the County Planning Department, English Heritage Education Department and the staff at Bolsover Castle.

ACCOUNT OF ACTIVITY

Introduction

This activity concerns an investigation into an environmental issue, in this instance the future development of Bolsover (an historic town centred around the castle). The method outlined below may be applied to any other area, although teachers are advised to choose an historic town which pupils know and perceive as being relevant to their lives.

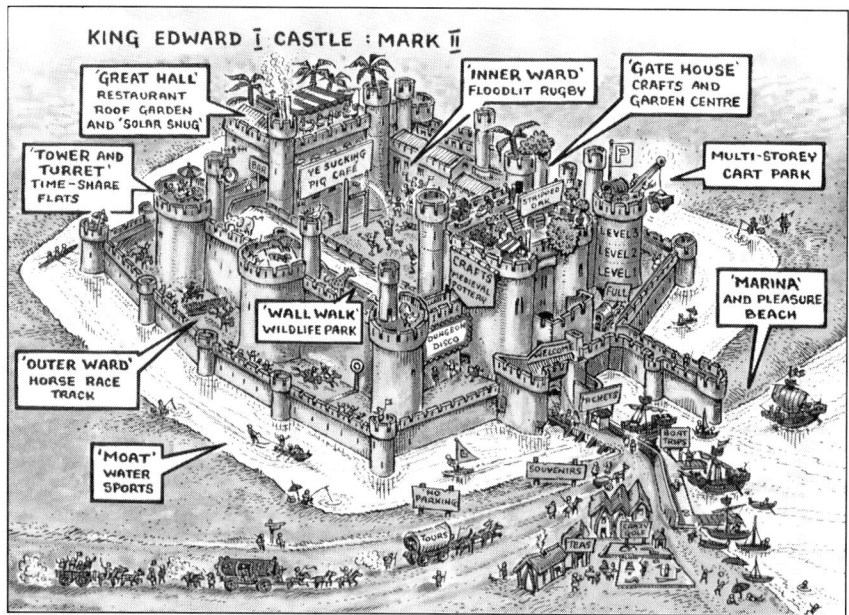

An enquiry is an appropriate way to plan an investigation at any key stage. Progression can be achieved by adjusting the scale and complexity of the enquiry and the extent to which the enquiry is pupil- or teacher-led.

Working with an enquiry approach to teaching and learning also provides an opportunity to:

- design activities for all group sizes;
- teach in a variety of styles;
- differentiate activities by outcome (since an enquiry is open-ended);
- enable pupils to work independently where appropriate;
- develop skills of investigation.

The activity focused on an attempt to answer the question 'What should the future development of Bolsover Town, Castle and locality be?' The enquiry could form the basis for a unit of work or be the subject of only one lesson. Clearly, the amount of time allowed for the activity will affect the planning that needs to be undertaken by the teacher.

Stage One

The work began with an investigation of the issues surrounding the future development of an individual listed building – in this case, the castle. Pupils were asked to provide simple descriptions by way of answers to such questions as:

- What is a castle?
- What is a castle used for?
- Is this a castle?
- What do I and others think/feel about this place?

The issues of the future development of listed buildings were introduced through means of the cartoon (opposite), and, in answer to the question, 'What could English Heritage do with Bolsover Castle?', the following alternatives were given: preserve it; conserve it; re-use it; re-interpret it; leave it alone; re-develop it; record and destroy it.

For pupils to be able to decide which of these options to select, they need to have a set of criteria which will inform their choice. These criteria could focus on the building's:

- function (What was/is this site/building used for? Is the function unusual or interesting?);
- construction (What is this building made from? What is its state of repair? How was it built? Does the construction make this building special?);
- design (Is the design appropriate to the building's function? What style/period is the building? Who designed it? What styles does it reflect? Does the design of the building make it special?);
- location (Where is this site/building? Why was this site or location chosen? How is this building positioned in relation to other buildings? Does the location of this building make it important for any reason?);
- value (Is this the only one of its kind? Is this site/building a good example of its kind? Who used it and what for? Is this the only example in the area? What is the building's aesthetic value?);
- cost (How much would any proposal cost? If this site/building was developed, would any other project suffer?);

- interested parties (Who would have to be consulted? Whose views would have to be taken into account? Who would pay/do the work? Who decides?).

It is important to note that the questions about the building's location help define the geographical work to be covered. However, the breadth of questions means that the topic has much cross-curricular potential.

Having posed the questions, the teacher (or pupil) will need to design activities to enable the pupils to gather the information necessary to answer them. This should allow the pupils to reach a conclusion about the best possible future use of the castle.

Stage Two

The next stage of the enquiry is to consider the castle in relation to the town and its locality. English Heritage is considering the possibility of organising a Town Scheme for Bolsover town (a Town Scheme is a partnership between the Local Authority and English Heritage to stimulate the regeneration of important historic towns). This scheme could assist the redevelopment of the town, possibly by promoting it as an historic market town for tourism. Bolsover already has a designated conservation area (Bolsover District Council has a map giving this area, called 'Bolsover Conservation Area') and several listed buildings.

Pupils should ask similar questions to those given above to help them explore what the future development of the town and its locality should be.

There are many ways in which pupils can gather information about the town, including an investigation of its present land use, researching opinions from residents and arranging discussions with the town council. One group designed a series of activities to help pupils undertake an environmental assessment of the town and an evaluation of the quality of the buildings. The tasks were:

1. Undertake a survey of the town and choose five views of a building that is important to the environmental quality of life. Take a photograph of each view. Mark the position of your viewpoint on the map.
2. Undertake a survey of the town and choose five views of a building whose removal would improve the quality of the environment. Take a photograph of each view. Mark the position of your viewpoint on the map.
3. Undertake a survey of the town and choose five buildings that show change in use or style. Identify buildings which are decorated to look old. Look for fake windows, new coach lamps, half-timbered integral garages, neo-Georgian bow windows, Tudor lettering and spelling. Look for changes to buildings. Identify replacement windows, extensions, blocked doors and windows, new roofing. Make annotated field sketches to show change. Mark the position of your building on the map.
4. Undertake a survey of the town and choose five modern or new buildings, of special architectural interest, that should be conserved in the future. Take a photograph of each. Mark its position on the map.
5. Undertake a survey of the town and choose five buildings, of special architectural or historic interest, that should be conserved. Take a photograph of each. Mark its position on the map.

Groups of pupils familiarised themselves with the town and then focused on the building or buildings of their choice in order to do the activity outlined above. Each group then had to make a presentation to the others, explaining their criteria for choosing that building and sharing their evaluation of the building, using photographs or drawings to illustrate their points. The officer from the Design and Conservation section of the County Planning Department was asked to comment on the groups' work and to use the pupils' newly acquired understanding, both of the area and of decision-making in this context, to make points about the process of listing buildings and designating conservation areas.

Outcomes of activity

This is an open-ended enquiry with no predetermined outcomes. The intention is to allow pupils to come to an informed decision about what they consider to be the best future for Bolsover. The range of questions asked goes beyond the traditional remit of the geographer, and the opportunity the activity offers pupils to take action make this a genuine cross-curricular piece of environmental education. In this instance, pupils could share their views with either English Heritage or Bolsover District Council in the form of a written or spoken representation.

… LIVING EARTH: A RESOURCE FOR LEARNING

HISTORY

History has an important contribution to make to environmental education, both in terms of what it reveals of the effect of past human behaviour on the environment and also in the ability it fosters to construct theories on the basis of evidence gathered and examined.

The two articles that follow present a broad spectrum of historical approaches: the first considers ways of organising an historical survey of a local area; the second takes an historical event and shows how it can be given contemporary significance.

Historical approaches to the environment

MARTIN L PARSONS

Aims
- to show that history has been shaped by the environment, as well as by kings, queens, battles and politics
- to allow pupils to develop the skills of the historian and to use material and information on their immediate environment to which they can easily relate

ACCOUNT OF ACTIVITY

Introduction

This project is based on the assumption that all history has been influenced by, or has itself had some influence on, the environment. There is much historical evidence in the environment, and this evidence can be used to show pupils how we can learn about the changes made to a locality.

The project has been used successfully with Year 5 and 6 pupils, but could, with suitable amendment of primary sources, be used equally effectively with Year 3 and 4 pupils; it lasts approximately one term, and each year's material may be used as resources for subsequent years. Inevitably, the references are specific to one school and its locality, Bradfield Church of England Primary School, Berkshire; the skills, methods and resources used are, however, easily transferable to any location, urban or rural.

There are at least three ways in which to approach this project:

- an overall study of a local area, developed on an annual basis and building on the previous year's work;
- the study of a specific historical event which has affected the area (this can be a local event or a national one with local significance, for example, enclosures, canals, the coming of the railways, road links, etc.);
- relating aspects of the National Curriculum study units to the locality, either by way of example, or as a 'way into the core topic'.

An overall study of a local area

If you develop a scheme on this basis, it is always simplest to start with whatever resources or stimulus materials are available to you. The best, and most convenient, resource that Bradfield School has is the school building itself. Bearing in mind that the intention is to develop this topic with each successive school year, a possible plan could be as follows:

Stage One – Investigating the history of the school and its relevance to and position within the village

Bradfield School

Resources available:

- the school building (change of layout/function, and reasons for these; building materials – were they local?);
- school log book (available from the local Records Office);
- local maps, both old and modern (available from the local Records Office);
- school artefacts (old registers, school bell, etc.);
- personal reminiscences of previous pupils (these should be recorded, with permission, and kept for future years);
- photographs ('then and now' photographs, in order to compare and evaluate witting and unwitting testimony. What the photographer set out to take is called the 'witting testimony', in this case, for example, a specific class at a specific school in 1900. (The 'unwitting testimony' is what the photographer did not set out to show, but which is available to others viewing the photograph, in this case, for example, the school uniform,

how girls and boys wore their hair, the weather, the ratio of girls to boys in the group, etc. Unwitting testimony can often be more useful than witting testimony.) Photographs can be gathered from a personal appeal in the local church/community magazine or from photographic collections in the local museum or reference library);
- reference library;
- Museum of English Rural Life, based at Whiteknights Park, the University of Reading;
- census of Bradfield Parish, 1831–91 (available from the Reading Reference Library and transcribed by staff onto a 'Grass' database for easy storage and accessibility. Photocopies of the actual census – which, for an area of this size, would amount to a few pages – provide an excellent visual resource for Attainment Target 3 and create a great deal of class discussion. If these sheets are laminated they can be used for a number of years, so the initial cost is worthwhile.)

The aim of this stage would be to show the link between the school and the village. This should also include past and present members of the school, both staff and pupils. The previous work done by some classes on the actual building (bricks, windows, etc.) can be used as an extra resource. Using the log book enables pupils not only to study school practices in the nineteenth century and compare them with today's (curriculum, punishments, common illnesses, etc.) but also to see how much the work and life of the village impinged on the life of the school in the past. For example, the log book will reveal days off for hay-making, 'acorn collecting', watching the Fair arrive, seeing the Volunteers' parade, etc.

The census will enable the pupils to put some flesh on to the skeleton of their research. Individuals mentioned in the log book will be found in the census, together with other members of their family and their address. This address can then be found and plotted on to a contemporary large-scale Ordnance Survey map. You may be lucky enough to receive old photographs of individuals who can be located in other sources. By its very nature, the topic will lead you out from the centre. The key to a good local study of this kind is to note these extra strands for future use, but to limit the present investigation to your initial objectives.

Stage Two

This next stage, and subsequent stages, will be determined by the information found and the questions raised during the previous stage. For example:

- there will certainly be references to the nature of the link between the school and the church, and the parish records are available in the Records Office if this line of enquiry is to be pursued;
- the census will refer to people being housed in the Bradfield Union (called Wayland) – records for this are also available in the Records Office, and these references will, in themselves, lead on to the reasons why workhouses were introduced (this is explored further in the second approach described below);
- pupils of the nineteenth-century school, and their parents, would not have ventured very far from the village. This raises the questions:
  - What was available to them in the local community?
  - How self-sufficient was it? What did it have by way of shops, public house, crafts, trades, etc?
  - How many of these services and shops are available today?

Bradfield Church

(References to local trades and occupations can be found in the census and also Kelly's Directories. These are normally available in the local reference library.)
- How did people travel to Reading or Newbury in the nineteenth century?
- Why did they need to go there?

Children's work from previous years should always be kept and used, both as a resource and as a display to provide an initial focus for the present year's work.

The influence of a specific event

All the sources mentioned in the previous approach can be used for this study. Some national events are recorded in school log books and parish records. However, others will require extra research into secondary sources. In our study area, two possibilities are immediately apparent as starting points:

Wayland

The workhouse records, board minutes, registers, etc. are available in the Records Office. Pupils could make a study of how Wayland was used in the nineteenth century and the

Bradfield Workhouse

changes of use in the latter part of the twentieth century (when it became a geriatric hospital and a home for mentally handicapped children). Secondary sources would have to be used in order to see the relevance of the workhouse in Victorian society: for example, in rural areas some inmates went into the workhouse on a seasonal basis!

It is very important that such a study is linked with the national events of the time. A class could easily plot the number of workhouses in the immediate area and so understand that the Victorians considered them to be very necessary. The moral issue of splitting families up could also be investigated and could lead on to a simple empathy exercise or role-play.

Using the census, school records and the workhouse records, it would be possible to trace the history of an individual or family within the community.

The War Memorial

The names of those people inscribed on the village War Memorial who died in the First World War can be found in the school log book and 1881/91 census. It would therefore be possible to investigate the life history of some of these soldiers from their birth to their death: the class could even use the census to plot where they lived on the village map. You would not need to go into great detail about the causes of the War, but a simple explanation would be necessary to put it into perspective. It would also be important to show that going to Flanders (or the Middle East) to fight a war would have been of great significance to both the individuals and the community, because so few people ever left the village. It would also be necessary to explain the conditions under which these men fought and the experiences they may have had, in order for the class to empathise with them.

Apart from the primary sources mentioned above, there are numerous secondary sources of this period which can be used. One very good example is *The Experience of World War One*: it contains excellent short reports of battles, maps, photographs, etc. as well as looking at the influence the War had on people at home. The maps would enable the pupils to plot the movements of those men mentioned on the memorial, and of their final battle.

The links between this topic and Geography (mapping skills), and English (war poetry, etc.) are obvious.

Relating the locality to the Core Study Units, Key Stage 2 (or vice versa)

One of the problems with this method is that the links can become very contrived, and the local aspect is lost within the plethora of other information and details. Such a course has, therefore, to be planned very carefully in order to provide a balance and to place enough emphasis on the immediate environment.

Some simple links in this area could include the following:

Unit 1: Invaders and Settlers
- The Romans can be linked with nearby Silchester and the Bath Road. Reading Museum has reputedly the best Romano-British collection outside the British Museum.
- The Anglo-Saxon settlements can be traced by their place names. Bradfield is also found in Domesday. Translations and original material are published county by county by Philimore. Wallingford was a very important Anglo-Saxon settlement; it still has its original defensive walls, and it is easy to trace the Saxon street patterns. Any place like this, or any example providing access to other invaders such as the Vikings, is always worth a visit.

Unit 2: Tudors and Stuarts
- Nearby Ufton Court and Englefield House can provide links with the Tudors.
- The town and museum of Newbury are useful for references to the Civil War, Donnington Castle, Wash Common battlefield site, etc. Members of the Sealed Knot may come into school in costume to talk about weapons and artefacts.

Unit 3: Victorians
This is an easy local link: education, society, rural problems, workhouses, etc.

Unit 4: Britain since 1930
Easy to do, but the local history does need to be seen in the national context. This can be done by:

- comparing the Victorian resources with life in the village since 1930 to show changes in lifestyle;
- investigating the members of the village who died in the Second World War (War Memorial);
- finding out if any London children evacuated to the village (if so, what did they do, where did they stay etc.?);
- looking at changes in the village's character brought about by developments in transport and communications;
- considering the changing role of the school: 1944 Education Act; raising of the school leaving age, new buildings, etc.

Unit 5: Ancient Greece
Difficult in this area!

Unit 6: Exploration and Encounters
- Some aspects of this can be seen as affecting the rural community (cheap grain from abroad, etc.), but it is very easy to contrive a link, and you should beware of making links too readily.
- One could go into the topic in another way and investigate the extent to which people in the area were affected by such explorers.
- Would the average person in a sixteenth/seventeenth-century village know about these voyages of exploration?
- There were no newspapers at this time, so how did people in this area get to hear about the explorers and merchant adventurers?

This can develop into an enquiry into the subject of communications. Explorers and others were travelling to America and other countries at a time when people in Bradfield rarely ventured the ten miles into Reading.

ASSESSMENT OF THE ACTIVITY

Many of the ideas listed here as part of our local school's study can easily be applied to any school situation. The emphasis of the study may change according to the location of your school, and you will have access to resources that are individual to your situation. Whichever way you decide to implement your local study, it is worth remembering the following:

HISTORICAL APPROACHES TO THE ENVIRONMENT

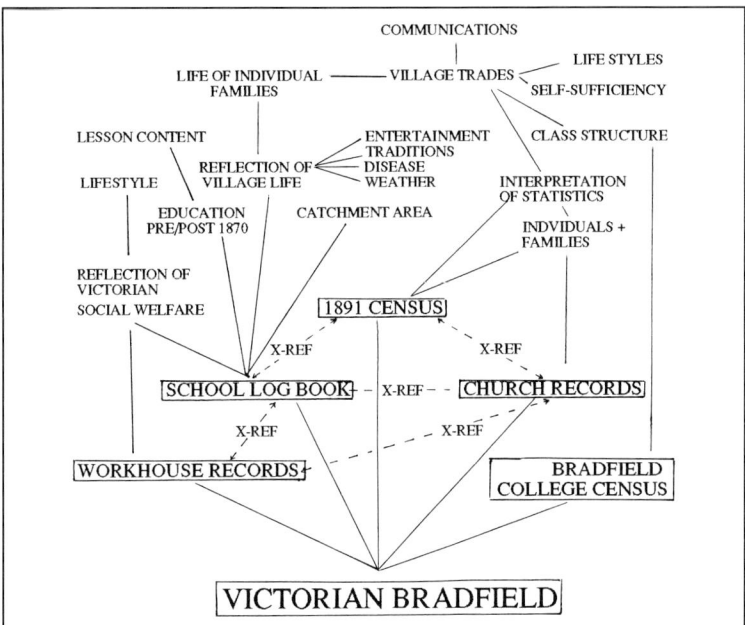

Local study planning chart © Martin L Parsons

- Do not be too ambitious. Start with something simple and develop it 'outwards'.
- Collecting resources will take time and requires forward planning. Build up a resource bank for use in future years. If done effectively, the major problem in a few years' time will be one of storage!
- Census material can be put on to a database, although this takes time. Try to get some parental help to transcribe it.
- When searching for this year's resources, take note of the references or whereabouts of material which will be useful in the future development of the study. These references can be stored on a staff database and will save a lot of time.
- Make the study enjoyable for yourself as well as for the pupils. Allow them to become historians and develop the skills of investigation and interpretation. Your role should become one of facilitating the process.

Reference

The Experience of World War One, J M Winter, Papermac

Martin Parsons is currently Lecturer in Education at the University of Reading with responsibility for PGCE History and for local history and modern history modules on the BA(Ed) course. He has run many INSET courses on the use of local study as a means of teaching History and has been very involved in the HIT (Humanities Information Technology) project, which developed IT for use in the local area. Although a secondary teacher, he has taught History to Years 3–6 as part of a joint Primary/Secondary Liaison project. He has written several books and articles, including the Foundation Skills History *series (1986) for* Letts Study Aids *and* GCSE Coursework Companion History *for the same publisher (1988).*

LIVING EARTH: A RESOURCE FOR LEARNING

Teaching about survival: the volcano

CHRIS KELLY

Aims
- to teach pupils to relate to the issues of migration, and particularly the situation of people forced to flee war and political turmoil
- to develop children's own social skills inside and outside the PSE curriculum

ACCOUNT OF ACTIVITY

Introduction
Controversial issues like evacuation and forced exile are often difficult for many children to address objectively, because the context may be surrounded by a set of media-inspired images that create prejudicial attitudes to the individuals or cultural or national groups involved.

This activity deliberately deals with such issues in the context of a fictional or historical event.

The work was first organised as part of a Humanities course in which Year 7 children had spent some 20 hours of lesson time involved in small group activities imagining how they would subsist in a technologically-simple society. In order to create a bridge between this extended simulation and the study of conflict between Celtic and Roman societies, the 'Volcano' scenario was devised. It was inspired by the idea of the eruption of Vesuvius and the dilemma faced by residents who survived the conflagration by escaping the path of the lava and taking their possessions with them. But which possessions did they take – and why? Were they useful, valuable, precious or merely immediately to hand? How would these possessions help or hinder their ability to survive and what effect would they have on their eventual fate?

For the unit, children worked mainly in pairs: the standard arrangement for this Year 7 class was for children to work at their own pace following a whole-class scene-setting activity. All children had a short story and a copy of an artist's impression of what the exodus might have looked like; they had printed worksheets on which there were outlines for written responses to the various decisions that the children had to make, and their justification for these; a set of 'crisis' cards for each pair to use (see Stage Two, below); and sufficient dice for each group to be able to use one briefly when they reached a given stage near the end. The whole unit took between one and two hours of class time, depending on the amount of time allowed for discussion and de-briefing at the end.

Stage One

Read or tell the story to the class, which concludes with the question, 'If you were one of the family escaping from the volcanic eruption, what would you take?' You may need to emphasise, first, that people wouldn't know for how long they would be away or if indeed they would ever be able to return and, secondly, that some items would be much easier to carry than others.

Individually, children choose the items they would take from the following list, taking account of a 'points' weighting on each item based on its weight/bulk, up to a limit of 20 points' worth.

Imagine you were one of the people escaping from the volcanic eruption.

What would you take? (Remember: you don't know how long you will be away!)

Choose from this list. Take as many things as you can – but not more than 20 points' worth. Don't let your partner see what you are writing for this exercise!

- a goat's skin bottle filled with water (2)
- a woven blanket (5)
- a joint of meat (3)
- a bundle of firewood (6)
- a sword (2)
- a knife (1)
- your younger brother, two years old (6)
- one of your goats (4)
- a shield (3)
- a spare tunic to wear (2)   (continued)

- a cushion (2)
- a bale of straw (4)
- a spare pair of shoes (2)
- a comb (1)
- needle and thread (1)
- some fruit (2)
- wine (2)
- a statue of your god (4)
- cups (2)

Write your list here:

My survival kit:
_____
_____
_____
_____
_____

TOTAL (not more than 20 points' worth) _____

Figure 1 Survival

Stage Two

In pairs, children then play a game (see below), in which each person takes a turn to read out one of the 'crisis situation' statements provided for them on pieces of card which are shuffled and picked for each player's 'turn'. The partner looks at their 'survival kit' and declares whether or not any item would have helped them survive the 'crisis', marking their 'Survival' outline sheet with a 'Yes' or 'No'.

With a partner, play this game. Take turns to pick any three things from the list below and see if your partner's survival kit will keep her or him alive.

Tick off the items your partner calls out.

Crisis situations
Write 'yes' if it helped you to survive, or 'no' if it didn't.

The streams have dried up and there's no fresh drinking water.

It's night time and you're freezing cold.

The animals you took are starving because the grasses and bushes are burned.

A shower of rocks the size of plums falls from the sky while you're away from buildings or other shelter.

Your animals are all dead and you need food quickly.

Your leg is cut and you need bandages urgently.

Figure 2 But would you survive?

Stage Three

After each player has had three turns, she or he fills in the worksheet (see Figure 3 below) to summarise how well she or he was prepared and whether she or he would probably have survived. Ask the pairs to discuss whether they consider their fate to be a matter of luck or good judgement in what they chose for their 'survival kit'.

If you wrote 'No' in one or two of the spaces, you might have survived but you needed help from someone.

If you wrote 'No' in three spaces, you would have been killed.

Choose which of these sentence applies to you and finish it off:

'I was killed because _____
_____
_____

'I survived but I needed help when _____
_____
_____

'I survived because I was ready for any problems like _____
_____

Discuss with a partner whether you think your survival was a matter of luck or whether it was due to how well you chose your survival kit.

Figure 3 After the game

Stage Four

As each pair finish, they join with another to form groups of four to decide what attitude they might have had to the people in nearby villages who had resources they would have needed (see Figure 4 below). This discussion may create some sharp disagreement at first. If necessary, allow a majority vote to decide on the group's decision. This indeed raises questions about corporate responsibility and group consensus.

The village has been destroyed, and the crops are ruined. There are two goats left, but not enough for the 60 people who survived from your village. Everyone meets together to decide what to do next. You have enough food and water for one or two days. You think the village in the next valley might have survived but you're not sure...

In groups of four, decide what you might do when you arrive at the next village. Remember you don't know how long you are likely to be there.

(continued)

Tick the option you choose.

Trade your weapons or other valuable items for food. ___
Beg the villagers to give you some of their own food. ___
Wait until night-time and then attack the village, stealing their food. ___

Give your reasons here:
_____
_____
_____
_____
_____

Figure 4 After the eruption

Stage Five

Once a group has made its decision, a die is thrown to show what happened to them when they reached the village in the next valley: the outcomes are given below.

Die lands on '1'
The other village has survived, and you can trade your weapons for food. They allow you to settle on land nearby to make a living, but only if you work for whatever food there is.

Die lands on '2'
The other villagers want to trade with you, but they don't want you to stay because food is short.

Die lands on '3'
The other village has survived, but they are expecting an attack from people such as yourselves. They have more weapons and warriors and have a 'watch' system so that any attackers will certainly be seen and probably killed.

Die lands on '4'
The other village has survived. They are happy to trade or even to give you food. When another disaster wrecked their own village a few years ago, the people of your village helped them to rebuild it and they consider that their homes will always be open to you.

Die lands on '5'
The other village has survived. The people have few weapons and just enough food to feed their own families, although there is a big stockpile of food kept under armed guard by the lord who lives nearby.

Die lands on '6'
The other village was destroyed in the eruption. There are no people or crops, just heaps of rock and ash everywhere.

The group members now discuss whether they feel they were right or wrong to have opted for their chosen alternative:

Did you make the right decision?
Discuss this in your group and write your answer, starting like this:
'We were right/wrong to ___, because ___.'

ASSESSMENT OF ACTIVITY

Clearly, the process and quality of discussion is a major outcome of this sort of work. The activities are sequenced in such a way that decision-taking begins as being personal and individual but becomes progressively more group-based and corporate. This is a classroom strategy that reinforces collaboration between pupils while exploiting opportunities for interactive games and for conflict-situations. By showing the delicate balance between luck and judgement in such situations, many of the children taking part realised the difficulties faced by people caught in situations of war, evacuation, famine, etc.

There is, of course, always a danger that some will see such an 'adventure game' scenario as unreal, which to some extent it is, but also as irrelevant. My experience was that, if children were de-briefed thoroughly (i.e. as a class they identified those elements that were real and those that were realistic), they could see its relevance to actual events taking place in the world today.

Chris Kelly has taught in primary and secondary schools in South London for 20 years, specialising in Humanities teaching. He has been involved in several curriculum development projects aimed at heightening children's awareness of political and environmental issues; these have been cross-curricular, with a particular emphasis on collaborative learning within a mixed-ability framework.

INFORMATION TECHNOLOGY

IT is essentially a tool which may be used either to interrogate data and present findings or to set up environmental enquiries which could describe issues, find reasons for them and demonstrate the effect of possible solutions. As the articles in Section 1 showed (pp. 25–32), there are software packages available which not only provide pupils with factual information on environmental issues but also give them the opportunity to investigate the human consequences and implications of decisions taken about these issues.

The two articles that follow combine these two approaches: in each case, the focus is on an actual product (a newspaper or a folder of work), but the process of researching, selecting and interrogating information is of equal importance.

Global environmental problems presented using IT

DAVID J WRAIGHT

Aim

- to develop a computerised folder of work based on environmental issues which will allow a group easy access to other pupils' work within the class (the content of this work will be based on environmental matters, particularly those concerned with atmospheric problems)

Resources

Going Global Magazine, from ACTIONAID, Old Church House, Church Steps, Frome, Somerset, BA11 1PL
Global Environment (BBC TV Programme or Video)
Various publications produced by British Petroleum, from BP Educational Service, Brittanic House, 1 Finsbury Circus, London EC2M 7BA
Various publications produced by the Central Electricity Generating Board (CEGB)
Various publications produced by Safeway, Tesco
Environment in Trust (Information Pack) from the Department of Environment, Room N19/14, 2 Marsham Street, London SW1P 3EB
Campaign reports from Greenpeace
Environmental Care from BNFL
This Common Inheritance, London, HMSO

Hardware: Archimedes A3000 or a network of machines.

Software: MAGPIE – © Peter Cole and Logotron Ltd 1992. This content-free programme provides the method of linking pages of text, diagrams, music and graphics into a folder of work, and is the ideal method of presenting the information. It is available from all good software distributors at approximately £60

Preparation required

Teacher familiarity with MAGPIE, and pupils' ability to use a variety of techniques of presentation, are the most important aspects of this work. Access to a number of A3000s is also essential, though the work could be carried out over a longer period of time using just two or three machines.

ACCOUNT OF ACTIVITY

Introduction

This activity could be undertaken with pupils at Key Stages 3 or 4; it is, ideally, cross-curricular in nature but could otherwise form part of a scheme of work in Science (AT5), Technology (AT5) or Geography (AT5). At least three one-hour lessons are required for this work, with computer management time in addition.

Stage One

The introduction took the form of a short video presentation and a brief talk from the teacher about global atmospheric problems. This covered a wide range of issues such as global warming, the greenhouse effect, ozone depletion, smog, hurricanes and other catastrophic weather situations. This introduction was brief and to the point.

Stage Two

From a prepared list of subject titles (global warming, rainforests, greenhouse gases, CFCs, high-level ozone, low-level ozone, the problems and benefits of the greenhouse effect, carbon dioxide, methane, climatic change, strange weather occurrences, hurricanes, drought, volcanic activity) groups of pupils then selected a subject which held a particular interest for them. (The method of selection will depend on how much freedom individual teachers wish to allow their pupils to have.)

Using the resource material, pupils started to work on their own pages of the folder. Pupils worked together, in groups or pairs, to produce information which could be used on the MAGPIE pages. The first step was to ensure that pupils only wrote the briefest of notes, mostly single words and then linked these together in a spider diagram or a family tree. Once they had done this, pupils put together simple linking sentences which formed the basis of the MAGPIE page. They produced these pages in rough first (since there was access to only two computers), the emphasis being to display the most important information. Discussion between pupils and teacher helped to decide the mode of presentation: this also offered the teacher the chance to check that the pupils' work was their own and not in fact copied directly from some other source.

GLOBAL ENVIRONMENTAL PROBLEMS PRESENTED USING IT

Working directly on to MAGPIE pages was the easiest method of presentation. Multi-coloured screens are easy to prepare with a choice of fonts. Other pupils used the applications 'Draw' and 'Paint' to produce diagrams and pictures which were then copied on to MAGPIE pages. Longer pieces of work produced by more able pupils were incorporated into the folder by using 'Edit' files. Once pages were complete they were copied into the master program: this was where good planning was important.

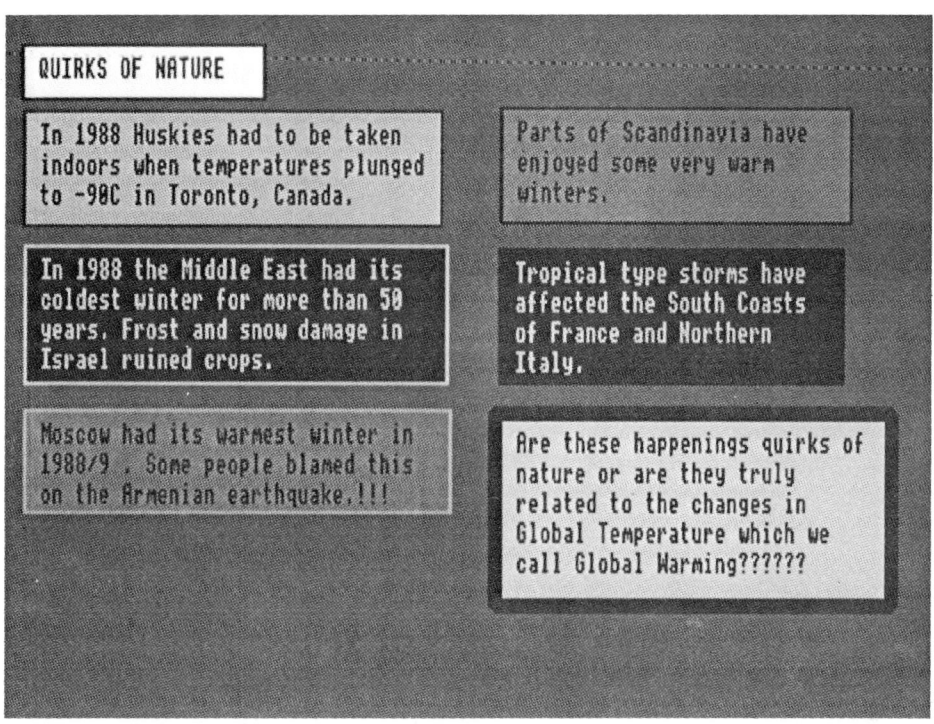

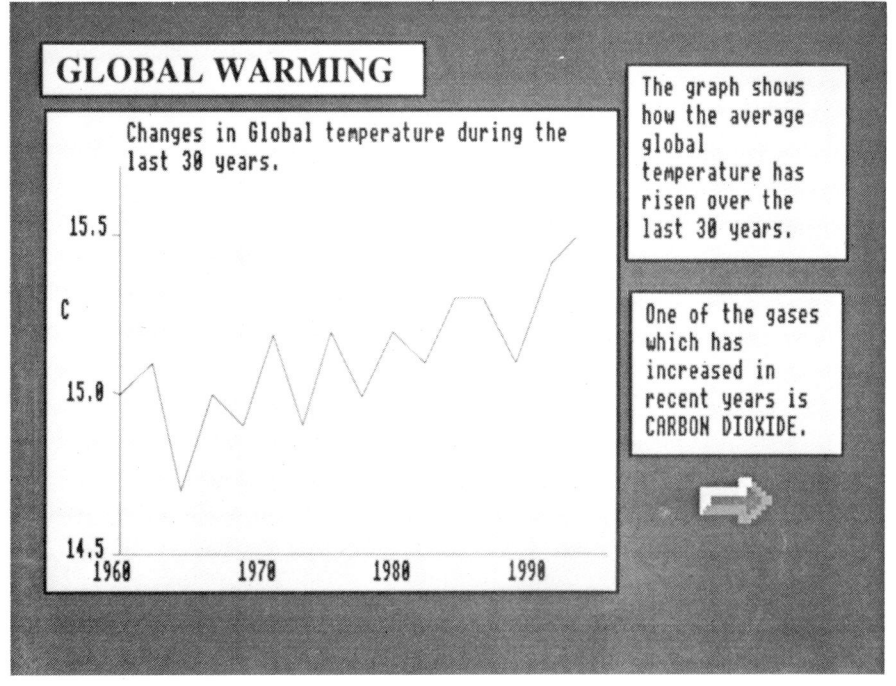

The folder itself required time and patience and involved pupils and teachers working together. Each group had identified links with other groups. Once the pages had been assembled into a folder, the links – in the form of screen 'hot spots' – were added.

The final folder provided an interactive resource which was used by pupils to put together their own folder of work on the subject. (Printing from MAGPIE is an easy process.) This was the first trial of this work, and the content was limited. Further familiarity with MAGPIE would allow the introduction of video sequences and music into the program.

David Wraight is responsible for Geography and environmental education at Ridgewood High School in Dudley. He has been a teacher for over 20 years and is especially interested in the environment and the use of Information Technology in the classroom.

Environmental newsday

SALLY WICKS

Aims

- to provide teachers with an insight into the contribution IT makes to the writing process and to fulfill some of the National Curriculum requirements for Technology AT5 and English ATs 1 and 2
- to enable pupils to simulate the creation of the front page of a national newspaper or a special supplement for younger readers on environmental issues

Resources

- *essential:* one computer to relay the news bulletins, as many computers and blank discs as needed according to the group size to enable them to produce their pages and a photocopier capable of reproducing enough papers for each pupil
- *optional:* digitisers, CD-ROM drive and discs, fax machine, tape recorders, video cameras and people to be interviewed.

Preparation required

- Use a computer program which allows information to be issued via screen or printer at timed intervals, such as as Extra (BBC), Hotline (BBC and Archimedes) or Simtex (RM).
- Create bulletins of a length and level of difficulty appropriate to the teaching group.
- Identify the class and organise the pupil groupings, supervising teachers and venue (an IT room and adjacent classroom with easy access to photocopying equipment is ideal).
- Liaise with colleagues and Senior Management Team and ask for help from parents or governors who may be willing to be interviewed in role or to fax a message.
- Notify the local newspaper who may offer the help of journalists on the day; at the very

least, they will report the event, and often they will work with the pupils, offering valuable insights into the real world of the media.
- If necessary, prepare help sheets for using the software and discs of useful clip art.

ACCOUNT OF ACTIVITY

Introduction

This is an activity which is ideal for pupils at Key Stage 4, but which is also suitable for pupils at Key Stages 2 and 3, since the complexity of the work remains under the control of the teacher. Ideally, it should take about one day to complete (some schools suspend the timetable for participating pupils for the duration of the activity), at the end of which pupils will have compiled folders of work, items of which may be relevant to English, Science, History, Geography and PSE. One school, at the end of their Environmental Newsday, presented the pupils' work in a file which contained drafts and finished articles about the threat to dolphins, water contamination in the Thames and the erosion of the Lake District landscape through the increase in tourism. Participating teachers then took the file, removed the items which were appropriate to their curriculum area and added others which were part of their GCSE syllabus or referred to work covered earlier in their course.

You may be familiar with the twice yearly newsdays organised by Campus 2000. These events involve a group of pupils who receive news items from the international news networks, select items and use the electronic mail facility to send them to participating schools. The schools use those bulletins to create newspapers which are then entered into a national competition for the best school newspaper.

However, not every school has a subscription to the Campus network and, even if it has, a school may prefer to design its own newsroom simulation. This is not a difficult prospect; there are a number of software packages (see above) which allow passages of text to be displayed on screen or as a print-out at timed intervals using a computer. The major advantage of creating your own text files is that the school has control over the bulletins created and may generate news items to meet particular curricular and pupil needs. Another advantage is that the school can decide the length of time the simulation is to run: a whole day may be devoted to the activity, or it may run within one or a series of double lessons. A final advantage is that files created are available to be adapted for future use.

Since 1988 the Berkshire Information Technology Team has run a series of newsdays, each with a different curriculum focus. One, a cross-phase project for secondary English teachers and language co-ordinators in feeder primary schools, aimed to introduce pupils to Media Studies. In another History project, teachers created newsroom scenarios to engage pupils in exploring events such as Pearl Harbour, the Anschluß and the Cuban Missile Crisis, and in examining the way in which such incidents were reported. Topically, the 1992 newsday had a European focus, with bulletins arriving in a variety of languages.

The Environmental Newsday arose from the desire to demonstrate the potential of IT as a facilitator of cross-curricular themes. An environmental focus to the newsday provided an opportunity to link the work of English, Humanities and Science departments in collaboration with the IT Co-ordinator.

Stage One

The procedure is straightforward but dependent on the resources available, the time given over to the project and on the way in which the groups have been organised. Essentially, pupils are briefed about the activity, receive information and news bulletins via the computer and other sources (telephone, fax, CD-ROMS, etc.) and proceed to draw up their newspapers, special supplements, tape or video broadcasts – or whatever form in which they choose to present their information. To do this, pupils work in groups of about six, the group size which has been seen to be the most productive. Some teachers may like to allocate specific roles to each participant: for example, editor, art editor, etc. Others prefer to let each group have time to organise itself. Another possibility is to organise groups so that one is a local newspaper, one a national newspaper, one a television station and one a radio station.

Whichever organisation of groups is decided, the activity should always start with a whole group briefing, the purpose of which is to explain to pupils what they will be producing and what activities they will be engaged on in order to do this. (It may be a good idea to organise the activity so that it follows work done on newspaper reporting as part of pupils' English curriculum, so that they are familiar with the various roles of newspaper production, for example, and with the various stages in the production of a broadcast or a finished article.) The briefing should also give a clear indication of the time to be allocated to each stage of the activity, so that pupils are aware of the various deadlines which they will have to work to: for example, if the activity is to take a whole day, they will have to have produced a first draft within three hours and they will have only a further two hours to work this into a finished product before the final session, in which the various products are shared and discussed.

Stage Two

Following the briefing, the teacher's role changes to one of facilitator or source of information, and it is up to the pupils to decide how they organise their own work. The basic

Front covers of two papers produced by Year 10 pupils, Sandhurst Comprehensive School, Berkshire.

procedure is that pupils start to receive news items and begin to create a front page or special supplement pages based on them. As more bulletins arrive via the computer, they will be forced to retrieve stored files, amend and add to them to produce polished finished articles. As part of this process, they will need to engage in research for background information and discuss the content and organisation of the final product.

ASSESSMENT OF ACTIVITY

One particular value of this newsroom simulation is that the activity is as much about the process as about the product: it gives pupils a living demonstration of the relation between product and process, and it also demonstrates that forms of note-taking other than 'typing up in best' may be more appropriate at earlier stages of the production process. Another is that at all times, the activity involves group decisions about priorities, angles taken on news items, etc. The learning is thus three-fold: about the environmental issues with which they are presented; about the computer skills needed to retrieve/receive this information and to re-present it in their own work; about the human skills required in working as a group.

Every teacher who has participated in this activity has commented on the motivation of the pupils involved during the day. It has had the additional benefit of producing evidence which could be submitted for assessment in different curriculum areas. Work submitted as part of a GCSE English coursework folder included the parts of the paper for which the pupils were solely responsible, their reflections on the activity and their assessment of what it had added to their understanding of the media.

Sally Wicks has taught English and Drama in Berkshire secondary schools for several years and has trained teachers in the same subjects. For the last five years, she has worked as an advisory teacher for the Information Technology and English team in Berkshire.

MATHEMATICS

Mathematics has an important contribution to make to environmental education in terms of the skills involved in the subject and of the opportunities it offers to construct models and test out hypotheses. These are issues of combined importance: accurate data, measurements and statistics can only be collected if pupils have the appropriate mathematical skills for the task; the analysis of this data and the construction of models arising from it can influence our understanding of environmental issues and inform the human decisions we make concerning them.

The two articles that follow show both aspects of this process in operation; on the one hand, children are shown engaging in simple measurement and data collection activities; on the other hand, they are gathering evidence which they may then use to make, or to suggest, decisions concerning their human environment.

Rivers

ALLAN LUND

Aims
- to study the physical characteristics and dynamics of a river or stream
- to allow children to test a number of hypotheses concerning rivers
- to use IT to store and present data

Resources
- software required: *Introducing Geography* (Rivers) – BBC Publications (a useful software program which accompanies the television programme of the same name and which introduces several key concepts to primary and older children); *Grasshopper* (Newman Software) – useful for spreadsheets; *Branch* (NCET) – this has a binary tree which is useful
- ranging poles
- metre rules
- 30cm rules, 20m tapes
- nets, hand lenses, waders, collecting trays, floats, stopwatch

Preparation required
You will need to give pupils some initial training in measurement skills and in collecting and analysing data.

You will also need to have drawn up a series of data sheets, on which pupils may record the results of their measuring.

ACCOUNT OF ACTIVITY

Introduction

If children are to appreciate that mathematics has a wide variety of uses in everyday life, across the whole curriculum and in their future work, and if they are to be able to use their mathematical knowledge in all these types of situations, then they need to experience maths in a rich variety of situations.

Mathematics in the environment is really applied mathematics in the majority of cases. Children use concepts and skills learned in the classroom and apply them in a different situation. We should not teach them in isolation, neither should we try to teach them when we get to our field centre, park, river, or place of visit. We can develop, practise and extend their skills. We can set problems or investigations for the children to apply what they know and what they can do. We need to show that various techniques have many uses. In a new situation, depending on the conditions of space, time, equipment or even weather, a child can use the most suitable technique.

In the following activity, pupils apply techniques of measurement and observation to a study of a river. The activity is clearly cross-curricular – there is scope here for work on Geography, Science, English and Information Technology, among other curriculum areas – but the focus here is on Mathematics. It is particularly suitable for work with Year 6 pupils, although the tasks could be simplified for use with Year 4 and 5 pupils (equally, they could be made more complex for use with pupils above this age).

Stage One

Use an appropriate software program to introduce the basic concepts which children are going to be handling as part of their fieldwork: contour lines, rivers flowing downhill, cardinal points of the compass, speed of flow, meandering. (*Introducing Geography* is particularly useful and fun here, since it introduces these concepts by means of a simulation exercise in which children survive a plane crash and have to regain civilisation within a certain period of time.) If computers are not to be used for this part of the activity, you will need to find some other way of introducing these concepts.

Explain to pupils what their task is to be. You could present pupils with the hypotheses which they will be testing now, or leave this until the final stage of the activity. There are three hypotheses which they can test and 'prove' with one set of data, and they are as follows:

- The fastest current is located in the middle of a river.
- On bends, the fastest current is located closer to the outside bank.
- More sediments are found on the inside of river bends.

Further hypotheses may be tested and 'proven' if several sets of data, taken at various points of the river, are used, viz:

- A river becomes wider downstream.
- A river becomes deeper downstream.
- The water speed of a river increases the further downstream it flows.
- The size of the pebbles found in a river decreases the further downstream it flows.

(A lot of preliminary work on these hypotheses should be done in the classroom, so that children are practised in the skills needed for both the Geography and Maths.)

Explain that pupils will need to enter data neatly and accurately for ease of later recall. One way of doing this may be to organise some preliminary exercises, for which pupils do not have to move out of the classroom: for example, they could measure their classroom and situate it in relation to the rest of the school, working out along the way their answers to 'real' questions, e.g:

- Given the size and shape of the room, is the furniture arranged economically? Plan and draw your ideas for change.
- How much would it cost to carpet your classroom in carpet costing £5.95 per square metre?
- If you had to make new curtains, how much material would you need? Can you calculate the cost of new curtains?

Children should also have lots of practice at this stage in the use of the database. They could, for example, compile class lists, lists of families, plants, tree studies, etc.

Stage Two

This stage is to be undertaken in the open and involves pupils in direct observation of and research into a river. They will be undertaking the following tasks:

- Measuring the river at various stages of its flow and seeing if there is any relation between width and depth.
- Measuring the speed of the river's flow in the mid-stream and by its right and left banks.
- Identifying the material found on the river bed and, again, analysing this in terms of its position (mid-stream/near bank) in the river.

For the first of these activities, pupils place ranging poles at one river bank, cross the river and then insert a second ranging pole on the other bank. They stretch tape between the two poles until it is taut and measure the river's width. Keeping the tape taut, they now measure the depth of the river at intervals of 0.5 metres in order to find the maximum depth.

In order to check the speed of the river's flow, pupils have first to choose the stretch of river on which they will be working and then place two sets of ranging poles ten metres apart. Standing in the river close to the left bank, they drop a float in the river and time how long it takes to travel the chosen distance. They need to repeat this three times in order to be able to calculate the average speed. Once they have done so, they should repeat the process for the middle of the river and the stretch of the river close to the right bank.

The pupils now retrieve material from the river bed at every 0.5 metres across the river and note what they find (e.g. mud, sand, pebbles). If they find pebbles, they should measure their length with a 30cm ruler and indicate where in the river they found them. Having done this, they should return the pebbles safely and carefully to the river immediately.

A final part of this river-profiling is to ask the pupils to sit quietly on the river bank and watch the surface of the water in order to judge how smooth or rough it is. They gauge its roughness on a scale going from 1 (still and flat) to 5 (rough and stormy).

With each of these activities, pupils must remember to record all their results on data sheets provided.

Stage Three

The final stage of this activity can be completed in the classroom and involves the children entering their findings on a suitable database and using them to provide their answers to the hypotheses which you presented them with earlier. How they choose to do this is obviously for them to decide, but here are some possibilities:

- A poster giving general information about rivers with specific reference to their research.
- A pamphlet introducing other pupils to the river and presenting their findings.
- An audio or video recording explaining and/or showing what they did.
- A 'River Safety' poster, applying what they have learned for the benefit of parents and other children.

Most of these options will be enhanced if the pupils make use of computers and/or word-processing facilities. More able children could try to make a working model of a section of a river.

Other possibilities

As discussed earlier, there are further hypotheses which pupils could test if they are able to take several sets of data at various stages of the river's flow. They could also take 'eco-samples' from the river. To do this, pupils stand in the river and push a net through the material on the river bed to see what they can find. A further refinement is to have one pupil standing with a net downstream of a rock; another pupil turns over the rock, and the first pupil quickly sweeps the net under the rock.

All creatures found in either of these activities should be placed immediately in shallow containers filled with water. Pupils observe these creatures, fill in details on their field sheets, make field sketches of the creatures – and then return the creatures safely and carefully to the river. With this data, they could add information about the life forms found in the river to the data discussed above.

Allan Lund is the headteacher of Anfield Junior School in Liverpool: he has taught in the maintained sector for over twenty years.

Plotting the position of local amenities

COLIN SEMPLE

Aims
- to teach pupils how to apply the skills of measurement to a real-life problem
- to teach pupils how to present data in graph, tabular and display form
- to give pupils an elementary understanding of town planning

Resources
- tape measure (5 metre or 10 metre)
- 1 metre trundle wheels
- maps of the local area
- OHP
- computers and appropriate software programs for display of findings

Preparation required
You will need to have prepared recording sheets on which the pupils may process their data and to have practised various methods of measuring before this activity so that pupils may select the one most appropriate to their task.

For the second stage of this activity, you will need to secure senior staff and parental permission to allow pupils to work outside the school grounds. Some practice may be needed in word-processing/graphical skills if you are planning to use IT to present the pupils' findings.

ACCOUNT OF ACTIVITY

Introduction

This is an activity, in two basic stages, which could be conducted as a group or paired activity: it is a demonstration of how classroom skills not only have significance for the immediate, school world of the pupils, but are also applied on a regular basis in the adult world. In this respect, the activity demonstrates how mathematical research can provide vital information for people making decisions of an environmental, economic or human nature, or – as in this case – of all three. The activity is appropriate for Year 3 to Year 6 pupils and will provide the basis for a week's work.

A word of warning: the subject of home and where you live may be a sensitive one for pupils, and this activity could lead to taunts aimed at pupils living in the 'poshest' or the 'slummiest' area. Two ways around this are to: undertake the activity only when pupils are doing field work away from their home/school area; be very specific about the kind of person for whom this research is being undertaken (for example, elderly people, or someone wanting to open a greengrocer's shop in the area, etc.).

Stage One

Explain to your pupils that they will be drawing up a picture of their environment which attempts to show the best location for private accommodation. Many pupils will have memories of moving house and of looking at new houses with their parents or guardians. Apart from the obvious consideration of price, how did they decide which area to consider? What makes one area more or less desirable than another?

One way to introduce pupils to the concept of amenities and to develop their understanding of location is to start with a survey of the school. Set pupils the task of discovering which classroom is ideally situated in relation to the amenities of the school. Either ask them to volunteer ideas about what these amenities might be (theirs may well turn out to be intriguingly different from your own!) or 'suggest' the following to them through guided questioning:

- The headteacher's room
- The medical room
- The main store room
- The secretary's office
- The infants' store room
- The kitchen
- The library
- The playground
- The toilets
- The staffroom

For each classroom, they now measure, or pace out, the distance from that classroom to each of these amenities and enter their results on a recording sheet. They also make a record of the time it took to do the measuring. For each of these records, they work out which amenity is furthest away and which is nearest. Finally, they add up the total distances and divide this number by the number of amenities. The classroom which provides the lowest figure is the one with the best location in the school.

Stage Two

Now explain that they are to apply this same technique to the area in which the school is based. Pupils first draw a sketch map of this area, using maps of the area with which you have provided them, or work from a map which you present on the OHP or chalkboard: it is up to you to define what size this should be. Working in groups of four, pupils now choose six houses from various locations within this area, and mark these on their map. They measure, record and produce a visual representation (picture or photograph) of the premises in question.

As before, you can now either present them with a set of amenities which people would like their houses to be near or you could ask them to come up with their own set of amenities which they think make a residential area attractive. If you decide to use a more objective set of amenities, you could again ask pupils to provide their own ideas by asking them to consider the needs of, for example, elderly people, parents with young children, people without private transport, etc. One such list of amenities might include the following:

- Telephone kiosk
- Post Office
- Post box
- Church
- Doctor's surgery
- School
- Shops
- Zebra crossing
- Park
- Library
- Public house
- Police Station
- Bus stop

Now provide them with a table or chart on which to plot their findings: their task is to measure how near each of their six houses is to these amenities. (How they measure this is, to a certain extent, up to them, but they need to remember the need for consistency of method.) Remind them of the need to present their findings clearly on the table: colour coding might be the best way of doing this.

Stage Three

Back in the classroom, pupils now collate all the information they have discovered and present it in tabular or graph form: if you have access to a computer and suitable software, this would be the best way to present the data. They should also explain how they arrived at their results. (The calculation is the same as in the earlier classroom activity: for each house, pupils calculate the total distances and divide this total by the number of amenities. The house with the lowest final number is the house with the best location.)

There are several ways in which pupils could display this information: they could present it as maps of the area for display on posters, etc. within the school; they could produce a pamphlet explaining their work and present this to the estate agents in the area; they could award medals to the houses with the best location; they could provide audio or video recordings of what they have done.

Other possibilities

In this activity, pupils will have not merely acquired a more detailed understanding of their immediate environment; they will also have engaged in a basic form of town planning, in the course of which they will have had to think about what makes a human community, what are the essential public services, what effect distancing an area from key amenities might have on the 'culture' of that area. A logical extension of this activity would, therefore, be to ask pupils to plan their own ideal community, to draw a map of it and to explain how they decided on that particular plan in a written statement (perhaps appended to the plan) or in an audio account.

Colin Semple, headteacher at St Paschal Baylon School, Liverpool for 20 years, has always found that Mathematics provided immense scope for work on the environment. The activities described here form part of the work undertaken at Liverpool Education Authority's Environmental Education Centre at Colomendey in Clwyd, where Year 6 pupils from the school spend a week every year, studying all aspects of the environment from tree and river studies to mini-beast studies.

MODERN LANGUAGES

Concern for the environment unites the young of Europe – and probably of the world – as much as pop music or despair at the failure of the older generation does. There is, therefore, a strong argument for saying that a subject which exists to further communication and understanding between nations has a duty to provide pupils with the communicative means to discuss such urgent matters with young people in France, Germany, Spain and other countries.

In addition to this 'moral imperative', the environment could be taught as a part of any of the seven areas of experience outlined in the National Curriculum for Modern Languages. The two articles which follow demonstrate how naturally lessons may be adapted to focus on the environment, one making it the subject of a research and debate activity, the other using it to develop and extend the basic language needed to describe where you live.

Environment and pollution in the target language

CHRISTIANE MONTLIBERT

Aims
- to teach pupils an environmental topic in the target language, studying largely (if not exclusively) authentic materials for language input
- to develop the maximum degree of pupil involvement and independent learning

Resources
- video of 'Lessives polluantes' broadcast by Antenne 2 and reshown on Olympus (three mins)
- soundtrack of video on audio cassette
- 'Restera-t-il un chant d'oiseau?', a song by Jean Ferrat (published by MFP, EMI)
- 'Publicités' – on pollution from Mary Glasgow Publications – *Thémathique*, 1989, Unit 1 'La qualité de la vie', 'L'environnement', 'L'énergie' and 'L'air que nous respirons', (pages 9 and 10)
- brochure on sources of pollution: 'Gaspillage = Pollution'
- evaluation questionnaire (including pupils' comments on the choice of topic, the methodology and resources used, what they have learned and, finally, their overall reaction to the project)
- photocopies of materials to be used and overhead transparencies for briefing, brainstorms and guidelines for some of the activities
- black/white board or flipchart
- OHP (if there is no white board, a screen/blank wall will be needed)
- bilingual dictionaries and one unilingual French dictionary (e.g. *Petit Larousse*)

- TV and video recorder
- tape recorders, junction boxes and headsets; if team-teaching is an option and a neighbouring room happens to be free, the listening/recording can be done in that room, with one teacher supervising
- tables and chairs set out for group work

Preparation required

- Locate suitable authentic materials in newspapers/magazines or even text books, recording satellite TV broadcasts and songs, preparing 'cloze' exercises, making photocopies and OHTs.
- Time tasks and activities carefully: some of them will operate on a 'carousel' basis.
- Prepare a succinct and clear introduction to pupils, stating the aims and objectives of the project.

ACCOUNT OF ACTIVITY

Introduction

This is an activity for Year 10 pupils which gives them the opportunity to work on a topic more usually taught at post-16 level. It is based on materials produced by Annie King (now at the University Language Centre, Cambridge) for use with non-specialist adult learners. The activity is a whole-class project which will cover four one-hour lessons: some tasks involve the whole class together (i.e. introduction, brainstorms), while others are based on self-selected friendship groups. There is also scope for individual work; extension work may be set for homework.

The project would fit very easily into the framework of 'The World Around Us' (Area C in the National Curriculum), and there are clear links to be made with Geography and Personal and Social Education.

Stage One

In March 1990, Dr Lid King (currently director of CILT, the Centre for Informaton on Languages Teaching and Research) came to my school (Boswells Comprehensive School, Chelmsford, Essex) for a series of four one-hour lessons with my Year 10 GCSE class. Dr King described this class as:

> *a good, but not exceptionally gifted group of 32 pupils. Prior observation showed that they were responsive, enthusiastic and used to working together in groups. Well acquainted with GCSE topics, skills and language.*

In the first lesson, Dr King and I briefed the class about what we were going to do: we were going to work in groups on the topic of 'l'environnement et la pollution' in French for four hours, using different tasks on a 'carousel' basis. The end product was to be a presentation to the whole class of their own group work.

The class then divided into self-selected friendship groups to brainstorm ideas: what was the expected language? For this task, they were given a copy of 'La pollution – feuille de l'étudiant' (see next page) – and asked to fill out the first column:

Qu'est-ce que vous savez?	Les images	Des mots utiles (Anglais → Français)	Qu'est-ce que vous entendez?

La pollution – feuille de l'étudiant

After ten minutes of brainstorming they compiled their lists, and the whole class reconvened to present their findings. These were noted down on the OHP for everyone to jot down, repeat and practise. Then the class watched the video, 'Lessives polluantes', several times without the sound; working in groups, they noted down what they saw (in French) or found out the words they needed and wrote these in the second column of 'La pollution – feuille de l'étudiant'. This task took 15 minutes. The class got together again to brainstorm more vocabulary and structures, which were written down on the OHP. Finally, we played the class 'Restera-t-il un chant d'oiseau?', by Jean Ferrat, and gave out the words of the song. song.

For homework, pupils had to complete the third column of 'La pollution – feuille de l'étudiant', a linguistic prediction exercise for which they had to think of the words which were likely to crop up in the topic and look up what the words were in French, if they did not already know them (for this they used a dictionary and the key-word list 'Les mots-clés/ Les phrases-clés' (see below)). They also had to translate the song into English.

LES MOTS-CLÉS/LES PHRASES-CLÉS

- La suppression de l'emploi du phosphate
- Cela provoque le phénomène d'eutrophisation qui se traduit par une prolifération des algues
- Le premier visé: Rhône-Poulenc, premier producteur français de phosphates
- L'UFC préconise l'emploi de lessives sans phosphate mais celui-ci est alors remplacé par d'autres composants
- Juger l'impact global de la formule sur l'environnement
- Certaines lessives avec phosphate sont vingt fois moins toxiques
- Ces composants (...) selon différentes études seraient aussi très polluants
- La Secrétaire d'Etat: 'Je voudrais demander à M Brice Lalonde d'étudier ce dossier:
    - en tenant compte de toutes les causes de pollution des lessives;
    - de ne pas limiter les mesures (...) au phosphate.'
- Inciter les fabricants à réduire sensiblement le taux de phosphate dans tous leurs produits

Stage Two

We corrected the homework first and then, as a class, checked the vocabulary and phrases learned; the next step focused on acquisition, and the format used was again a 'carousel':

- video of 'Lessives polluantes' (the group watched this with the sound on and prepared lists, identifying sounds heard and checking afterwards with a 'texte visuel' prepared earlier);
- sound sets (audio cassette with 'Lessives polluantes' video soundtrack only);
- sound (cloze text on the song with the verbs removed); make sure you have collected in the original words used for homework before starting this task!;
- written texts (exploitation task on OHP in French from *Thématique*, as well as a brochure on sources of pollution);
- a game whereby pupils had to match visuals (photographs and illustrations) to text (statements describing a condition, etc.).

Each group had about ten minutes to spend on each activity before moving on to the next. For homework, the class had to devise a puzzle/test, revise the vocabulary and phrases and bring in pictures from magazines connected with pollution and the environment.

Stage Three

The aim of this lesson was to consolidate what had been learned; it was left up to each group to decide what to produce for presentation to the rest of the class.

After pupils had tested each other in pairs on their homework, the groups concentrated on their 'display'.

Stage Four

The last lesson focused on the completion of the tasks and their filmed presentation, in French, to the whole class. Among the forms of display chosen by the class there were the following:

- posters on ecology and pollution (see photo);
- a TV discussion with mother, daughter, ecologist and industrialist following an accident to the daughter;
- a rap poem/song;
- a radio interview with school children on pollution and its prevention.

For homework, pupils wrote a newspaper article on the environment after completing the exercise on 'La pollution: actions et conséquences'. This is a sheet with two sets of images, the first of which shows an 'Action' (a car driving with a dirty exhaust, a man smoking, etc.), and the second of which shows the 'Conséquence' of this action. Having matched up the consequence to the action, pupils have to write about them using 'si' (for example, 'Si vous jetez les médicaments, vous polluez l'eau') and then draw their own sets of images.

Other possibilities

Teachers do not need to use the materials mentioned here; they can prepare their own or record more recent broadcasts (TV or songs). They can also use commercially produced packs on the topic, such as *Thématique* or CILT Post-16 Dossier on 'L'environnement'. They can also liaise with Geography teachers and transform their materials to fit the target language. Why not teach that part of the Geography syllabus all in French/German/Spanish/ etc., if the school has a 'Language For All' policy, as ours does?

ASSESSMENT OF ACTIVITY

The pupils' interest and their ability to work independently were key factors in the success of this project. Dr King and I found the class extremely responsive: the room was a hive of activity where a lot of useful English discussions were taking place among the pupils ('Yuk, that's algae', 'My dad works at Rhône Poulenc', etc.). The checks on remembered vocabulary/phrases were quite extensive, and the 'carousel' worked extremely well, with the pupils identifying a surprising amount from the video (less from the audio cassette); the song 'cloze' exercise was done very quickly and accurately, and during Lesson Four, while it did not appear that the groups were on target at all, they still managed to complete and present their work with varying but real success. We were very impressed by the articles produced for the last homework, and marks were allocated and used for evidence and record of performance.

In their evaluation of the project, the majority of pupils said that they had found it interesting and therefore relevant, even though it was not, strictly speaking, a GCSE topic. One pupil commented: 'The choice of topic was not only interesting, but we learned things about our environment that we haven't even discussed yet in English. It was a good project, as it gives us a break from the real French lesson, but we keep on learning in a fun sort of way.'

Pupils learn better when they are asked to consider what they learn, why they should learn it and how they should learn it. In this respect, the subject of the environment ('the main problem at the moment', as one pupil put it) is ideal: it commands the pupils' attention and offers a suitable and flexible means to involve pupils actively in their learning.

Christiane Montlibert is currently Assistant Head of Modern Languages at the Boswells School, Chelmsford. She has given talks at ALL (Association for Language Learning) French Days on Creativity and the Environment and has attended CILT conferences on Autonomy, contributing to CILT's publication, Letting Go, Taking Hold *(1992). She has worked for the NCC on the use of the target language and has contributed to the 1993 NCC video on the same subject.*

Verschönung eines städtisches Wildnises

DUNCAN SIDWELL

Aims
- to teach students the language to suggest how a derelict site can be renovated, so that they may then develop their own solutions to a similar case
- to engage students' creativity and to involve them in problem-solving and group work

Resources
- OHT of the derelict site (see page 215)
- OHT of outline solution for renovation (the class work)
- individual work sheet of second derelict site

Vocabulary

anlegen	reinigen
abreißen (Zaun, usw.)	renovieren
ausgraben	reparieren
bauen	verschönen
demolieren	verwandeln
einführen (Tiere, Pflanzen)	
ersetzen (durch)	der Abfall
füllen	der Bach
herausreißen (Schienen, usw.)	der Baum
machen (flach machen, usw.)	der Bauernhof
pflanzen	der Biotop

das Blumenbeet	der Rasen/R-platz
die Brücke	die Schiene
der Busch	die Schlackenhalde
das Café	das Schwimmbad/Hallenbad
die Fabrik	der See
das Feld	der Sportplatz
der Fußballplatz (Tennis-, Spielplatz, usw.)	das Sportzentrum
die Garage	die Straße
das Gebäude	der Teich
das Gras	die Terrasse
die Hütte	das Tier
das Kanal	der Zaun
der Picknickplatz	verfallen
das Pfad	vernachläßigt
die Pflanze	

The vocabulary gives an idea of the range of possibilities, but the following could be suggested:

- factory – demolish
    – or convert to a sports area
- derelict garage – convert into a café
        add a terrace; tables, chairs
        fence for safety by stream
- canal – clean, plant
- slag heaps – landscape, plant
- railway line – take up
- repair/renovate – bridge, fence
- lay out – car park
        play area
        paths
- create – flowerbeds
        bushy areas
        picnic area
        sports pitches
        urban farm
        biotope
- dig out – lake for sailing (and club house)
        lake for fishing
        pond (plant life, birds)

ACCOUNT OF ACTIVITY

Introduction

Although the basis of this activity is an imaginary derelict site, the subject is sufficiently common to enable students to identify strongly with it and to be personally motivated in the work. One way of guaranteeing even greater motivation would, of course, be to base the activity on a local area known to students; if the work results in a written statement, this could be sent to a German school with which your school is twinned or, individually, by students wanting to write to pen-friends.

This activity can be used with Year 10 to Year 13 students, depending on the level of the class, the way the activity is presented and structured and the range of vocabulary employed. Often the verbs can be mainly generic or similar to the English ('reparieren', 'demolieren', 'machen', 'bauen', etc.) rather than less well known terms (which are nevertheless more appropriate to the subject) like 'ausgraben', 'anlegen', 'ersetzen', etc. Similarly, the phrases used to propose changes can again vary in their level: 'Man könnte . . .'; 'Wir könnten . . .'; 'Wie wäre es, wenn man . . . würde'; 'Wir haben gedacht, daß man . . . könnte'. Students can report back at various levels, too: one possibility, on a higher level, would be to use the perfect tense ('Wir haben einen See ausgegraben'; 'Wir haben gedacht, daß man . . . machen könnte.'); on the other hand, a more simple report could describe the renewed area ('Es gibt jetzt einen . . .'; 'Statt einer . . . gibt es ein . . .'; 'Man hat . . . demoliert.').

Stage One

Present the OHT of the derelict area (an example, which may be photocopied, is given below) and explain the purpose of the lesson: you can do this in the target language, using the following kind of phrases and writing up those which are new and which will be needed when the students work further on the activity:

– Das ist ein Wildnis/vernachlässigtes Stück Land.
– Es ist nicht schön/Es ist häßlich.
– Wie kann man es schöner machen/verschönern?
– Man könnte einen Park/Sportplatz anlegen.
– Man könnte es in einen Garten verwandeln.
– Habt ihr Ideen?
– Was könnte man machen?

Then begin presenting, and accepting, ideas from the class:

— Wenn ihr Vorschläge/Ideen habt, könnt ihr das auf Englisch sagen.

(The best idea is probably to steer the class quite strongly at this stage.)

As ideas are given, present the vocabulary, ensuring that students repeat it a number of times and note it:

— The factory? Ja, das ist eine Fabrik. Was könnte man mit der Fabrik machen? Man könnte sie demolieren. Man könnte sie in ein Sportzentrum verwandeln. Ja, statt der Fabrik könnte man ein Schwimmbad haben/bauen.

(The students will have to use the object pronoun if the questions are posed in this way. A way around this, which is however less flexible and natural, would be to change this to: 'Was könnte man hier machen (pointing)?' 'Man könnte die Fabrik demolieren.')

Treat the various parts of the site in the way suggested above; as you do so, sketch the changes on to a blank overlay, placed over the OHT of the derelict site.

Stage Two

When you have noted all the changes on the blank overlay, you will have an image of the 'städtisches Wildnis' as it will be once it has been converted to its new use. (If the OHT from which you have been working is now too covered in writing and drawing, sketch a clean one which incorporates all the changes that have been made, or use the illustration below, which may be photocopied.) Now stand back and go over the 'städtisches Wildnis' again, using either the present tense, the perfect tense or the future tense, depending on the level at which the class is working:

— Also. Es ist fertig.
— Was hat man gemacht, um das Stück Land zu verschönern?

- Welche Ideen haben wir gehabt, um das Stück Land zu verwandeln?
- Was haben wir/hat man hier (mit der Fabrik) gemacht?
- Was könnte man mit den Schienen machen?

Stage Three

The class could now use a worksheet of the *existing site* and:

- label it;
- prepare a report of what will be done.

Alternatively, or in addition to this, they could use a worksheet of the *renovated site* and:

- label it;
- write a report of what has been done;
- take turns to present the report verbally.

Stage Four

Give the class a new worksheet with another derelict site. Run through the possible solutions to this renovation. The ideas should go beyond the original ideas used, this time including a shopping centre, housing, petrol station, school, or a combination of any or all of these.

Stage Five

Divide the class into groups and give them the task of working out a solution to the renovation of the new site. Encourage the groups to work only in the target language, using the phrases used earlier:

- Was könnte man mit ... machen? etc.

Students report back verbally and/or in writing.

Other possibilities

A good activity, and one which is really an essential part of the learning process, is to create communicative activities around the theme. This can be done at any stage, provided the students have a firm hold on the vocabulary required.

Example

Provide pairs of students with two cue cards (examples of these are given below: these may be photocopied).

Card A has two illustrations:

- a derelict site with a number of buildings, etc. with words (nouns and infinitives) indicating the changes to be made;
- an illustration of the area after it has been improved.

Card B has only the illustration of the derelict land.

The language in this communicative activity would involve the basic phrases:

- Was machen wir mit ... ?
- Was könnte man mit ... machen?

- Wir haben ... demoliert/gebaut/angelegt/eingeführt, etc.
- Wir werden Bäume/Pflanzen ... etc.

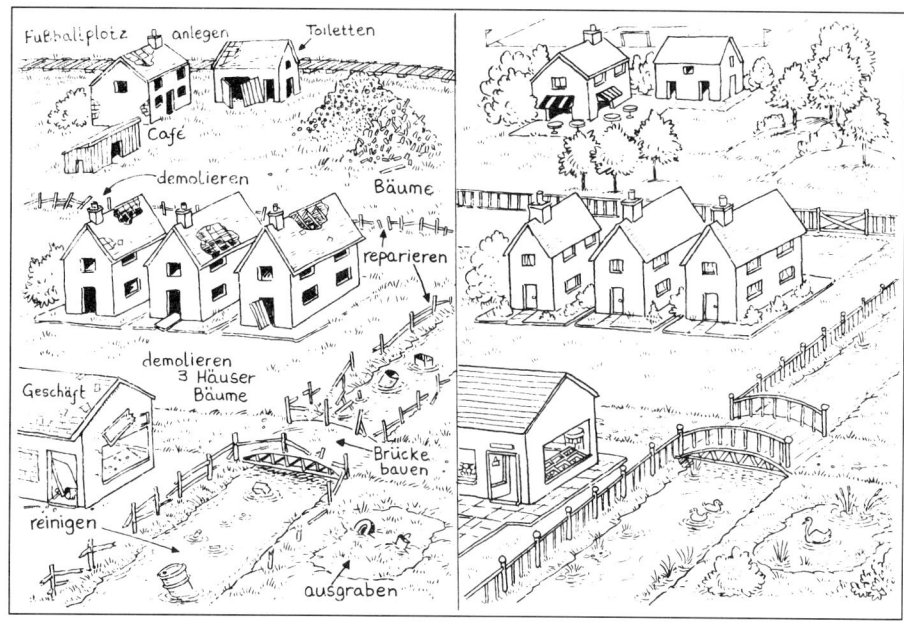

Card A **Card B**

Duncan Sidwell is a General Adviser of Leicestershire LEA, where he has responsibility for Modern Languages. He has worked in all phases of education, including adult education, in which he has a special interest. He is the author of a number of textbooks, including Du und Ich, Toi et Moi *and (with Penny Capoore)* Deutsch Heute *for Thomas Nelson.*

MUSIC

As with the other expressive arts, music can play an important part in developing pupils' imaginative understanding of environmental issues and enabling them to articulate a personal response to these. There are two case studies in Section 3 which describe performances or events designed to heighten awareness of the rainforests: in each, music has a key contribution to make. Several other contributors talk about the powerful effect of organising 'sensory bombardments' which may involve seating pupils in darkened rooms and playing recordings of the sounds of the rainforest to them.

Music is to be performed as much as to be listened to, however, and the article which follows presents five activities which are based on the environment. They are of interest in themselves, but it is difficult to read them without wanting to build some other event or performance around them.

Five musical projects on the environment

PETER GAMBIE

THE ENVIRONMENTAL RAP

Age range: from 9+
Resources: Keyboards, drum machine, sampler
Project Length: c. 10 × 35-minute lessons

This activity is appropriate for use with children from Year 5 upwards. It requires keyboards, and a drum machine and sampler make useful additions. The project may run for about ten 35-minute lessons. As with all these projects, it would be best studied as part of a Humanities contribution to environmental education.

At its simplest level, rapping is a patter song spoken to the sort of rhythmic backing found on all modern keyboards. At its most complex, it may involve sampled sounds, bass lines and melodies and regular metrical changes to the underlying rhythm.

There are many reasons why rap is a good activity to organise with children. One is that children respond to it at many different levels, limited only by their skills and imaginations. A second is that children are readily motivated by something they perceive as being in a popular, contemporary style. Thirdly, it can offer an opportunity for vocal contributions to all children, even those boys who are suffering the random pitch-shift of breaking voices. Finally, it is a powerful tool for crusading messages, giving children an opportunity to express their own opinions and feel that they are valued.

Stage One

For children unused to rapping themselves, the project could start with a rap that the class creates as a group. (I've experienced no difficulties doing this with 12 and 13 year olds.)

- Play one or two examples to the class to start with – alternatively, use one of the many good commercial recordings available. (The American duo, Salt 'n' Pepa, are particularly good.)
- Explain to the class that they're going to create their own rap.
- Start a keyboard 'Swing'/'Big Band' rhythm at a reasonable tempo.
- Tell the class to click fingers, or clap, in time with the beat.
- Tell them that you'll start the first line and that they will (one child at a time) compose the remainder. If you feel uncomfortable with this, there's always one extrovert in every class!
- Start with your first line (on a subject they will work with easily), for example, 'I went to my maths class the other day . . .'.
- Now pray that someone will come up with a suitable next line! You'll probably have to add/remove a few words to make the line scan.
- If no one manages a second line, add your own, like 'The teacher was shouting, so I said "Hey!"'
- Continue, until you have a four-line verse.
- Divide the class into groups and ask each one to write a verse.
- For performance, use a single keyboard for the backing. Start with the verse composed by the whole class, follow this with each group's individual contribution and finish with a repetition of verse 1.

Stage Two

Your class should now feel confident with the principles of rapping, so invite them to compose something less banal on the subject of the rainforests. You need to establish whether the children already know enough about this subject for the purpose, or whether they need further input, in which case you could ask for assistance from those with the necessary resources, if you are not confident of the facts yourself.

- After initial discussion, groups should compose four verses and a four-line chorus. It's a good idea to play them a steady beat every five minutes or so, so that they can assess whether their words are fitting correctly.
- Invite experiment on different backing rhythms. If you've a drum machine, use it – the same words will frequently fit different patterns, thereby totally altering the character of the music.
- Suggest a short bass pattern (3/4 notes) to be played between each line. (A, C and D, with D as tonic, is often a good starting point for improvising.) Experience suggests that this is about as far as 12 or 13 year olds can go in a five-week topic.

Stage Three

Obviously, more able pupils will be able to go beyond what is indicated above. Here are four examples:

- GCSE students may wish to compose their own piece in this genre (in which case, the

lyrics could be submitted as part of English coursework).
- A melody may be added, for example, to the chorus.
- Rhythm patterns may be altered during the piece.
- More sophisticated equipment, such as samplers and multi-tracking, may be used to produce a more complex and professional final composition.

A RADIO PROGRAMME

Age range: from 12+
Resources: Keyboards, tape recorders
Project Length: c. 10/12 × 35-minute lessons (5/6 weeks).

This is a class topic, appropriate for Year 8 pupils upwards; the final outcome is a 30-minute recorded radio show, involving speech and music. The project has the particular advantage of combining the persuasive strengths of the media and music. The aim is to give children an insight into many aspects of the world of radio.

Stage One
- Ask the pupils to give their thoughts on the content of a radio programme (news, music, adverts, weather, interviews, phone-ins, etc.).
- Select (or ask the class to vote for) a production team of four or five people. These pupils will plan and co-ordinate the entire programme.
- Describe the theme of the project as a 'Rainforest Special'. Give pupils any necessary background information on the issues involved yourself, or ask a teacher from another department to help. Alternatively, if you've enough time and material, an even better arrangement is to allow pupils to research the subject themselves, using colour supplements, text books, etc. If you use this method, it is a good idea to have a reporting session which involves the sharing of statistics and views.
- Divide the class into an appropriate number of working groups (the number will depend on how many sections the programme contains) and ask each to decide which part of the programme they wish to work on.
- Provide each group with the relevant information concerning their contribution (the adverts could be about 'green' products, the weather slot could involve global warming, etc.).
- Suggest a minimum level of music to be produced by each group – perhaps each section needs a jingle or a theme tune; adverts require more than that.
- The production team should initially devise a 'running order' (they will often respond to the imposition of a realistically rigid structure, with every section being timed to the nearest second). Following that, they should monitor the progress of each group and help to generate unity (for example, by encouraging similar styles of jingle).
- It may be necessary to assign (or invite the children to choose) certain key individuals – a presenter, DJ, etc.
- Practise, rehearse and record!

Stage Two
Once you have completed the programme, encourage the children to take a more critical look at the media, noting their influence and power. We are all aware of the strengths of the

transmitted word, whether through newspapers, television or radio, and it is important for our pupils to be equally informed. (You might also choose to draw a basic ambivalence of attitude here to the attention of pupils: we need to harness the media to help us spread the message of rainforest destruction, but at the same time we may regard them with some cynicism for the role they play in encouraging consumerism.) Finally, having completed your radio show, why not contact a local radio station and suggest that they transmit all or part of your programme!

MUSIC TO GENERATE EMOTIONS

Age range: 9+
Resources: Various instruments
Project length: c. 8 × 35-minute lessons

This activity is appropriate for Year 5 pupils and above and requires the use of a range of classroom instruments; it should take eight 35-minute lessons to complete. The main musical purpose of this work is to illustrate the affective nature of the art form. At the end of the topic, each group will have composed a piece in two or more contrasting sections, which either illustrate or generate emotions (or both).

Stage One

- With the class, consider the affective nature of music. Start, perhaps, with film music (particularly horror film music), indicating the different responses when the music changes (or when the sound is turned off on the television).
- Another effective way of doing this is to ask a pupil to act out a short kitchen scene, in which she or he tests a knife for sharpness. For the first 'take' of the scene, play background music which might suit a soap: for the second 'take', change this to horror music (perhaps by using the inside of a piano). The pupils should be able to see how the accompanying music alters their perception of the action.
- Examine the structural elements of dramatic music with the children, helping them to hear how atonal passages – dissonances, sequences becoming faster, higher or louder, etc. – produce effective sounds.
- Invite pupils to explore instruments to find suitable timbres. On electronic keyboards, there may be particularly relevant tones. Other instruments may be played effectively in unusual ways, such as using a prepared piano.
- Ask the class to explore sound texture, in groups, and give them every opportunity and encouragement to compose a piece where many instruments are being played at the same time.
- Tell the children about some aspects of the rainforest where direct human tragedy is involved (or persuade a knowledgeable colleague to do so): for example, indigenous peoples losing their villages. Invite the pupils to relate to this and to compose a piece which reflects the emotions that would be felt, for example contentment leading to anger, frustration and depression, and happiness leading to sadness.

Stage Two

- Use other art forms to enable the pupils to express their feelings.
- GCSE pupils may well work on this stimulus and find it particularly satisfying. Personally, I

have found that pieces in an abstract style work particularly well to stimulate emotions. Pupils need to be given considerable freedom for experimentation here, using instruments in unusual ways – using polytonality and atonality, breaking away from limiting rhythmic structures, and using other art forms are all possible. Once a particular focus has been found, it may be effective to combine the music with an abstract poem, in a ternary structure. It is worth pointing out that both words and music are of equal importance – a useful bi-product of this project is the fact that the poem might be submitted as part of GCSE English coursework.

POLYRHYTHMIC COMPOSITION

Age range: from 9+
Resources: Classroom percussion instruments
Project length: c. 8 × 35-minute lessons (4 weeks).

This topic is appropriate for Year 5 pupils and above; it involves the use of classroom percussion instruments and will take about eight 35-minute lessons. The project may be undertaken as part of a programme developing children's understanding of rhythm and rhythmic notation, and it may be freely adapted to include notational elements. Its position in a programme of rainforest instruction is somewhat tenuous, although the Burundi drummers of Central Africa live in an area of tropical rainforest. At present, their habitat is under threat, and with it, their culture.

Activity

- Show the children how varied rhythm patterns can be by, for example, playing parts of Stravinsky's 'Rite of Spring', followed by a march or a pop record. Then try some simple clapping games.
- Divide the class into four groups. The first will clap in 6/4 time, the second in 5/4, the third in 4/4 and the last in 3/4. If a fast tempo is achieved, a fairly complex texture results. Instruments may be substituted for clapping. To make this more complex, groups should clap on the first and last beats of their bars.
- A second exercise involves considerable mental agility and co-ordination – so try it at home first! The class is to clap successive bars of 5/4, 4/4, 3/4, 2/4 and 1/4, strongly accentuating the first beat of each bar, clapping the other beats quietly and repeating the pattern continually (i.e. ONE, two three, four, five, ONE, two three, four, ONE, two, three, ONE, two, ONE, ONE, two, three, four, five). Work up to a pulse of around 200 beats/minute with the clapping only on the first beat of each bar. To make this more complex, use percussion instruments and divide the class into two groups to perform this as a round.
- A third idea involves seating children in a circle, with a large pile of percussion instruments in the middle (if there are not enough instruments for all pupils, they may clap, use pencils or rulers on chairs/tables, etc.). If you've a reliable pupil who can keep a steady pulse, give him/her a suitable dominant instrument such as a bass drum. Otherwise, take this role yourself. Start an underlying pulse and invite individual children (or groups) to collect similar types of instruments from the middle. (You might, at the end of this, have four children with cymbals, eight with wood blocks/claves, six with tambourines, etc. sitting together.) Dictate a different rhythm pattern to each group, by playing it yourself. Develop

this idea by adding dynamics and/or introducing more rhythm patterns.
- A final possibility involves dividing the children into five groups and assigning different types of percussion instruments to each. Tell them that they're to play in a ten-beat repeating pattern and that they are only to play on a specified beat, which you will indicate. Write (or say) something like 2, 7, 10, 6, 3. This indicates that the first group will play on the second beat of the pattern, the second on the seventh, the third on the tenth, etc. Once they have understood this, change the beat on which each group plays, either by calling out new numbers or by altering your written instructions. To develop this, speed up the piece and/or have pupil conductors.
- In the case of all four exercises, record them and play back the results to the pupils, instructing them that they are to compose their own polyrhythmic compositions, which may use some of the ideas they've already explored.
- Apart from the ideas already given, invite the pupils to use repeated rhythmic ostinati but, to give variety, tell those who use such patterns to use several different ideas during the piece, rather than continuous repetition.
- Show the children how to give their piece a structure with a suitable beginning and ending. For example, adding in one instrument at a time at the start with a similar fading out at the end provides a suitable shape.

When the pieces are finished, relate them to African drumming by playing recorded music. You may then like to show the complexity and sophistication of such music, comparing it with the relative simplicity of Western rhythmic patterns. Through this, it is possible to explore common misconceptions about African tribal peoples and their music. Many children, particularly in predominantly white schools, have an unfortunate stereotype based on 'savages' and unsophisticated life-styles. It is salutary for pupils to see that 'sophistication' is a relative term and that our own rhythmic complexities are, in comparison, extremely simple. You may, if you wish, also like to allude to the influences of Afro/American music on contemporary pop music, showing a direct line to tribal music. Finally, an indication of the possible loss of such cultures through rainforest destruction will provide an appropriate ending to this topic.

GAMELAN

Age range: 9+
Resources: Pitched and unpitched percussion instruments
Project length: c. 8 × 35-minute lessons

This is a project for Year 5 pupils and upwards, which may be used as part of work on the pentatonic scale, on tonality and/or as a continuation of the previous topic on polyrhythm. The project will take eight 35-minute lessons and requires pitched and unpitched percussion instruments. As with the previous project, the relevance to rainforest education is somewhat tenuous, lying in the threat to an indigenous culture posed by rainforest depletion (the forests of Indonesia are under threat). This tenuous relevance nevertheless demonstrates that environmental destruction involves immediate human cultural loss, although it has been reported that one of the most satisfying aspects of the Gamelan – the natural, uninhibited pleasure taken by the performers – has already disappeared, now that it has become a tourist attraction for Westerners and merely a source of income for indigenous peoples.

Activity

- Play children some Gamelan music. Explain that the Gamelan is an orchestra largely comprising gongs and xylophones and that the type of music produced is based on the interdependence of the players, complex rhythmic patterns and enjoyment.
- Introduce the pentatonic scale (C, D, E, G and A or F#, G#, A#, C# and D#) to the pupils, along with terms such as ostinati and drone. Simple improvisations may be explored in small groups with one individual playing a melody while others play drones and/or ostinati.
- As a digression, allow the children to compose their own five-note scale and to compose a piece. This should show them that tonality influences style.
- Remind the pupils of their polyrhythmic compositions and ask them to recreate these with both pitched and unpitched instruments, using the pentatonic scale, adapting the music where necessary.
- The Gamelan itself is a co-operative endeavour, so to recreate it involves the whole class playing together and, at times, pupils swapping instruments or stopping playing for a while. (A performance may last from a minimum of three minutes up to ten minutes.) It is essential that pupils pause to listen, since the overall effect is easily missed when playing.
- Begin by setting a moderate pulse which has its own in-built texture. For example, don't have a single instrument constantly playing a beat – use several instruments alternating and combining. It is important here not to set anything with a recognisable time signature, so avoid thinking in fours. The polyrhythm composition pattern in ten beats may help to provide such a pulse.
- Give pupils (or groups of pupils) rhythmic or melodic patterns to repeat (the pentatonic scale obviously works well here). Once they've picked up the pattern you've taught, encourage them to improvise on it and then develop 'conversational phrases' with other instruments.
- Once the class is used to working in this way, they should feel able to start without any teacher input, especially when beginning rhythmic/melodic patterns. When this has been accomplished, they should be encouraged to stop occasionally, to listen and also to move to another instrument during performance. Each child should aim to play at least two different instruments during a piece.

Peter Gambie trained as a music teacher at the Dartington College of Arts. Throughout his teaching career, Peter has sought to reflect a concern for the environment in his teaching, bringing his pupils to an awareness of environmental issues through music. He is currently Coordinator for Performing Arts at Horndean Community School.

RELIGIOUS EDUCATION

In God's kitchen

Religious Education is the natural forum for examining the moral dimension of debates on environmental issues. One of the main concerns of the subject is to investigate the quality of the relationships between peoples, cultures and countries and to determine what moral considerations should inform them; another is to look at the ways in which various peoples and cultures have expressed their relationship to the world and to whatever being or force they recognise as the basis of life.

In both these respects, the environment provides a natural focus, either as the context in which human life is played out, or as the legacy handed down from one generation to another. It has an added part to play in RE, because it provides an obvious motive for investigating the beliefs and attitudes of other cultures and times and for demonstrating that tolerance should be applied to the natural world as much as to its human inhabitants. The articles that follow show both aspects of the subject in operation.

A three-year cycle to celebrate Easter

VALERIE PACEY

Aims
- to give infant children an experience of the religious celebrations in their community
- to give infant children an opportunity to share the beliefs and enthusiasm of adults
- to use the immediate environment of the school grounds as the focus for an experience of religious celebration

ACCOUNT OF ACTIVITY

Introduction

This article describes an infant school activity, which was organised by staff, parents and children. The activity was planned and experienced as a three-year cycle and focuses on the Christian celebration of Easter. In the way it was organised, as much as in its actual content, the activity also serves to demonstrate that the moral and spiritual development of every child in school, and every family in the school community, is central to the development of the school's environmental education.

An infant school lays the foundations of all the different areas of learning and experience, but at the same time faces the problem that children of this age do not draw a distinction between the different subjects. For these reasons, the curriculum has to be especially carefully planned, so that none of these subjects are neglected.

Infants do not experience school as a separate part of life from all other experiences, and it is therefore important to involve the wider community as far as possible in order to reinforce the local aspect of Religious Education and to make the learning more effective. In this school, parents and friends of the school from all faiths work alongside teachers to plan a chosen calendar of Religious Education events. By sharing adult beliefs, skills and enthusiasm, and the interests and concerns of each other, children learn how religions celebrate important festivals.

The activity was planned as a three-year cycle, which divides into the following three parts:

- A 'walk through' Easter customs and practices.
- An Easter festival.
- Preparing for Easter.

Stage One – A 'walk through' Easter customs and practices

This part of the cycle was planned to convey a sense of the ways in which Easter is experienced in various cultures, and to use the school grounds as the particular stage on which this activity was to be set. The local aspect of Religious Education was thus combined with an experience of its diversity: adults and infants would experience possibly unfamiliar forms of the Easter celebration in the familiar context of the school grounds.

This 'walk' involved the preparation of further activities and products. The Christian Friends of the School helped the teachers in all classrooms to produce:

- miniature Easter gardens;
- peace eggs;
- Easter cards;
- Easter songs with percussion;
- Easter bonnets;
- home-baked hot cross buns.

The walk through the school grounds was planned to take place one morning, and examples from the work each class had undertaken on Easter traditions were set out along the way. All the children – a class at a time – walked through the attractive environment and had a chance to consider, and experience, this work. This experience was enhanced by children and adults demonstrating other Easter customs:

- egg rolling (from France);
- egg tapping (from Greece);
- decorating an Easter tree (from Germany).

Along the way, everyone paused to listen to:

- Easter music played by wandering musicians with guitars, recorders, and percussion;
- a story about new life (with everyone joining in the actions);
- Easter poems.

Stage Two – An Easter festival

In January, parents and friends from all faiths, teachers and governors, met one evening to plan the festival. This was a celebration of fellowship rather than a formal meeting: there was music, singing, guitars, a choir, poems, stories and readings, the chance to move to music, and the sharing of food and drink. This experience produced the following plan, which was presented in the school grounds in the form of six tableaux.

- **The Last Supper**
  The daffodil and primrose hill became the Garden of Gethsemane. The children made three crosses.
- **A dance in front of the trees and hills**
  Parents and children in black, brown, and grey costumes depicted the sadness of the Crucifixion in a dance. Some carried dried flowers, dead bulbs and leaves, while others trailed a floating purple drape. The dance ended near the crosses.
- **The empty tomb**
  The copse with the bluebells and wood anemones was the background for the empty tomb. The stone was rolled away to the guitar and percussion accompaniment of 'The Angel Rolled The Stone Away'.
- **Butterfly garden**
  A butterfly garden became the place where Mary met the gardener.
- **Lake Tiberias**
  The pond area became Lake Tiberias with little boats floating on it. A net was pulled over the nearside fence – and produced no fish. A net was pulled over the far-side fence – and brightly shining foil fish shimmered in the net. Everyone sang: 'Peter Is Fishing In A Little Brown Boat' while alongside on the grass there was a picnic scene with a glowing fire. Fish were being cooked for breakfast.
- **Jesus meets his disciples**
  By the side of the sundial Jesus met his disciples, and everyone was happy. Parents and children with flowers, garlands and pretty costumes danced to music.

Stage Three – Preparing for Easter

The significance of Easter is enhanced by the celebrations and traditions that lead up to it. This stage of the activity incorporated these occasions into the preparation for the festival. For Shrove Tuesday (Pancake Day), families designed and made creative frying pans and pancakes to share the fun of pancake racing in the playground. In the classrooms afterwards, the story of 'The Pancake Bell' heralded a 'Day of Happiness'. Everyone endeavoured to have a 'smiling face', wore badges of smiling faces with pride and sang:

> *If every girl had a smiling face*
> *And every boy had a grin,*
> *Wouldn't it be a wonderful world,*
> *For all of us to be in?*

For Mothering Sunday, pupils made a card for the grown-up who looked after them. For children in the Reception class, the card was based on the letter 'V', the vase of violets in the *Letterland Scheme* published by Thomas Nelson.

For Palm Sunday, newspapers were collected so that all children could make palm trees. Each class was told the Palm Sunday story by their teacher. Children and adults walked in procession around the grounds, singing Easter songs, waving their palm trees and following 'Jesus' on his donkey. 'Jesus' tied up his donkey to a tree, led everyone into the hall and told us the story about how the donkey felt on Palm Sunday.

Easter time is a time for reflection, and adults and children remembered friends in Tinaud, a Romanian village the school had adopted. Gathered together, we recalled the day when a mini-bus disappeared down the drive, laden with our gifts of old shoes, pens, buckets, bowls and toys. Later, a lorry took old desks, chairs and a sink to furnish a classroom. Christians from the village who made music and prayed with us have visited Tinaud, prayed and made music and helped the Christians to build a church in Tinaud. Leaders from Tinaud are going to visit the school to meet members of the school community. We hope that their children will become friends with the pupils.

ASSESSMENT OF ACTIVITY

Using the school grounds in this way provides a nature haven in which the children can experience the sheer delight and wonder of the many varied aspects of creation. Yet it also enables them to experience the way Christians might remember different parts of the story of Holy Week, Easter and other important events. The school and its environment provides much for children to reflect on in Religious Education. Children can observe, care for and protect the world of nature, which many would see as God's world. The environment enables children to understand food webs and the interconnection of life – that birds eat caterpillars, and caterpillars eat leaves, or that the heron eats the fish from the pond and the fish eat the plankton. The interaction between humans, animals and plants is also apparent in the environment.

For example, parents and children in our school have created a wet area near the pond and brought aconites, snowdrops, violets and primroses from their gardens to plant there. Children take care not to throw rubbish in the pond, because they know that if they do, the water will become polluted and stagnant, and they will not be able to catch the fish, see the waterboatmen, watch the dragonflies hover over the umbrella plant or see the frogs jump into the long grass. The children respect their environment by not dropping litter or picking wild flowers or trampling on seed beds or treading on aconites ... In the distance the woodpecker hammers on the tree trunk ...

In an environment like this, learning to be at peace with one another should come naturally.

> *Valerie Pacey is the headteacher of the County Infants School at Nettleham, near Lincoln. Her enthusiasm to develop the school environment for children has involved her in widening the school's circle of friends. These friends have shared their beliefs, skills, gifts, knowledge and time. The school community is valued and is moving towards a position where all faiths work together for the benefit of the children.*

A planet fit for the future?
LORRAINE RIMINGTON

Aims

To enable pupils to:

- become aware of environmental issues;
- realise that they have a responsibility to and for the environment and other forms of life;
- recognise what these responsibilities might be and how they can fulfil them;
- make sense of the world around them and their place in it so that they can respond positively;
- explore the responses of Christianity and two other world religions to environmental issues.

Resources

Bible: Genesis 1^1–2^4, 2^4–3^{24}, Judaeo-Christian creation stories

The Hindu creation story from *Skills in Religious Studies, Book 1* (Heinemann, 1988)

The following titles in the *Checkpoint* series, published by Hodder & Stoughton: *Conservation and Pollution* (John Foster, 1984); *Animals and Man* (Francis Leigh, 1979) and *Nuclear Issues* (R and S Usher, 1990)

The following charts from the Pictorial Charts Education Trust (see Section 1, pages 85–87): *The Ozone Layer, The Greenhouse Effect, Tropical Rainforests, Air Pollution, Sea Pollution, River Pollution, Acid Rain, Land Pollution, Recycling, Hunger – the Myths, Hunger – the Causes*

Magazine and newspaper articles on environmental issues

Numerous RE and PSE text books focus on environmental issues, animal rights etc., especially the following:
Moral Issues in Six Religions (edited by W Owen Cole, 1991) and *Contemporary Moral Issues* (Joe Jenkins) in the *Examining Religions* series (Heinemann)
Guidelines for Life (Mel Thompson, Hodder & Stoughton)
World Religions and Ecology series (Cassell/WWF)

Preparation required

Obtain two appropriate Hindu creation stories and suitable accompanying texts (alternatively, prepare your own information sheets). Provide A5, A4, A3 paper, coloured pencils, stencils, felt tips, video tapes, etc. and adequate funding if practical work is to be done, e.g. raising seeds, horticultural work.

ACCOUNT OF ACTIVITY

Introduction

This unit of work comprises a number of tasks to be completed over a period of about 16 weeks. Together, they offer a sequence of activities which consider the environmental implications of both the stories and the teachings of the major religions. The work is appropriate for Year 10 or Year 11 pupils: the specific focus is on the City and Guilds Foundation programme, but some of the tasks are appropriate also to GCSE Religious Studies. Some tasks demand individual work, while others can be completed in pairs or small groups. Class discussions and debates can be organised.

Outline of activity

The activity revolves around six tasks which are delivered as part of the City and Guilds Foundation programme, but which fulfil the requirements of the Lincolnshire Agreed Syllabus for Religious Education. The first three tasks can also be adapted to form part of an assignment on the natural world for GCSE pupils taking the MEG 'B' syllabus in Religious Studies.

The tasks are presented as a developmental sequence: effective work on the later tasks can only be undertaken if the earlier tasks have been successfully negotiated. The tasks need to be progressive in order to fulfil the stated objectives, but it is possible to present them as individual units over two or three weeks. They require careful monitoring to ensure that all pupils pace themselves sensibly and make appropriate contributions to the work.

The mode of delivery and the skills-based assessment are particularly suited to mixed-ability classes.

Task 1
Design a strip cartoon which gives one account of creation in Christianity, Hinduism or Judaism.

Task 2
In small groups, discuss what these stories say about the way the Earth and everything on it should be treated.

Task 3
In the same groups, produce a written account of how these stories might affect the way that Christians, Hindus and Jews live.

Task 4
Design a poster on one or more aspects of pollution which:
a) shows the harmful effects pollution has on the environment and on humanity;
b) suggests ways in which we can reduce or prevent such pollution to make the world a cleaner and safer place.

Task 5
Produce a visual display which shows the importance of the world's rainforests and the ways in which they are being harmed.

Task 6
Produce a book for children which helps them to:
a) understand which animals are facing extinction;
b) why this is happening;
c) what can be done about it.

Other possibilities

Tasks which might develop from this work include a study of the Jewish and Muslim dietary laws, animal husbandry in different religions, vegetarianism, land conservation, animal protection agencies and environmental organisations. The possibilities are endless.

Given appropriate time and planning, it is also possible to engage in practical horticultural work, so that pupils can produce something which will enhance their school environment and that of residential homes, etc., in the community.

In Cordeaux High School, we are sowing and raising our own seeds so that flowers and hanging baskets can be planted and placed in the school grounds. We are also creating a scree bed at the front of the school and a wildlife garden.

Below are some examples of work produced by Year 10 and Year 11 pupils:

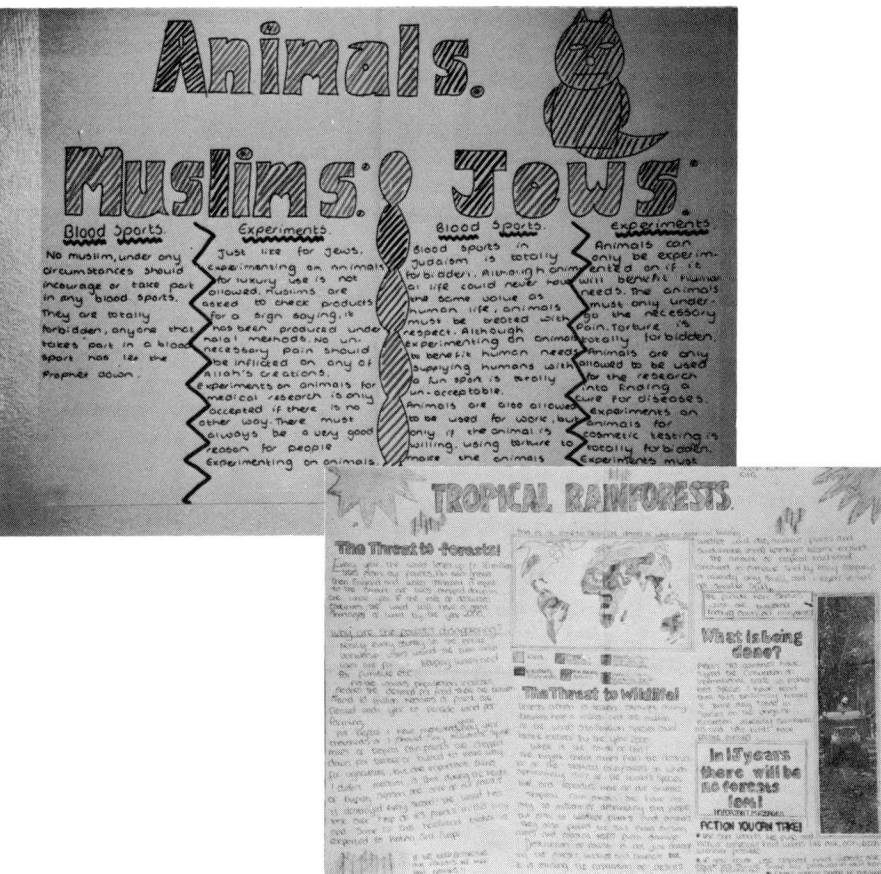

ASSESSMENT OF ACTIVITY

This activity meets the curricular requirements for Religious Studies in terms of knowledge, understanding and evaluation, while providing an environmental focus which pupils perceive as directly relevant to their own lives. Pupils appreciate the fact that they have greater control over their work and that they are responsible for the research necessary for many of the tasks. The work encourages teamwork, builds up self-confidence and is particularly appropriate for lower ability pupils, since there is less pressure to complete content-based tasks. The result is that the work that comes in tends to be varied, well presented and interesting to assess.

> *Lorraine Rimington is currently head of Religious Education at Cordeaux High School, Louth, Lincolnshire. At Cordeaux, 'green' issues are built into the syllabus at Key Stage 3, and there are specific units of work on the environment in both Religious Education and Religious Studies at Key Stage 4. Lorraine is also a member of the City and Guilds team at the school and shares responsibility for the environmental context, 'Tending animals, plants and land', which is part of the Diploma of Vocational Education taken by all Years 10 and 11 pupils at Cordeaux.*

LIVING EARTH: A RESOURCE FOR LEARNING

SCIENCE

"The picture's pretty bleak, gentlemen. ... The world's climates are changing, the mammals are taking over, and we all have a brain about the size of a walnut."

Scientific method provides a framework for researching the way in which the environment works, the human impact on it and the way in which environmental problems may be solved. This method may be applied equally well to the investigation of an exotic plant species, the pollution from a chemical works or the energy efficiency of an engine.

For a long time, science was naively seen as the source of all environmental ills. As our understanding of the complexity of environmental issues grows, we have come to see that scientific enquiry and investigation are in fact neutral and that it is how we choose to apply our scientific understanding and where we decide to concentrate our future scientific research that is crucial. The two articles that follow show how vital a part Science has to play in increasing our understanding and exciting our curiosity about the world in which we live.

What's the science behind that nasty smell?

MAGGIE HANNON

Aims

- to reinforce pupils' understanding of ecosystems, chemical change and weather
- to enable pupils to apply their understanding in a real context
- to provide a means by which pupils can explore the interrelationships between aspects of science
- to allow pupils to develop further their ability to carry out investigations which draw on their understanding

ACCOUNT OF ACTIVITY

Introduction

This project demonstrates how a local phenomenon may be incorporated into a school's or department's curriculum planning. The actual subject of investigation was obviously specific to the school in which it was undertaken, but the principle of using local phenomena for general scientific enquiry is of more general application. In a similar way, such an activity lends itself to treatment at a variety of levels and with pupils of different ages.

This description focuses on the work of a Year 10 mixed-ability group (the activity itself predated the arrival of National Curriculum Science).

Stage One (find a problem)

The school in which this project was undertaken is set in open ground between two villages. Across the road from the school is a farm which grows large quantities of vegetables which are shipped up to London wholesalers. Not far from the school on the other side is a sewage works. The increasing population in the area is putting great strain on the sewage works, and the system sometimes cannot cope. (Even in 1992 there were stories in the national press about the overflow of sewage into the local backwaters.)

Occasionally a nasty smell would well over the school for days at a time. There were several theories about the cause of the smell. The two most popular were that it came from:

- the sewage works;
- the crops on the fields across the road (e.g. cabbages left to rot because the weather conditions hadn't allowed harvesting).

Stage Two (interrogate this problem)

This problem provided many opportunities for pupils to consider the place of 'service' and 'commercial' activities in society. The potential of the discussion for a broad range of scientific enquiry was immediately apparent: there was, for example, the uncertainty of the explanations, and the relationships between conclusions/explanations and scientific evidence. Sixth formers worked in collaboration with the sewage works. They studied the reactions which could produce smells, the ways in which these could be monitored, siting measuring devices, taking measurements, using knowledge of the devices to work out, quantitatively, possible levels being produced at source. Key Stage 4 pupils used their understanding of metabolic or decay reactions in sewage works (or the crops) to link it to observations and suggest how the problem might be addressed. Year 9 pupils could identify possible sources of the smell and investigate these, making use of their developing ideas about photosynthesis and respiration, surface area and so on.

Stage Three (hypothesise)

It was impossible to predict *when* the smell would arise: previous years' work had suggested it was more likely to arise in wintry, wet weather. I told the group that we would do some work when we noticed the smell and set them to brainstorm reasons for the smell. Suggestions included:

- people imagined the smell/had faulty sense of smell;
- the sewage works became overloaded and were unable to cope fast enough with the treatment;
- cabbages (or other named crops) decayed in the fields;
- something was being put on the fields (e.g. a pesticide);
- the smell was always there, but it was only noticed when the weather conditions were right.

As a group we discussed these possibilities and identified those which we could investigate with the resources we had available. The class's responsibility was to do some thinking/research about factors which might be involved. We divided the tasks between the small groups and set some dates on which to report back. Pupils were used to this way of working and knew the rules of operation. Some lessons were identified as opportunities to use class time to carry out work on the project, but pupils were expected to work outside these times as well and to plan for the efficient use of their time in lessons. This meant that those who wanted to carry out laboratory investigations needed to organise themselves so that they used lesson time for doing the investigation. Groups were responsible for planning, carrying out and evaluating the work and reporting back to the class. Each group had to consult with me before embarking on its work, and also to consult as it worked.

Pupils' investigations included: the factors which affected the rate at which vegetables decayed; the kind of products which resulted from decay; how smells travelled; people's sensitivity to different smells.

The class made a record of weather patterns, of when various crops were planted and of the varying demands on the sewage works. In addition, there was some sampling of people's perception of whether there was a smell.

Stage Four

There was a break from this investigative work when the smell arrived: pupils checked the crops, visited the sewage works, sampled people's perception of, and reaction to, the smell, etc. Their evaluation of the findings failed to produce a clear answer, but the balance of opinion was that the smell was caused by rotting cabbages and the 'right' wind conditions.

Other possibilities

This project could have led to work at a higher level on the reactions involved in the sewage works and/or in the decay of plant material. It would also have been possible to investigate in greater detail the rates of such reactions and how they could be altered. Finally, the project could have developed into a much grander project involving the local community and consultation over, for example, plans to re-site the sewage works or new housing. Similarly, the project could have been used at Key Stage 3 as a vehicle for acquiring (rather than revising) knowledge and understanding of the processes involved.

ASSESSMENT OF ACTIVITY

The project had great relevance, because it was a local and important issue (at least when the smell was there). The difficulty lay in finding sufficient lines of investigation which pupils could follow. The project lent itself well to work with a mixed-ability group, because pupils could undertake investigations at different levels. It gave plenty of fuel for debate at the end and real opportunity to weigh up the advantages and disadvantages of the farm and the sewage works. There was also debate about the implications for the community of the sewage treatment plant and the farm. This allowed pupils to compare and contrast the sewage plant (which served the local community) and the farm (whose produce was transported elsewhere).

One of the main difficulties of the project was that we were never able to find out what was in the smell. The sewage plant, in conjunction with sixth formers, had set up a monitoring device, but it had not produced conclusive results.

Maggie Hannon taught Science in Wiltshire and Berkshire before being seconded to the Secondary Science Curriculum Review as regional Project Officer for the South-East of England. She has been involved in assessment and, as part of the CATS team, has worked to develop Key Stage 3 SATs. An active member of the Association for Science Education, she is currently Senior Inspector in Liverpool.

LIVING EARTH: A RESOURCE FOR LEARNING

Acid rain: how are different stone building materials affected?

JANET COOK

Aims

- to help the children appreciate that many of the environmental issues they hear about do actually have a direct effect on us in our local environment
- to discover the pattern that acid plus carbonate produces fizzing (effervescence)

Resources

- Basic scientific equipment, e.g:
  - petri dishes or beakers;
  - pipettes;
  - weak acid (for example, 0.1 M HCl);
  - universal indicator and charts;
  - spatulas, forceps or spoons;
  - safety goggles;
  - cloths.

- Water samples, e.g:
  - rain water, pond water;
  - river water, sea water;
  - tap water, distilled water;
  - hard water, soft water.

- Building materials, e.g:
  - brick, gravel, breeze-block;
  - marble, sandstone;
  - concrete, chalk;
  - limestone.

- Books, leaflets, slides.

- The local library, the school library (the School Library Service will provide boxes of topic books, if requested in advance).

Preparation required

If possible, organise the collection of water samples from different sources and different areas of the country (it is important to have samples from rural areas as well as industrial areas): pupils could collect these over a summer holiday. Collect a range of building materials and write to local environmental groups (e.g. local branch of Greenpeace) and to the Department of the Environment with requests for information – or ask your pupils to do so.

ACCOUNT OF ACTIVITY

Introduction

This is a project which is appropriate for Key Stage 3 pupils, although some of the work (that on indicator species, for example) can easily be developed for students of A level Biology. It allows pupils to investigate the scientific basis for acid rain, and to examine its implications both in terms of the construction industry and of the broader environment.

The activity is introduced in the form of a whole class discussion, from which the teacher draws out key points and notes them on the chalkboard. Pupils then form small groups or pairs to carry out the practical work and reach their own conclusions, which they then report back to the whole group in a concluding class discussion.

Stage One

The following diagram is a useful starting point for this activity. Teachers may use it to inform their planning, and they may choose to make a version of it explicit to their pupils, in order to share the objectives of the activity with them.

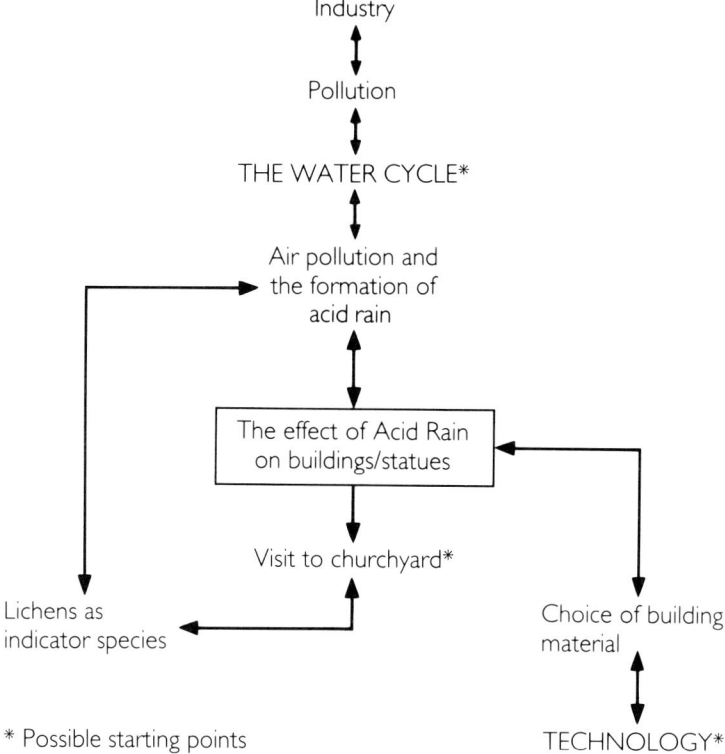

* Possible starting points

This diagram represents a number of routes into the chosen activity. Depending on your teaching programme, you could tackle each route independently or study all aspects in the scheme.

The first route, via the water cycle, is a classroom-based project. A general group discussion on the use of water – how much we use, what we use it for, where dirty water goes, how it is cleaned, how it is used outside the home, in industry, etc. – should enable you to establish the necessary links between industry, pollution and the water cycle, and lead on to a discussion of the formation of acid rain.

The second route, again classroom based, involves the children bringing in samples from home. This route considers the choice of building materials in the light of the environmental conditions to which these materials will be exposed: in this respect, the route has a strong Technology focus. Discussion of building materials available could lead to a series of experiments – how strong is the material? how is it affected by heat, water, sunlight, acid, etc.? – and could then lead on to consideration of the way in which acid rain erodes certain building materials.

The third route is an environmental one which requires a visit to a suitable local churchyard. This could easily be set as a homework activity – with pupils having to visit and observe the presence of lichens on the gravestones, the erosion of statues and decorative detail on the masonry – or it could be arranged as a class outing. If the latter option is chosen, you will have to seek parental and school authority permission. Back in the classroom, pupils will research the subject further and undertake experiments, which will (with your own in-put) lead these field observations back to the discussion of acid rain and pollution.

Stage Two

Whichever of these routes you choose, there are two possible classroom experiments:

a) Testing the pH of the water samples.
Using the samples collected, or an existing school collection, pupils test and compare the pHs of various water samples and then discuss them in terms of their source and the industries in the area.

b) What is the effect of acid rain on different stone building materials?
Pupils test the reaction of the materials they have collected, or an existing school collection, to a weak acid solution (representing acid rain). Follow-up discussion about what pupils observed, what the material looked like before and after exposure to the solution, etc. should establish that the acid eats away certain materials.

This might be an appropriate point at which to introduce the following scientific equation and to explain that the stone materials eroded by acid rain are those which contain carbonate:

ACID + CARBONATE → WATER + CARBON DIOXIDE + SALT DIOXIDE

$2HCl + CaCO_3 \rightarrow H_2O + CO_2 + CaCl$

The actual experimental procedure for both these exercises is straightforward, viz:

Testing the pH of water:
– Pour 10ml of water sample in test tube.
– Add 2–3 drops of universal indicator.
– Read off pH chart.
– Tabulate results.

How are different stone building materials affected by acid rain?
– Place a small sample of material on to petri dish.
– Cover with 5ml acid solution and observe results.
– Add another 5ml acid solution and observe results.
– Tabulate results.
– Rinse building material under tap, and place in waste bucket.

Stage Three

To conclude the practical work and to involve pupils in using what they have discovered, you could set them problem-solving exercises, for example:

- If you were a builder and your only building materials were limestone and marble, would you choose to build in:
  a) Sheffield;
  b) Cornwall;
  c) Los Angeles;
  d) the Australian bush?
- What materials would you choose to build with in the following situations?
  a) a new factory building for a pickling company;
  b) an extension to a dairy farm.

Other possibilities

With older pupils, you could organise further practical work as an extension of the experimental work, to show that:

- the effervescence which will be observed when the acid eats away at the carbonate is carbon dioxide gas;
- the reaction between the acid and the carbonate neutralises the acid.

The following extension activities do not involve practical work:

- Pupils could design posters to display the findings from their experiments.
- Pupils could design posters with appropriate messages (for example, 'Stop Acid Rain').
- The class could hold debates on the rights and wrongs of building an industrial plant in a well-known countryside beauty spot.
- Pupils could design board games based on the subject of acid rain, e.g. 'Go back to Start – you've polluted a stream', etc.

For other ideas of continuation work, refer back to the scheme flow diagram on page 242.

Janet Cook taught Integrated Science and A level Biology in a comprehensive school for eight years before leaving to start a family. Since then she has been involved in home tutoring, examination writing and GCSE marking and moderation.

SPECIAL NEEDS

No area of the curriculum should, of course, be closed off to any pupil, but there is evidence that teachers have sometimes shied away from discussing environmental issues with those pupils whom we still refer to as having 'special needs', because they have considered the issues too complex to discuss easily.

The two articles that follow show that it is not the conceptual complexity of a subject which is at issue but the way in which that subject is presented. Far from being 'beyond' these pupils, the environment is firmly within their grasp. Indeed, several of the contributions to Section 3 of this book have specifically referred to the immense contribution that special needs pupils have made to whole-school initiatives and to their delight at contributing to the general debate and proving themselves to be of practical value. Environmental issues affect everyone, regardless of age, gender, creed, race or intelligence.

Understanding Antarctica

LYNN STUART

Aim
- to increase pupils' awareness of the special environment of Antarctica and to show how this continent may be protected

Resources
- a globe, atlases/maps of Antarctica
- rough paper, pens/pencils
- pictures and photos

Preparation required
If you require further information about Antarctica before you start the activity, or if you want to suggest to your pupils that they write themselves for further information or in a gesture of support, the following two addresses are useful:

World Park Antarctica
Greenpeace UK Ltd
30/31 Islington Green
London N1 8XE

WWF UK
Panda House
Weyside Park
Godalming
Surrey GU7 1XR

ACCOUNT OF ACTIVITY

Introduction

This activity is appropriate for Year 4 to Year 8 pupils and may be undertaken as part of National Curriculum English (where it fits work required for AT1, Speaking and Listening) and Geography (where it fits work required for AT3, Environmental Geography). It is designed for use with pupils in Special Needs classes (and can be used, in Special Schools, at ages beyond those given above).

The whole class works together initially, then breaks into smaller groups of five or six pupils, coming together again at the end for the final activity. You need a chairperson (pupil/teacher) for the final activity. There is the possibility of individual/pair work for extension activities.

Stage One

Before starting the activity, write the following on the chalkboard or OHP:

> *Men wanted for hazardous journey. Small wages, bitter cold, long months of complete darkness, constant danger, safe return doubtful.*

Make seven cards, large enough to be displayed – and seen – from the back of the class, with the following information on them:

Card A: Antarctica is a *continent*.
Card B: Antarctica covers one tenth (1/10) of the world's land surface. It is 56 times larger than Great Britain.
Card C: The land is covered with ice one mile thick.
Card D: In winter, it gets as cold as −89 degrees.
Card E: In winter, the sea around Antarctica freezes. This makes the ice area twice as big.
Card F: In some places in Antarctica it has not rained for two million years. It is the driest place in the world.
Card G: The ice on Antarctica is made up of 9/10 of the world's fresh water.

Stage Two

Ask the class to suggest what the job description on the board is about. When they have given their ideas, tell them this was Ernest Shackleton's actual advertisement for expedition members in 1908. Ask the class to provide any more information they might have about Antarctica – explorers, climate, wildlife, etc. The point of this initial activity is to indicate that Antarctica has not been fully explored yet and that not a lot is known about it.

Turn over each card: a pupil reads it and then the class explore its implications, which you could then summarise on the board. Teach or establish vocabulary as it comes up, and convey key concepts, e.g.:

Card A: You will need to establish the meaning of 'continent'; do this via discussion of 'land' and what land is.

Card B: Try to get ideas of what 1/10 is; establish that it is very large; gather ideas about what the land might be like – mountains, rivers (glaciers) – and about what might be under the land (this introduces idea of minerals, oil, etc.).

Card C: Try to convey the idea of a vertical mile; what might live on/under/around it in the sea.

Card D: Get pupils to imagine the degree of coldness – all liquid frozen; think of protection needed by animals and of what humans need to stay there.

Card E: Importance of rain for plants; implication for plant life in Antarctica; what animals might eat.

Card F: What is fresh water; who/what needs it and why? Tell the class that 39 countries in the world reckon some or all of Antarctica is theirs. Why could they possibly be interested? Divide the class into two groups. Tell Group A that they want to be there, encourage them to think of everything they could get out of Antarctica. Tell Group B that they are opposed to the idea of Antarctica being developed in any way and want it to become a World Park; encourage them to work out reasons why they might want this.

If the class cannot cope with this as a group activity, ask them to suggest ideas and write these on the board. Focus on:

- mining and drilling to see what mineral resources there are (coal, gold, oil, etc.) and how this could be seen to lead to wealth, research, military bases, source of fresh water;
- impact on the environment of drilling equipment, men, supplies (already some areas are littered with old machinery, human debris – cans, etc. – disturbing the breeding grounds of wildlife), pollution – refer to Exxon oil disaster in Arctic, Braer disaster in the Shetlands.

Hold a United Nations Earth Summit and ask each group to present arguments, through the chair. Try to get some sort of overview and class conclusion.

Other possibilities

Research into Antarctica could lead to studies of particular animals/birds, how they survive, their adaptations, etc. It could involve examination of the food chains of the environment and how both of these are threatened by environmental disasters like the Exxon disaster in the Arctic or the Braer in the Shetlands. For those interested in the history of the region, there is ample scope for research into early expeditions and reading about, for example, Scott of the Antarctic or the unsupported 1992–93 transcontinental crossing by Sir Ranulph Fiennes and Dr Michael Stroud.

ASSESSMENT OF ACTIVITY

When this project was undertaken with 13 to 16 year olds in a Special School, pupils seemed to experience difficulty with three main areas of the work:

- understanding what a continent (land mass) was;
- understanding that land is a resource and that what is in the land may be more important, economically, that what is on the land;
- confusion between the Arctic and the Antarctic, and between frozen sea and frozen land. It helped to point out that there were other differences, for example in terms of the animals living there. The joke that follows helped, once it was explained:

Q: Why don't polar bears eat penguins?
A: They can't get the wrappers off.

Lynn Stuart works for the Service for Communication Disordered Pupils in Northumberland, supporting children of all ages in a variety of settings. As Lynn Hutchinson, she has published material aimed at developing reading and comprehension skills. In addition to teaching communication skills, she is involved in improving access to the curriculum and helping to translate knowledge and concern into individual and personal choice.

Preparation required

Prior to the session, students should collect photographs that, in their eyes, represent their way of life, their family and the area where they live. You will need to keep on reminding them to do this!

Account of activity

At the beginning of the session divide students into pairs and ask them to compare the photographs they have brought in with those of their partner. Each student then notes similarities and differences. Without prompting from their partner, ask the student to form a general impression, on the evidence of the photos, of the other's life and customs. She or he then tests the hypothesis with the partner. Following this, encourage one or two pairs to report their discussion to the group. Students should concentrate on those areas where their initial impression has proved wrong. There may well be a number of sources of misunderstanding, but most can be traced to the absence of a caption or guiding text. Invite students to add their own captions to their photographs. Allow further discussion to ensue in small groups on the manner in which photographs are changed by accompanying text; how it encourages the viewer to 'read' the photo in a certain way.

Now distribute a selection of images of the 'Third World', largely drawn from Asia and Africa (available in the pack, *One World, Many Worlds*), in turn to small groups of two or three students. Each group should ponder the photographs and record in written form the feelings inspired in them by what they imagine to be their content. After allowing a brief period of discussion, append short, factual captions to the photographs (written on the back of each photograph in the pack). Students who have 'read' economic distress will be confronted with evidence of new housing projects. Some will refuse to believe the captions provided by the tutor, because they conflict so strongly with their own expectations about the images. In the light of these captions, ask each group to revise their texts if they consider it necessary.

Adult Basic Education and 'Third World' issues: some practical ideas

JOE CARTER

Aims

- to provoke discussion, group work and writing by looking at the relationship between industrialised and developing countries
- to challenge some of the commonly held beliefs about life in developing countries
- to describe the experiences of some people from developing countries who live in the United Kingdom
- to encourage a much more dynamic, interrelated understanding of the concerns that bind rich and poor countries to one another

ACTIVITY 1: THE POWER OF A CAPTION – USING PHOTOGRAPHIC IMAGES TO UNDERSTAND THE 'THIRD WORLD'

Resources

- the 'Images' section in *One World, Many Worlds* (ALBSU, 1987)
- pen and paper
- cameras would be useful for follow-up activities

To conclude the session, students mount the photographs on card with the 'before' and 'after' text to compare readings. The written work produced during the session, both individually and in small groups, may form the basis for the general practice of literacy skills.

Other possibilities

After discussion on the influence of the text that goes with photographs, students could consider the effect of positive and negative captions, provided in the pack, for each image. For example, students might compare the following alternatives to accompany an interior shot of a woman's house: 'Dona Martina and her family are fortunate to have moved to a new brick-built house donated by the local council.' and 'Dona Martina has left her friends and family behind in her move to a new brick-built council house in Baixa.' Students may then write their own positive and negative captions either to the photographs they had brought in or to those found in newspapers and magazines. This stimulates a productive awareness of the nuances of words and the impact they may have.

In the past, one unexpected and very welcome development of this session has been the growth of a small photography project among some of the students. Dissatisfied with their own snaps, and the ill-informed public images of so-called marginal cultures in Britain, a number of students have sought to remedy the situation by producing their own images and their own texts.

Assessment of activity

It is important to keep planned objectives in mind in sessions like this which have considerable potential for heated discussion among group members. On one course, too much discussion interfered with the production of written work at each stage of the activity. Some students were understandably irritated by this. It is worth noting that if the activity is to achieve its outcomes, discussion must, with the agreement of the students, be short and to the point.

ACTIVITY 2: THE LANGUAGE OF FOOD – IMPROVING BASIC SKILLS IN AN INVESTIGATION OF FOOD AND TRADE

Resources
- the 'Food and Trade' section in *One World, Many Worlds*
- pen and paper
- blank playing cards

Preparation required
Ask students to read closely the labels and packaging of food sold in their local supermarket or corner shop, in order to establish the country of origin. If time is short, make a pack or cards with the names of a representative selection of foods written on them. On another pack, write the countries of origin for each food.

Account of activity
Split students into two small groups of five to play 'The Map Game'. The materials for, and rules of, the game are contained in the pack. Without actually speaking to one another, each student must reconstruct a map of the world that has been carved up into a number of segments. A player can communicate with another player by offering a piece of map if she or he thinks it will be of assistance in putting the map together. The aim of the game is to

develop recognition of graphical conventions, a co-operative group spirit and critical awareness of why some parts of the map are familiar and some aren't.

On completion of the game, the students reassemble in one main group. Remind the students of their preparatory task. Any problems in deciphering labels should be aired at this stage, e.g. size of lettering, abbreviation, etc. Then explain the two sets of cards which denote a food and its country of origin. Students form pairs to identify the country on a world map. Organise a group discussion in response to these three questions:

- Which cards are new to the pack?
- What would have been on the shelves 20 years ago?
- Does the name of each food come from the language spoken in its country of origin?

One of the possible activities arising out of this discussion involves work on the history and development of vocabulary. You could ask students to brainstorm words used in English which they know originated in other languages or other countries. Those students who possess a certain cultural bilingualism and who are at home in more than one culture have a key contribution to make to this exercise and are better placed to spot words which have entered English from external sources. Ask students to write down reasons why they thought words from other countries had been assimilated into the English language. This can lead to a critical perspective on Britain's relations with non-European countries, often promoted by students with personal experience of colonialism.

Other possibilities

The pack puts forward a number of routes you could take from the starting point provided by this activity. Students may be interested in investigating the changes in dietary habits revealed by the discussion of the first two questions in the activity above: this can be led into by reminiscences of what students ate as children. The activity establishes a basis for work on the relationship of everyday foods to the terms of trade that obtain between Britain and non-European countries. Students might wish to consider the pricing of goods from abroad. Numeracy tasks could be included in an examination of the ways in which the price for imported goods, particularly for those from the 'Third World', is kept artificially low. Discussion of the development of English vocabulary could lead to consideration of the influence of American English on British English. In addition to the names of foods, other American words and expressions are, of course, present in the language. Questions of cultural influence, linguistic change and national identity are good stimuli for students' writing.

Assessment of activity

Activity 2 leans heavily on game-playing to warm students' interest in the topic. Some groups may feel games are childish and not an appropriate learning aid. It is therefore advisable to check their preferences beforehand and explain the game's objectives thoroughly at the beginning of the activity.

Joe Carter has taught, and organised the provision of, basic skills to adults since the early 1980s, mostly in South London and in both the voluntary and the statutory sectors. He is currently a lecturer in the Return to Learning department of Westminster Adult Education service.

TECHNOLOGY

Like science, technology is often considered the source of all environmental problems. This view overlooks the obvious fact that the subject is essentially neutral; it is the use to which humans decide to put it that determines whether it is to be of benefit or harm.

The overt reference to the environment in the curriculum Orders for Technology reflects what is increasingly happening in the world outside, where industries are, at an early stage, building environmental considerations into research and development and subjecting all new designs to a 'cradle-to-grave' analysis of their impact on the environment. While it would be foolish to imagine that technology will, on its own, get us out of the environmental problems that our past technological excesses have brought about, there is every likelihood that a more environmentally-aware use of technology will lead to fewer such problems in the future. The two articles that follow show the educational benefit that may be derived from combining pupils' enthusiasm for 'hands-on' design work with a sense of the environmental purpose to which their work may be put.

'Imagine the amount of advanced technological expertise that went into producing this lot'

The outside school environment

CAROL HUGHES

All men are designers. All that we do, almost all the time, is design, for design is basic to all human activity. The planning and patterning of any act toward a desired, unforeseeable end constitutes the design process. Any attempt to separate design, to make it a thing by itself, works counter to the fact that design is the primary matrix of life.

V. Papanek (1991) Design for the Real World

Aims
- to improve an aspect of the school's outdoor environment
- to develop and extend the ability to use language related to design with special reference to people and their environments
- to describe the materials, structures, mechanisms and processes involved in a Design and Technology task

Resources
- construction kits (BauSpiel and Lasy – only obtainable from Spectrum Suppliers – Lego, Dacta and Duplo, Mobilo, Meccano plastic and metal are all recommended)
- tools: bench hooks, hack saws, hammers, single hole punchers, PVA wood glue, vices, jigs, screw drivers, wire cutters, drills and drill bits, rulers and nails
- found or recycled materials: cardboard boxes, cardboard tubing, cotton reels, egg boxes, etc.
- resistant materials: square sectioned timber, dowel (various sizes), plastic tubing (various sizes)
- general classroom resources: elastic bands, drawing pins, Plasticine, paper clips, paper fasteners, masking (double-sided and ordinary Sellotape), PVA glue
- various types of card or paper
- paints

(It would be useful to contact NES Supplies, Commotion, Heron, TTS and Sheffield Educational suppliers for obtaining most Design and Technology equipment.)

Preparation required

You will need to have a plan of the school and the outlying area; and pupils will need to have some knowledge about how to use simple hand tools such as scissors, saws, drills, etc. Make sure that you are fully acquainted with all safety issues (an excellent document is *Be Safe*, published by the ASE, but most LEAs have policy documents concerning the use of tools in the classroom).

ACCOUNT OF ACTIVITY

Introduction

Much of what is currently done in the primary curriculum area of Design and Technology involves designing and making artefacts as part of a theme or project in Science, History or Geography. The project described below focuses centrally on Technology and involves pupils in a real and relevant situation: the outside environment of their own school. If all the various activities are undertaken, the project could take a half term or a full term to complete, depending upon the depth at which you wish to develop the activities.

The environment of the school is often a neglected area for technological activities, and yet it is the immediate environment in which the pupils 'play' and could be considered as a place where children acquire much of their social, linguistic, scientific, mathematical and geographical knowledge. Using this environment as the central stimulus of a project will focus on the following key areas of a technological activity:

- designerly thinking (the ability to imagine change and bring about that change and to externalise imagining into reality through drawings, models and plans);
- technical skills (the skills and knowledge of the different tools, materials and equipment needed to realise designs);
- communication skills (the ability to work in a group, in which the skills of communicating ideas, negotiating decisions and sharing individual knowledge and expertise in a group are enhanced);
- planning (the ability, within a group, to plan the use of time, resources and tools);
- problem-solving (the ability to identify real problems and to find alternative solutions to those problems through discussion, research, evaluation and negotiation);
- spatial awareness (the appreciation that the space in which pupils learn, play and socialise can be changed for certain needs and reasons; the ability to translate those changes through design realisation in the form of annotated drawing, plans and models; the ability to work with plans and maps and to learn about scale, symbols and contours).

In addition to these skills – which are specific to the Technology curriculum – the project will also develop pupils' mathematical skills (measurement, shape and size), their scientific knowledge (of materials, structures, mechanisms, plants and animals and habitats), their investigation and research skills and their communication skills.

The activity may be organised as a whole class activity or as an activity conducted in groups, once the original problem has been raised in a whole class discussion. It is a project suitable for Key Stage 2 pupils, but well within the reach of pupils at Key Stage 1 as well. Pupils at Key Stage 1 could focus on one of the activities and expand that activity.

Stage One

In the form either of a class discussion or group brainstorming activities, ask pupils to consider the questions:

- What is wrong with the school's outside environment?
- Why does it need to be changed?
- What changes would you like to make?
- Why would you like to make the changes?
- Where would you like to make the changes?

The following are likely to feature among the reasons which children will volunteer:
- safety (there are areas of the grounds which are dangerous or offer health hazards);
- boredom (there's nothing for pupils to do at playtime and lunch times);
- aesthetic appearance (the grounds look unattractive);
- there's too much litter around;
- room (there are too many restricted areas in which they cannot play);
- there are no facilities for the housing of domesticated animals or habitats that would attract wild animals;
- there are no trees or plants to provide habitats for birds, insects or butterflies or ponds for fish, water creatures or insects.

In turn, when asked to consider what they would like to see this outside environment used for, pupils might suggest some of the following: an area where special play apparatus could be safely placed for the pupils to use; a quiet area; an area where you can sit.

From this initial brainstorming, explain to the pupils that their task is to come up with a design for an improvement to one particular aspect of the school's outside environment.

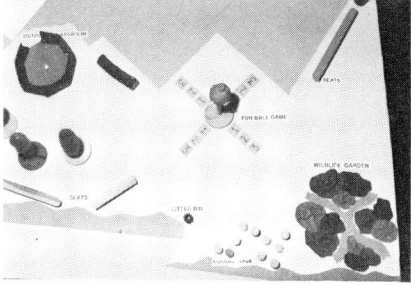

The whole class can either focus on one specific area of enquiry, or groups could choose different areas as their particular area of research. Some teacher guidance is necessary at this stage, and it might be a good idea to identify those areas on which pupils might most profitably focus. These might be:

- play areas (this would involve discussion of types of apparatus, etc.);
- habitats (this would involve looking at gardens, ponds, bird tables, etc.);
- trails (this would involve consideration of smell, texture and colour);
- communal areas for seating (this would involve identifying area for seating and different types of outdoor seating available);
- sports (this would involve identifying the types of sports activities that usually take place in the outside environment);
- litter control (this would involve identifying the problem of litter control and different methods of dealing with it in an environmental way);
- wall and floor markings (this would involve identifying the types of markings required to play different games both on the floor and the wall, such as hopscotch and aiming games).

(For each of these areas of investigation, a list of tasks and questions to consider is provided later in this article.)

Stage Two

The next stage of the project is for pupils to investigate and evaluate their own environment and, from their evaluations, to identify the changes that will need to be made to improve it. This in turn will involve them in making decisions and choices about the changes to be made and about the materials they wish to use to realise their choices.

On a plan of the school (you could photocopy this for each group to use individually), locate those areas of the outside environment which are already in use. Ask pupils to identify areas in the school environment where other facilities could be located. The pupils could at this stage design a sheet giving their reasons for placing these facilities in these areas; they could present their draft ideas on photocopies of the school plan, and the whole class could discuss the advantages and disadvantages of placing facilities in certain areas.

There are a number of ways in which pupils could organise this initial research. They could:

- take photographs of the environment, or record it on video;
- use maps and architect's drawings;
- draw sketches;
- devise questionnaires and interviews to use with different groups (dinner supervisors, the younger and older children in the school, the staff, the caretaker and the parents);
- look at the environments in other schools to see how they differ from their own;
- send questionnaires to schools in other countries with which they may be linked in order to identify how their school environments are designed.

This preliminary work will extend and enhance their research, investigation and observation skills and will identify the real reasons for changing the outdoor environment.

Stage Three

From the initial research and investigations of the first two stages above, pupils should now be moving to their idea of how the environment can be changed and identifying the practical implications of that decision.

- How much is it going to cost?
- How will they find the money for this?
- Who is going to do the work? (In terms of financing the project, you might need to consider outside agencies like the local LEA, The Playing Fields Association and the County Council.)
- How can the environment be changed?

Hereafter, the project centres on the realisation of the chosen design, and the order of the activities will depend on the particular design and the needs of the group working on that design. The actual form in which pupils present their design thoughts and communicate their ideas will, likewise, depend on what form seems most appropriate to those ideas, but is likely to involve one or more of the following:

- pencil design drawings;
- paintings;
- crayon drawings;
- cllage;
- mock-ups which use: construction kits, resistant materials, found or recycled materials or a combination of all of these.

As the teacher, you will need to provide input into this design process, and it may be a good idea to do this as a series of whole and group presentations. This input will be:

- technical (e.g. how to use saws, drills, scissors, vices, clamps, gigs and hammers; how to join items by means of card triangular corners, strapping, string, elastic bands, nails and dowel);
- explanatory (describing the construction kits, their use with other materials such as wood, plastics, metals, recycled or 'found' materials);
- analytical (considering, talking and testing the different properties of materials in terms of their colour, shape, form, texture, strength and resilience);
- evaluative (assessing the design in terms of both process and product, making an aesthetic judgement).

For each of the possible areas of investigation identified in Stage One above, the following questions and points to consider could be given to pupils.

Play areas
Task
To design and make a model or annotated drawing of a piece of apparatus for use in a play area in the outdoor school environment

The following questions could be used to stimulate designerly thinking:

– What is used now? Is it suitable? Is it useful in developing certain skills and team work?
– As far as a new piece of apparatus is concerned, who would use it? What would they use it for?
– What age children will use the equipment? Can the equipment be versatile so that children of different ages can use the equipment?
– Where would it be placed?
– What types of equipment are there on the market? Where can I find out about these types of equipment?

- Are there any rules or regulations concerning the types of play equipment used in a school playground?
- What safety factors need to be considered if equipment is to be placed in the playground?
- Does the environment require lighting? If so, where?
- What kinds of play equipment do you enjoy playing on?
- What can you do on play equipment?
- What kind of play equipment would be safe for our playground?
- Do we need to have a theme for the play equipment, such as animals, homes, castles?
- Would you prefer a variety of different themes?
- Where could the play equipment be positioned?

Habitats

Task
To design and make a plan or model of a wildlife area

The following questions could be used to stimulate designerly thinking:

- Where is the best place for the area?
- What plants could be used?
- How could birds be attracted to the habitat? A bird-feeding station? Nesting boxes? Berry-bearing trees (rowan, berberis, hawthorn, holly)? Where is the best place for these?
- How could insects and butterflies be attracted to the area? Which plants attract insects and butterflies? (Blue Ensign are attracted to candytuft, apple mint, dame's violet and *Buddleia davidii* (butterfly bush); Orange Tips are attracted to Michaelmas daisies, lavender, honeysuckle, lilac and primula; Orange Tips, Small Tortoise Shells and Red Admirals are attracted to evening primrose and jasmine; stones and rocks will attract insects, but need to be placed appropriately; large logs attract insects and hedgehogs.)
- What types of wild flowers can be grown (packets of wild flower seeds can be bought from local seed merchants or garden centres)?
- What size will the flower beds be? Where will they be positioned? Which plants will be placed where? What will the flower and bush beds eventually look like? When will they need to be planted? Can a plan or design be drawn to indicate their positions? Who will tend the garden areas? Will you need a system or rota of children to cultivate and tend the gardens?
- Where could a pond be safely positioned (away from trees and in a natural hollow)?
- How accessible will the pond be so that children can pond dip safely?
- What types of ponds are available on the market? How much do they cost? How could a pond be constructed? What types of creatures and plants need to be placed in the pond initially?

Trails

Tasks
To design an 'I Spy' trail for other classes
To design and make a booklet or pamphlet for a colour, texture or smell trail

The following questions could be used to stimulate designerly thinking:

- Which areas in the school environment could be used for a smell, colour or texture trail? (Colour and smell trails that include the use of plants are not advised because the colours and smells will change throughout the year.)
- Colour trails: which colours will you concentrate on?
- Texture trail: which textures can be identified in the outside environment? (Children may need to make an initial search of the environment and could perhaps take rubbings of the objects available to identify the different surfaces.)
- If you are going to design a pamphlet which explains your texture trail, how can the pamphlet be attractive and interesting? How could it be designed so that the instructions are clear? What layout could be used? What kinds of lettering could be used? Does the pamphlet need illustrations? Could the pamphlet be word-processed? Could you use a computer graphics package for the illustrations?

(The pupils will need examples of pamphlets and different lettering to help them make their final design.)

Communal seating
Task
To design and make a model of types of seating for the outside environment

The following questions could be used to stimulate designerly thinking:

- Why do you need to have seating in the outside environment?
- Where could the seating be located? What kind of seating could be used? What could the seating be made from?
- Do you need to consider the size of the children who will use it? What colours could be used? How functional does the seating have to be? Does the seating need to be permanent or could it be removable?
- Could the seating be designed using a theme, such as animals or plants?

School sports
Task
To design areas where the usual sporting activities take place and design and make a plan, annotated drawing or model of facilities to cater for the favourite sports activities of pupils in the school

The following questions could be used to stimulate designerly thinking:

- Do areas need to be set aside for school sporting activities? Which sports are played?
- Various sports require markings to show boundaries, specific shooting areas, etc. Are the positions of the markings for specific sports in the most convenient places? What size area is required for these markings? Will there be enough space for the markings to be drawn? Can these play areas where the markings are drawn be used at times other than during sports' lessons?
- Can you design a game and different markings for that game?

Litter

Tasks

To design and make a litter bin that would stop the litter from flying around the playground

To design and make a litter picking up machine

The following questions could be used to stimulate designerly thinking:

- Are the litter bins used? How could the litter bins be designed so that they are used?
- Are there enough litter bins?
- Are the litter bins placed in convenient positions?
- Do the litter bins *retain* the litter or do they leave as much litter outside as inside?
- Is there a system for recycling paper, plastics or aluminium cans?
- What methods can be used to collect litter from the environment which are safe for the collector?
- Can you invent a machine that will pick up litter?

Wall and floor games

Task

To design games where interesting markings are required for the walls or floor of the playground.

The following questions could be used to stimulate designerly thinking:

- What kinds of games can be played on a hard playground floor or wall? Do these games require markings? What shape will the markings be?
- What kind of games could you invent and design? Will these games require equipment such as balls or stones?
- How could simple games like hopscotch be designed to be exciting?
- Could the games have a theme, such as animals, imaginary creatures or space?
- Could the games be used to develop an outdoor learning environment?

References

DES (1990), *The Outdoor Classroom Building, Bulletin 71*, London: HMSO.

Dunn, S and Larson, R (1990) *Design and Technology: Children Engineering*, The Falmer Press.

NPFA (1980), *Towards a Safer Adventure Playground*, London: National Playing Fields Association.

Ross, C and Ryan, A (1991) *Can I Stay in Today, Miss? Improving the School Playground*, Stoke-on-Trent: Trentham Books Ltd.

STEP, *Key Stage 1 and 2 Design and Technology*, Cambridge: Cambridge University Press.

Wilkinson, P E (1980) *Innovation in Play Environments*, London: Croom Helm.

SMP Playgrounds Ltd
Pound Road
Chertsey
Surrey
KT16 8EJ

Wicksteed Leisure Ltd
Digby Street
Kettering
Northamptonshire
NN16 8YJ

(Both of these companies produce interesting catalogues illustrating different types of play equipment.)

Carol Hughes spent over 20 years teaching in primary and middle schools before taking up her present position in 1991 as senior lecturer at the University of Derby, where she is the curriculum co-ordinator for Technology. She is currently engaged in research into children's use of the computer in a Design and Technology task and, for a future PhD, into the different ways in which children design in a Design and Technology activity.

Litter

SALLY WICKS

Aims
- to investigate the problem of litter in the school and the surrounding neighbourhood
- to display the findings of this investigation and to provide possible solutions to the problem which will include a publicity campaign designed to raise awareness of this issue

Resources

- an appropriate software program which might provide a means of bringing together a variety of material – word-processed articles, databases, digitised and computer-drawn images, i.e. a multi-media package such as Hypercard (Apple Macintosh), MAGPIE/Genesis (Archimedes)
- video camera and recording equipment
- imagination, time and energy!

Preparation required

Staff discussion, across curriculum boundaries, to assess ways in which different subjects might contribute to the project.

Training for teachers and pupils in the use of the software and hardware which are to be used in the project.

ACCOUNT OF ACTIVITY

Introduction

This is a Technology activity which has immense cross-curricular potential: indeed, the example upon which this article is based started life as an attempt to bring together work which had a common focus but was undertaken in different curricular areas. This example included work done in English, Art, Geography, RE and Maths. Similarly, although the original example involved Year 7 pupils, there is no reason why pupils above and below this age range may not deal with the same issues in the same way.

The sharing of research findings is an important element of this activity, so it is not a good idea for each pupil to attempt to do everything, even at Key Stage 2, where this might be possible. The activity is essentially a group activity, although it is important to allocate roles clearly within each group, so that individuals may tackle different aspects of the topic before combining their efforts into a group presentation. Organised in this fashion, the project will take about six hours to complete, although this will depend on how used pupils are to working in this way, the number of machines available, etc. The alternative, which is that the whole group performs all parts of the project together, requires more time to complete.

Stage One

Present the tasks to pupils in the form of a Project Brief: there may be campaigns in your area or nationally (e.g. Litter Week) to which this brief could be linked. This part of the project should clearly take the form of a class discussion, which will give pupils the chance to brainstorm ideas around the subject which they can take with them into their group work and also enable you to clarify the three basic stages of the work involved. These are researching the problem, alerting the public and providing solutions.

Stage Two

In order to identify needs and opportunities, pupils will have to research the problem of litter and present their findings for others to interrogate. To do this they will need to have given some preliminary thought to the presentation of these findings:

Pupils should aim to research answers to the following questions:

- How big a problem is litter in the school and neighbourhood environment?
- What type of litter is there, and where is this mostly to be found?
- Where are the refuse containers?
- How often are they emptied?

Explain to pupils that *how* they set about finding the answers to these questions will to a large extent determine the way in which they will present their findings later.

Access to computers is particularly important at this stage. Pupils should use a word-processing program to produce a questionnaire designed to find out people's attitudes towards litter, and a database or specialist software like Junior Pinpoint/Pinpoint (Archimedes) to enter the data that emerges from this. They should also use an appropriate form of data collection to order the information they have gathered from their answers to the questions above.

Pupils now interrogate the database to establish:

- what the different types of litter are;
- where litter is found;
- what the worst areas for litter are.

They then display their findings on a suitable form of graph, or draw a map of the area under investigation which shows the same information.

Stage Three

Further tasks which they might perform could be to:

- design rubbish containers suitable for use in the school buildings, grounds and local area;
- produce materials for a publicity campaign which will raise awareness of the issue of litter (this campaign must cover radio, television – viewdata and commercials – posters and newspaper advertisements).

Pupils now have to generate their own design proposal in order to implement their own solutions to the problem they have analysed and perform their chosen task. You may need to explain that this design proposal should include, in addition to the proposed solution, an analysis of the problem itself, reasons for their choice of solution and an explanation of their choice of materials. You will need also to remind them of the continuous need for evaluation at each stage of the activity; this evaluation process should include a final overview which sums up what they have done and assesses whether the outcomes are those they had planned at the outset, whether the outcomes are satisfactory or whether they need to start again.

Outcomes

An immense variety of outcomes is possible. These may be actual products (nets for litter bins, maps of the school site area, posters, pamphlets, 'sculptures' or other artistic creations using and commenting on litter), or there may be performances or broadcasts (video recordings, taped discussions, interviews and debates). The cross-curricular potential here is obvious.

Digitised image and artwork from The Holt School, Wokingham, Berkshire

ASSESSMENT OF ACTIVITY

In the school where this project was first trialled – the Holt School, Wokingham, where it was organised by Diana Jackson, the IT co-ordinator – pupils' responses on their evaluation sheets commented as much on the skills the pupils had acquired (keying information in, using a mouse, handling a video camera) as on the content of the activity (litter sculpture, separation of recyclable litter from non-recyclable litter, etc.).

Staff responses were favourable, although many complained about the lack of time and resources to complete the work satisfactorily. There was also a problem with the software chosen which used up more memory than the school's computers could readily handle. Generally, however, the feeling was that the project had been more than worthwhile and had built on pupils' interest in the environment and extended their understanding of the subject.

Sally Wicks has taught English and Drama in Berkshire secondary schools for several years and has trained teachers in the same subjects. For the last five years, she has worked as an advisory teacher for the Information Technology and English team in Berkshire.

section three

WAYS OF
WORKING

'People, Places and Plants': an environmental education scheme

SUE BENNETT

INTRODUCTION

The Norton School is an 11 to 16 comprehensive school of 750 pupils. It is situated in the Teeside conurbation: housing surrounds the school to the north and west, Holme House Prison is on the south side, and to the east is the busy A19 trunk road and the chimneys of ICI Ltd.

Over a number of years, the Norton School has developed a policy of environmental education, involving the whole school. The main focus for this policy was the school itself, its grounds and the area surrounding it. Pupils were asked to evaluate their immediate environment and they found that there was much that could be improved:

- there was too much litter;
- the school playing fields were featureless – a green desert;
- an existing pond had become silted up;
- there were few wild flowers or trees, and few habitats for wildlife;
- there were few walks for the local community.

Following this evaluation, efforts were made to reduce the litter and the vandalism, and pupils developed a programme which included sowing wild flower seeds, creating hedges as wildlife 'corridors' and planting bulbs and trees. The hope was that this would improve the immediate surroundings of the school and make them more visually pleasing.

This local work is, of course, on-going, but it has led naturally to a longer-term attempt to develop the pupils' interest in the wider environment and, eventually, to embrace whole world issues. A clear opportunity to do this presented itself in 1989, when the school was invited by Living Earth and the Centre for International Peace-building to take part in the 'People, Places and Plants' project, which involved a link with Lenana High School for Boys in Nairobi. Both schools would benefit from the support and advice of The Royal Botanical Gardens at Kew. Key sponsors which made the early work and visits possible included Barclays Bank Community Relations Department, Unilever Plantations Ltd and the Commonwealth Foundation.

THE LINK WITH LENANA SCHOOL

Lenana School is situated in the suburbs of Nairobi. The school has about 870 boys, aged between 13 and 21, and draws its pupils from all over Kenya. Pupils are selected from applicants after they have completed the national examination, the Kenya Certificate of Primary Education.

As the first part of the project, both schools were to engage in practical environmental work on a plot of land, to exchange information about their progress and compare their very different environments. In the Norton School, almost every department became involved, either with the practical work or with the equally important work of helping pupils to understand more fully the background of the pupils in the twin school. This included studying and, where possible, experiencing the physical and cultural environment of two very different countries – Kenya and England.

The 'People, Places and Plants' project has proved to be a catalyst for the establishment of many contacts outside the schools, as well as for the growth of activities within it. These activities are too numerous to detail here, but a brief description of specific events and schemes should convey the flavour of the project and explain how the momentum has been maintained.

COMMUNICATIONS BETWEEN THE TWO SCHOOLS

For a twinning arrangement of this kind to succeed, good and frequent communications are obviously essential, all the more so if your twin is so far away, and in such a different environment. Pupils and staff have to be able to talk easily to each other and exchange ideas and information. Letters are the obvious means of achieving this, but the geographical distance makes this a form of communication lacking in immediacy. Telephone calls are costly and need to be used sparingly. Obviously there are electronic links, such as fax, computers and modems, but the exploration of these possibilities highlighted differences between the two schools. Information Technology is regarded as an essential part of the school curriculum in England, whereas in Kenya there are other elements, such as the teaching of agriculture, which have far more importance. This was brought home when the Norton School sent a sum of money to Lenana to assist with the purchase of a computer, only to be told by Mr Maneno, the Principal, that he could not justify spending that money on something which had as yet no established place in his school curriculum, whereas the trees which the boys had planted in the school compound as part of their environmental and agricultural practice, were dying through lack of water! Accordingly, the money was spent on a pipeline to the affected area.

Some direct means of communication turned out to be impractical. The use of a modem was ruled out, and, although faxed materials *are* sent, Lenana has to go and collect them from a Post Office. Direct communication of this kind proved a problem, but real, physical contact between the two schools had always been considered essential and would bring huge dividends.

EARLY EXCHANGE VISITS

The first exchange visit took place in 1989 and was a vital element in the forging of a permanent friendship between the two schools. Two members of Lenana staff visited Norton for two weeks, and later in the year two teachers from Norton went to Lenana. Both occasions provided opportunities to exchange materials but, more importantly, they enabled teachers to exchange ideas in extended contact with each other, and for each to see at first hand what the other partner was really like.

The two members of staff from Lenana remarked on how well supplied with books and writing materials the Norton School was, not to mention equipment such as computers and technical machinery. The pupils at Norton are much younger than those at Lenana, which caters for the 13 to 21 age range, although some boys stay longer. There were obvious differences in teaching methods and learning processes, which the visiting teachers were able to observe closely, since work on the 'People, Places and Plants' project was going on in many subjects and had a high profile within the school.

When two teachers from the Norton School went to Kenya in October 1989, they found that Lenana School had an established reputation for environmental work, with Mr Maneno, the Principal, the driving force behind the project. Mrs Wakesa, who had visited Norton, was an enthusiastic partner. A small group of 20 pupils and interested staff had begun work on the school's chosen area of land within the spacious grounds. The number of pupils working on the project later increased to 40, and the Humanities and Agricultural Departments were committed to the work of the project. Other departments were expected to join in as the project gathered momentum. The school itself was very short of basic classroom resources and had limited technical resources for recording and collating data. They did, however, have a good supply of gardening equipment, to enable them to engage in practical work in their immediate environment. Environmental issues are *real* issues to many of the Lenana pupils, who come from a rural environment where soil erosion, the water supply and fuel shortages are serious problems.

Both groups of teachers were overwhelmed by the welcome they received. Greatly stimulated and enthused by their visit, they played an important role on their return in spreading that fervour among the staff and pupils, who had enjoyed the experience of being hosts in their respective schools.

THE OFFICIAL LAUNCH OF THE PROJECT AT THE NORTON SCHOOL

The launch of the project afforded an early opportunity for the school to make contact with people and organisations outside and to let them know about the project and the plans to develop it. An exhibition showing the kind of work that each department was able to contribute to the project gave other staff and pupils, as well as people from outside, some idea of what was currently happening and what was being planned for the future. Many donations of money and equipment received later had their origins in the fact that, on the day of the launch, people could see that both pupils and teachers were enthusiastic and deeply committed to the success of the project.

The launch day had a high profile. There had been careful preparations beforehand, with a press release giving notice of the event, and large numbers of invitations were issued to existing and potential friends of the school. Lord Hesketh, Parliamentary Secretary of State for the Environment, officiated, and the presence of Dr David Clark, Shadow Minister of the Environment and Mr Frank Cook, MP for Stockton, demonstrated the high level of interest in environmental matters. Local government officials were also present, together with a large number of representatives from local industry and other interested bodies. One of the highlights of the opening ceremony was an amplified telephone call from Lenana joining in the event and sending their good wishes.

THE PEPPERCORN PROJECT

Until 1989, there was a British Rail Freightliner Depot adjacent to the Norton School grounds. When this was dismantled, the school sought permission to develop part of the land for conservation purposes. Negotiations with British Rail, who owned the land, were concluded towards the end of 1990, and a nominal rent of one peppercorn was agreed.

The area of land is just over four acres. It was very tired and clearly in need of care and attention, but it had potential as a valuable resource for the local community. A period of investigation of the site, and consultation with local people, followed. Pupils and teachers visited Billingham Beck Country Park, an area of formerly rough ground which has been developed as a community resource and an area of great environmental quality. The advice of the wardens proved invaluable.

Pupils were involved in the planning of the site from the beginning. The process of development involved many practical skills. A scale drawing was made of the precise area. It was then marked out on the ground. The topography was studied, and a photographic survey was made. It was necessary to make an analysis of the climate, the soil, the existing habitats and to study the aspect of the whole area. An aerial photograph was obtained. In the classroom, findings were converted into computer models, a 3D model and a photographic collage. The local community was consulted, and the history of the area was investigated. Throughout this planning and investigating stage, there was a continual review of progress.

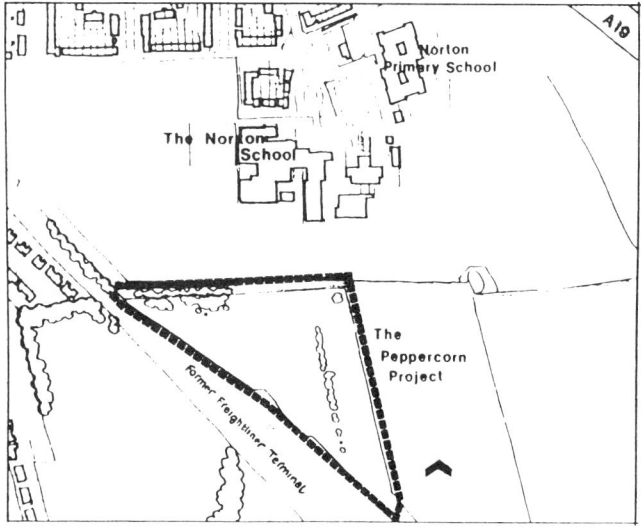

Location Plan 1 :1250

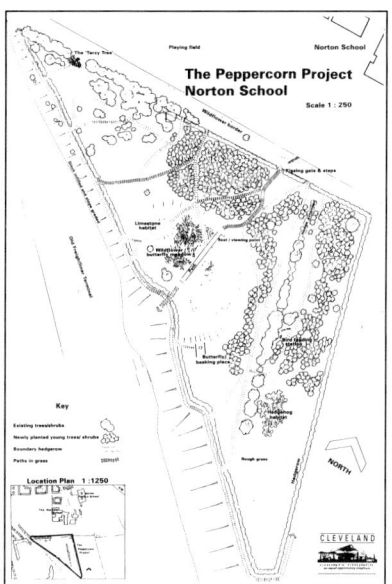

The area has been a hive of activity and has generated much interest in the local community. A boundary hedge has given the area an identity, and provided a habitat for wildlife. A wildflower meadow has been sown, and 2000 trees have been planted. Dolomite paths have been laid to provide access to the site, and a 'kissing gate' has been installed. Rank grass has been strimmed and removed. A bird-feeding station has been installed, and hedgehog habitats established. Recently, as a result of canvassing for large pieces of stone, pupils were invited to visit a quarry in County Durham, and the required stone was donated by the firm. As new work on the present site moves towards completion, negotiations are in hand for the rent of a further six acres of land between Peppercorn and Holme House Prison.

From this description, it is obvious that there is much scope for work across the curriculum. The Year 11 Modular Studies group, under the care of the Special Needs department, has been central to the scheme. They form the core of the planning team, and their development as the project progressed has been marked. Work is included in a Modular Scheme for a City and Guilds Certificate. In English, pupils have recorded the appearance of the area through the seasons, in poetry and prose. Mathematics pupils were involved in the measuring of the site. Science groups undertook the environmental audit, including soil analysis. Pupils in the Design department modelled the area, producing a 3D display. The investigation of the life of the area over the years was prepared by pupils in the History department, and a time capsule was prepared for burial on the site.

The Peppercorn Project has been an important vehicle for the link with Lenana. Each school has worked on an area of poor quality land and has undertaken conservation work. In the case of Lenana, they have collected the seeds of endangered species from a wide area of Kenya and have planted and cared for them, while Norton has engaged in creating a supply of wildflowers and seeds, by growing them on the Peppercorn land. This work provides a basis for continued collaboration.

REGULAR SCHOOL ACTIVITIES, INCLUDING FUND RAISING

Although large-scale events, such as the official launch of the project, are important, the real strength of the link with Lenana lies in the fact that it has permeated the whole school structure and now plays a part in the curriculum of most departments. It fits in well with the demands of the National Curriculum in many subjects and certainly complies with guidelines for environmental education:

> *First hand experience is an essential part of helping pupils to develop a personal response to the environment and to gain an awareness of environmental issues'*
> and
> *'School linking helps to raise in pupils an awareness of the interdependence of*

local and global environments and challenges their prejudices about other people.'

(Curriculum Guidance 7, *NCC*)

There is no space here to explain how each department engages in work on the project to comply with the requirements of the National Curriculum in their own subject, but the brief account of the Peppercorn Project above indicates the ease with which this may be accomplished. When a project is established as a whole-school initiative, with the school management committed to it, it is easy for departments to incorporate it in their own curriculum planning: indeed, in Norton the work is often seen as 'putting flesh' on to the 'bare bones' of statutory requirements.

Fund raising is of vital importance if both schools are to continue to develop the link. The Norton School has used the project work to enter several competitions, and this has resulted in a number of awards, of both hardware and funds. Local firms and organisations have been helpful and sympathetic, and the school has received cash and materials and, more importantly, expert advice and practical help. A 'road-show' of slides and a talk by a team of pupils has raised awareness in the local area. They have visited firms, church groups, other schools, even teachers' courses, in order to spread the word about the project.

Fund-raising events have also been held in the school, for special purposes such as the visit of a small group from Norton to Lenana in 1991 and for the hosting of a larger exchange in July 1992.

A word must be included here about the employment trainees, who have been based on the school site and who have wholeheartedly taken part in various aspects of conservation work, whether it be the restoration of school furniture, the planting of bulbs or trees with pupils, or assistance with the laying of paths and landscaping work on the Peppercorn site. It has been a valuable opportunity for children to work with adults, and the commitment of the members of the team and their organisers has been remarkable and a most valuable part of the project.

The project is always kept in the forefront of the school's consciousness by the use of whole-school and year-group assemblies, and by having two prominent notice boards in the main corridor regularly changed and up-dated. Parents' and pupils' newsletters also help to spread information, and visitors to the school may read of the latest happenings on an information board in the entrance hall. Having such a high profile helps to keep up the momentum.

RECENT EXCHANGE VISITS (KENYA 92)

In February 1991, a small group from Norton visited Lenana. Two girls and one boy were accompanied by a teacher and one of the employment trainees from the group who works at Norton. They received a warm welcome and found that arrangements had been made to fill every minute with interesting activities and excursions. Apart from taking part in school activities, and being able to exchange many views with staff and pupils, they visited a good number of the sights of Kenya, such as the Rift Valley, safari parks, and the coast near Mombasa. At the end, they returned exhausted but exhilarated, and with new ideas and new fervour for the continuation of the link.

'PEOPLE, PLACES AND PLANTS'

DJ Simon Mayo presents the cheque to Claire McGarvey and Scott Stewart, both 15

Grand work wins praise

A CLEVELAND school received congratulations from 3,000 miles away yesterday for a project on its doorstep.

Schoolchildren at Lenano, in Kenya, added their long-distance message to other plaudits for the 750-pupil Norton School at Stockton. The two are twinned.

Deep into conservation work for several years, Norton are the regional award winners in a community innovation programme launched by insurance group Scottish Widows.

The entire school is working on a project which will change four acres of wasteland owned by British Rail at a former freightliner depot into a community site with trees, wild flowers, plants and other attractions.

Scottish Widows sales manager Sandy Lamb said: "We were particularly impressed to find the whole school taking part in this. It is very encouraging."

A cheque for £1,000 to help finance the work was handed over by Radio One breakfast show presenter Simon Mayo.

He said: "The project helps to create a spirit of enterprise in young people and brings them into contact with wildlife."

• About sixty people attended a public meeting which will start moves to give a new lease of life to a surviving relic from thousands of years ago.

Bassleton Wood, on the western edge of Thornaby, is to be designated as a community nature reserve.

Mike Pratt, county council senior project officer, said the idea was to get local people involved in preserving a gem in the Tees green urban corridor.

One determined idea was that there should be a visit by Kenyan pupils to Norton the next year. This scheme became known as 'Kenya 92', and both schools set about the business of raising funds – in Lenana's case, mainly for transport costs, while Norton needed a large sum for the purposes of hospitality and entertainment.

As July approached – the month that had been earmarked for the visit – activity became feverish on both sides. The size of the party was to be 15 pupils and three teachers, and plans were made to accommodate them with the families of Norton pupils. A programme of lessons, events and visits to places of interest was drawn up. The Kenyan pupils worked very hard to raise the money needed: they obtained pulses and vegetables and cooked large amounts of food which they sold in the city. Their parents made considerable sacrifices, and friends helped out. The nine boys from Lenana, their Principal and a teacher were to be joined by six girls and a teacher from the Precious Blood School in Nairobi. The two schools had worked together for the annual Drama Festival in Nairobi, performing items of music and drama from their culture. Although Norton had had no previous contact with the

Precious Blood School, it was thought that the visit of a mixed group would be beneficial to all parties. This idea proved to be more than correct, and the visit would not have been the same without the girls.

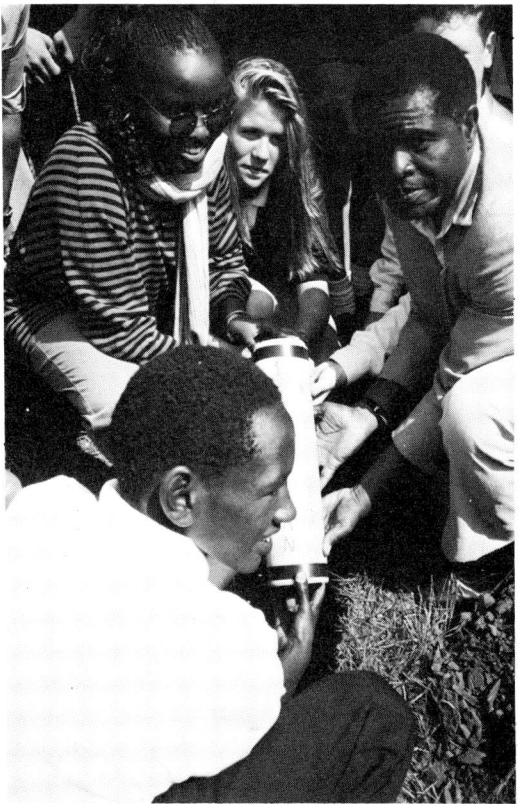

Burying a time capsule

The group arrived in the early hours of the morning of 4 July 1992 and were met by their hosts. The two weeks that followed were hectic, but unforgettable. The Kenyan visitors were quickly absorbed into their host families. Early natural hesitation, on both sides, vanished almost overnight, and pupils and parents later commented that their visitor had become a member of the family, a son or daughter, a sister or brother. As the programme unfolded, the host families were very concerned on behalf of their guests, worrying at the pace of the action, and the levels of fatigue. They were very possessive of their own time with the Kenyans and expressed the desire for more.

At a poignant last assembly, the visiting party entertained the school with song and dance, gave parting gifts by which they would be remembered, and two of the boys (with a well-developed sense of humour) presented the school with 100 peppercorns – as rent for the Peppercorn site for the next 100 years! There was real sorrow at parting, but determination on all sides that somehow they would meet again. Some of that sorrow has been assuaged by a flood of letters passing between Nairobi and Norton and by renewed promises of lasting friendship. It is hoped that the Precious Blood School will join in the environmental work and become a full partner in the project. All parties are looking forward to the visit by Norton pupils to Nairobi in 1994. In the meantime, the momentum will have been maintained by a staff exchange in 1993.

CONCLUSION

Clearly, 'People, Places and Plants' is now well established in Lenana and in Norton. In attempting to analyse the success of what was quite a difficult undertaking, several points come to mind. First, in both schools there is strong leadership by a member of the management team. This has given the project official 'status'; it has also facilitated the efficient running of the project, whether in the dissemination of information or new ideas, or the development and fostering of precious outside contacts which have been vital in terms of the work done so far. Secondly, the interest and commitment of teachers and pupils have also been invaluable in the planning of schemes within the project. Thirdly, it has proved easy to include the project legitimately in the curriculum of both schools. Fourthly, good communications, in a variety of forms, have been absolutely essential, and the exchange visits have obviously been of the greatest importance here.

All this would, however, have had little effect if the pupils could not see the relevance of the project to their own lives. It is *their* enthusiasm, and the whole-hearted support of their parents, that has made the project what it is, both in Nairobi and Norton: a continuing success story.

> *Sue Bennett was, until her recent retirement, head of Humanities at the Norton School, Cleveland. She continues to exercise her interest in the environment – and in environmental education in particular – through voluntary work and writing. She expects to remain involved in the 'People, Plants and Places' project.*

Our wildlife area – from bare earth to outdoor classroom

RALPH SLANEY

INTRODUCTION

The idea for this project originated with a discussion between the headteacher and myself about improvements that might be made to the school environment. Each of us had separately considered developing some kind of wildlife area, and we put the idea to the rest of the staff at the next staff meeting. After some discussion, it was decided to create a pond and butterfly garden on the school field which we all felt would prove a valuable additional outdoor resource for the whole school.

We originally planned to create the wildlife area at the far side of the school field near a row of mature trees, but when the idea was put to the school trustees, who own the field, they decided that a location nearer the school would be better. The reasons for this were two-fold. First, there would be fewer leaves to clear out of the pond each autumn, and secondly, there would be less chance of vandalism (although this is not a great problem in the area of the school).

As chance would have it, a firm of builders was building an extension to the school at that time; this extension, together with the old building, would enclose the project area on two sides, so making it easier and cheaper to fence in.

Two other advantages of this plan were that it could be provided at relatively little cost and that it would also provide an opportunity for the children to help plan and create an addition to their own environment. As far as the curriculum was concerned, the staff and governors envisaged children working in the wildlife area as an extension to their classroom activities, finding and identifying living things, carrying out research and solving problems.

In the event, the planning and making of the wildlife area provided many opportunities in other areas of the curriculum. Children were able to solve real problems in Maths involving estimation, measuring and calculating surface areas. There was also a lot of map work such as drawing plans and making scale drawings and scale models with which to generate designs for the pond area. There were opportunities to carry out research on food chains, food webs and other aspects of ecology. Some of the children became very interested in the conservation aspects of the project, and this led to a lot of work on endangered species, the human effect on the environment and the consequences of our actions, such as picking wild flowers.

FINANCING AND PLANNING THE PROJECT

Once the project had been agreed and the site of the wildlife area decided on, the next stage was to apply for financial help. We were fortunate to be able to fund the project almost entirely from grants and gifts, obtaining two grants, each of around £200, from Lincolnshire County Council and from English Nature. These roughly covered the cost of the pond liner and the fencing. The sand which we used for lining the pond was donated by one of the parents, and the plants were given by friends of the school.

Then came a period of waiting. First we had to wait four months for the builders to finish the extension and then a further four months until the ground was fit to dig the pond.

However, some of this time was usefully filled by the children in Class Three (Years 3 and 4) getting involved in planning the pond area and studying food chains and food webs so as to decide on which plants and animals we should try to introduce.

Early in the summer term, the children from my class went out and marked the position of the drains with wooden pegs and string. Having spent some time designing the size and shape of the pond, they marked the place where it was to be dug in a similar fashion.

PUTTING THE PLAN INTO ACTION

The actual digging of the pond was achieved one Saturday morning by a party of willing volunteers which included parents, governors, children and myself. An appeal for volunteers to bring their own spades and wheelbarrows was successful and, when plied with coffee (adults) and orange juice (children), they even managed to dig us a long jump pit at the same time. Having spent some time in consultation with various authorities about what shape to dig the profile of the pond (the argument was between a smooth profile or a shelved profile – the latter is generally preferred because it enables children to stand on the upper shelves in wellington boots without slipping), the decision was taken out of our hands by a County circular which stipulated that it should be shelved for safety reasons.

The next task was to line the pond with sand to prevent damage to the liner when it was filled with water. The children picked out all the stones, and a very obliging parent, who is a builder, gave us two loads of sand with which to line the pond. When I had added my old bedroom carpets cut into strips, the pond was ready for its butyl liner and water.

It is amazing how quickly a new pond colonises itself; within two days we had water boatmen and great diving beetles swimming around. I have stood by the pond and seen these flying in, though goodness knows where they come from or how far they fly – future possibilities for children's research, perhaps?

It is also amazing how quickly word of a new pond gets around a village like ours. Very soon we had people calling at school to say, 'We heard you had made a pond and wondered if you would like these.' They would then produce buckets and plastic bags full of yellow iris, water soldiers, young frogs and so on. Some of these wonderfully generous people had no connections with the school at all, and I should like to take the opportunity to thank them here and now for their help. In addition to these gifts, we have also purchased extra water plants such as lilies, king cups and other marginals.

Already the pond was beginning to look green and populated, and I now began the laborious task of laying paving slabs around it. Most of these were left by the builders in school as the result of another fruitful conversation with the foreman. If you ever read this, Alan, we won't forget your cheerful, willing help and our thanks must go to you, too.

The whole area, which is about 16m by 10m, has now been fenced in by outside contractors, and a gate with a padlock has been added. These are other safety features which are strongly recommended for peace of mind and for the safety of children who might play on the school site outside school hours.

FUTURE POSSIBILITIES AND PLANS

We have now got to the stage where the hard work has been done and we can see how the area will look when greened over. We are in the process of buying mixed hedging to plant around the outside of the fencing in order to provide additional habitats and to keep out dogs and balls! We still have to provide seating and work tables for children to work at and we are in the process of applying for a further local authority grant to help with this. We envisage a facility which will not only provide an extra 'outdoor classroom' for the school, but will also be a pleasant place to visit and a place where children can be exposed to a multitude of things which an indoor classroom can never provide. Eventually, we hope that the children's work in the area will include the creation of written nature trails which will be produced and researched by the children for other children. These can then be saved in school as yet another resource.

PROJECT OUTCOMES

On the negative side, the project has involved an enormous amount of time and effort to get it to its present stage, and we anticipate problems maintaining the area in the future. The project has changed slightly from the original idea of a pond and butterfly garden, because we have reduced the butterfly garden to a few plants and added an extra area of wild flower meadow instead. This is partly for ease of maintenance and partly to give a larger work area for children to use. Even so, however, there will be a need for regular mowing and strimming, tasks which cannot safely be done by children and which will require access to these types of machines.

On the positive side, there have been many beneficial results already. We have created a fine addition to the school environment and what will hopefully be a permanent resource for the school. The involvement of the children in the project has provided opportunities for work right across the curriculum, and has given them a sense of pride and achievement and ownership. In addition, we feel that we have provided another small but safe habitat for some of our rapidly declining wildlife.

The whole area seems all set to become an attractive and peaceful little environment tucked away in a corner of the school. The children have a place to meet and to work with wild creatures and plants, a place in which to learn how to respect and live alongside other forms of life. In times like these, this is surely one of the most important lessons which we can teach our children.

A FINAL WORD OF ADVICE

Perhaps the most valuable resource you can get for a project like this is good advice, preferably before you begin digging! We approached the County Advisory Service, English Nature, various reference books, circulars and the area manager responsible for grounds maintenance before starting work. We also had a certain amount of experience to call upon because I had been involved with a number of similar projects in other schools.

In addition, we were fortunate that we happened to mention the project to the foreman of the builders working on the extension. This led to an interesting conversation.

'How big is this pond of yours going to be then?' he asked.

'About five metres by four. Why?' I replied, expecting him to be impressed.

'Oh well, you realise there will be two underground drains going through that area?'

He must have seen something in my expression, because he promised to tell me exactly where they ran before he left at Christmas for his next job!

As it turned out, there was plenty of room between the drains for the pond, and a crisis was avoided. However, the presence of the drains did mean that we could not bring in a mechanical digger for fear of fracturing them. The moral is clear. Check very carefully for underground services before digging your pond! In our case, it was only this chance conversation with a builder which saved us.

Ralph Slaney has taught in primary schools in Cleveland and North Yorkshire and is currently deputy headteacher at Mrs Mary King's Church of England Primary School, Lincoln. He previously worked as an advisory teacher for rural school support on the Eskdale Project on the North Yorkshire moors, which gave him an opportunity to become involved in developing wildlife areas in a number of different schools.

'A Tree for Life' Project

RICHARD BURROWS

INTRODUCTION

This project began in autumn 1988 as a joint venture between the village primary school and the Colsterworth and District Gardeners and Allotment Holders' Association. Colsterworth Church of England Primary School has around 130 pupils on roll, aged from four to 11, and arranged into five classes. The school is set in pleasant grounds in the village of Colsterworth, Lincolnshire, some eight miles south of Grantham, just off the A1 trunk road. Colsterworth has a population of approximately 1800.

The origins of the project lie in a desire to stimulate a wider environmental interest and greater awareness among young people, and in a response to the widespread destruction of trees following the 1987 hurricane. It entails the collection, sowing and germination of the seeds of native deciduous trees, with healthy saplings ultimately planted out at various local sites. An essential element is the encouragement of a sense of 'ownership' for the children, whose own saplings, germinated from seed they themselves collected, will literally become their own 'Trees for Life'. Considerable emphasis has also been placed upon recognising the importance of trees for the support of wildlife, and, indirectly, human existence. The project offers tremendous potential in terms of raising awareness and shaping attitudes. Such a community-based initiative, aiming to improve our immediate environment and awaken an early interest and commitment towards conservation, has generated immense enthusiasm among children, parents, staff, governors and the wider community.

LAUNCHING THE PROJECT

The idea for the project originally came from Doug Campion, a local resident and member of the Colsterworth and District Gardeners and Allotment Holders' Association. His idea was discussed with staff and governors, before being launched with a letter to parents, which explained its aims and objectives. We constructed our 'Tree for Life' compound alongside a shed adjacent to the school which we used to store project-related materials. Before we started collecting seeds, we held a special assembly at which the project was formally introduced to the children. Our own posters depicted a 'Tree for Life' and illustrated the different seeds which the youngsters were encouraged to collect.

Now that the project was launched, we had to set about collecting seeds. Children collected seeds with parents at weekends and when they were taken out as part of the school activities. The aim of the project was to focus on the seeds of indigenous trees. Some of these we collected ourselves (certain species – horse chestnut in particular – were especially popular with children; in addition to these we prompted them to collect seeds from oak, ash, beech, hazel, silver birch, hornbeam, alder and field maple); the wild service tree also contributed berries – this is a native tree (*Sorbus Torminalis*), a rather 'shy' and not particularly prolific tree which is found throughout the UK and which is related to the mountain ash and whitebeam. We kept the seeds in paper bags which we named and stored in a cool, dry place. Reference books were hurriedly consulted: clearly this was going to be a learning experience for all concerned.

Meanwhile, we began the important business of publicising the scheme, writing letters to the National Tree Council, the Forestry Commission, the Woodland Trust and Lincolnshire County Council. A minimal input from School Fund augmented sponsorship by the local Gardening Club, which was boosted by a significant private donation.

THE PROJECT TAKES OFF

Sowing began in October 1988, with children planting seeds under adult supervision and with the enthusiastic participation of volunteer helpers. We used a coding system to label each pot, entering details (including dates of planting) in a register. This enabled us to keep

an accurate record of all participating children and the species of seeds which they had sown. Pots were then sunk into peat in our specially prepared compound. We sowed around 500 pots in our first season. For the next phase of the project, we contacted local organisations, farmers and landowners who might be willing to allow planting on their land. One important criterion was that youngsters and their families should have ready access on future occasions.

Now that the project was up and running, we eagerly awaited the first signs of new life in the compound the following spring. In anticipation of this event, we designed 'Tree for Life' Germination Certificates which were commercially produced and used a different coloured tree symbol for each species successfully germinated. Earlier, we had been delighted to secure the involvement of a local author and broadcaster, Eric Simms, who is an authority on the British countryside. Mr Simms kindly agreed to be patron of our scheme and, in this capacity, he presented the inaugural set of Germination Certificates at a special assembly in May 1989. At the same assembly, we distributed lapel badges promoting the scheme to children.

This celebration of successful germination re-awakened the children's interest and enthusiasm for the project, and, as saplings grew, the children 'potted on', a task in which they were supervised. This continued through the summer months, with volunteers watering seedlings.

About a year after the launch of the project, we finalised plans for the first planting-out ceremony. In November 1989, with the support of Anglian Water, our first eight trees (oak and hazel) were planted out during National Tree Week at a site on the shores of Rutland Water. Family representatives from each of the children involved were present, to make it more likely that children would revisit the planting site in the future. Children, parents, governors, staff and representatives of the village community witnessed this auspicious beginning to the project.

When planting out, we prepare holes, enriched with compost where needed. A shelter protects saplings from rabbits and adverse weather conditions. A mulch mat on top of the soil prevents weeds growing immediately around, using up valuable water. It also helps stop moisture loss by evaporation. The shelter is firmly attached to a stake.

LIVING EARTH: A RESOURCE FOR LEARNING

FUNDING THE PROJECT

As more and more young trees have been planted out, the funding implications have become increasingly significant. We have secured generous sponsorship after much hard work by project organisers and are particularly indebted to: Fitchett & Woolacott Ltd (Nottingham); Lincolnshire County Council; Ruddles Brewery; Smiths Coaches of Corby Glen; Lincolnshire Agricultural Society; Colour Processing Laboratories (Nottingham); the printers, Barnes of Humby, and commercial artist, Elaine Laws for their support. More recently we launched a 'Become a Friend' scheme, and individuals received a 'Tree for Life' car sticker in return for a donation. We also now promote the scheme through selling our own merchandise – pens, pencils, notebooks, rubbers, badges and bookmarks.

In autumn 1990, we won first place in a competition organised by the Council for the

Part of the exhibit for 'A Tree for Life' at the Lincolnshire Show, 1991

Preservation of Rural England and second place in the Lincolnshire Village Ventures Competition, which was a considerable boost to morale. In 1992, we received a further donation from a gentleman living in Sussex! Mr Len Wright, once of Colsterworth, had read of the project and raised several hundred pounds to supplement funds.

This financial support has been vital to the success of the project and has come from publicising and promoting the scheme extensively. School and village newsletters provide regular updates; local radio and newspapers have featured the scheme; articles have appeared in county and national publications. Most interest is generated through our local displays. We have a permanent display at Sacrewell Country Park, near Peterborough, where some project trees are planted. We have displayed at the local library and at Lincoln Cathedral. For the past three years we have set up a display at the Lincolnshire Show, courtesy of Lincolnshire Agricultural Society. This has led to both sponsorship and further offers of sites for planting out.

CURRICULAR OPPORTUNITIES

The project is now successfully established to the extent that teachers are able to draw on it as and when they wish. One of our busiest times relates to preparations for the display at the annual Lincolnshire Show. Using a whole-school approach, each year a different theme is chosen to illustrate the project. Last year, children's work on the four seasons featured on and around our own hardboard 'tree' at the centre of a marquee. The scheme has enormous potential for the curriculum. We have drawn upon the scheme to enhance children's experience in the area of religious and moral education and, as far as specific curriculum areas are concerned, excellent work has been produced in Craft, Science, Mathematics, Geography, and Information Technology. Art and language work have also drawn heavily on the project. Children have written poetry, descriptive passages, newspaper articles and produced their own video documentary on the project. Speaking and listening activities featured prominently on the days of the Show, with children briefing visitors on our project while encouraging them to enter an environmental quiz which they themselves had devised. Assemblies which have focused on the project have included drama presentations by children. Art work has allowed the children to explore a wide range of media and techniques in illustrating and responding to trees and the variety of life which they support. For the 1991 show, children produced our own 'Tree for Life' ceramic mosaic.

Secondary attention falls upon the project in the autumn term, when preparatory and follow-up work takes place with regard to seed collecting trips. This work is planned by the individual teacher. Otherwise, the scheme represents a tremendous living resource to have on one's doorstep and one which is drawn upon to supplement or initiate a unit of work as the teacher sees fit.

ASSESSMENT OF THE PROJECT

A vital ingredient of our success has been the establishment of an organising committee, comprising two members of the Gardening Club, Doug Campion and Marion Miller, who, in consultation with the headteacher, took responsibility for the direction and organisation of the scheme. Doug Campion and Marion Miller have worked tirelessly for four years, and their commitment has contributed significantly to the project's remarkable success.

Obviously a similar project could have operated on a lesser scale without significant external support. In our own case, however, virtually all the extra work generated by the project has been undertaken by volunteers from within the community. We consider ourselves the fortunate beneficiaries of their experience and enthusiasm. Such an ongoing commitment is clear evidence that the project has struck a chord with many interested adults.

Technical and organisational difficulties have inevitably arisen as the project has developed. With two dry summers, watering trees at isolated sites has not proved to be possible, but the majority of trees are growing very well nevertheless. A warden scheme, whereby volunteer parents check sites at given intervals, has helped to monitor progress. Deer have caused some problems, and special tree guards have had to be fitted at some sites. Certain species, especially beech, have been very difficult to establish. It has proved far more difficult than anticipated to obtain access to local sites for planting. Consequently, the aim of planting trees in and around Colsterworth has barely been achieved, and we have had to travel many miles to some of our sites. However, the enthusiasm for the project that has been shown by conservation-minded landowners and managers supporting us from further afield has been ample compensation for this.

The project is an important feature of life at Colsterworth School and, through sensitive handling and promotion, we have gained the interested support of our parent body. At the same time, we have been careful to prevent the project taking over the wider curriculum to the exclusion of other activities: this could have produced over-kill and led to the children becoming jaded and disenchanted with the project. However, we do recognise that we are engaged in something special which has captured the imagination of many and will, we hope, inspire a generation who will respect and value their natural environment.

Marion Miller and Doug Campion, with helpers

As costs mount, we have cut back on sowing this year and only children new to the school have been encouraged to collect and plant seeds. For one thing, the compound is already bursting at the seams! The considerable success of the project has hinged upon the unstinting efforts of a relatively small group of local volunteers, many of whom are retired. One wonders for how many more years these gentle folk will willingly persist in bending aching backs to dig holes in the frozen earth on the chilly, windswept shores of Rutland Water, or elsewhere? The spirit may be willing... In any case, we shall not be turning away further youthful volunteers!

CONCLUSION

At a recent social evening, the project's patron, Eric Simms, gave an illustrated talk on the history of tree cover in Britain. Project supporters listened with interest, aware of the increasingly acute need to take positive action to reverse the trend of deforestation. Members were updated on the progress of the project in a social context, many of us aware that our own lives have been considerably enriched through working to inspire and influence our youngsters.

We have now been up and running for four years. Over 500 trees have been planted out at 17 different sites. These include farms and a farm trail, a nature reserve and country centre, a golf club, a cemetery, land fronting a local factory and the local National Trust properties – Woolsthorpe Manor and Belton House. After each occasion the children involved have been presented in school with their own gold 'Planting Out' certificates to celebrate the beginning of the life of their own tree in its new habitat. At these presentations, parents are welcomed, to reinforce the significance of the event. We hope that these occasions will be held in the children's hearts and minds and that their 'trees for life' flourish, blossom and mature as they will, too, in the years to come.

Richard Burrows has taught in primary schools in Lancashire, Hertfordshire and Lincolnshire, where he is now headteacher of Colsterworth Church of England Primary School. He has made his personal interest in the environment a focal point of his teaching over the 20 years he has been in the profession.

THE RAINFOREST EDUCATION PROGRAMME

The following events took place as part of the Rainforest Education Programme, launched by Living Earth in 1990, with sponsorship from Midland Bank, in order to create a strategy and to develop resources to help teachers deliver education about rainforests in UK secondary schools. The first part of the Programme involved consulting teachers in order to discover the scope for rainforest education, particularly in the context of the emerging National Curriculum. This consultation was achieved by inviting Midland Bank's network of 800 associate secondary schools to participate in an environmental education questionnaire survey.

A national weekend workshop was then organised which brought together subject specialists from across the curriculum in order to initiate a national programme of curriculum development. The workshop identified the 'special event' as an effective way to introduce and develop a cross-curricular environmental topic within a class, year group or whole-school group, and a series of pilot programmes were carried out in a selection of schools to test this thesis. The plan was to suspend the normal timetable for a period of time in order to immerse pupils in a highly sensory experience on an environmental topic. Subject specialists would later capitalise on the interest and enthusiasm that had resulted from this special event and use these to develop the topic within their normal programme of teaching.

Four schools were given £1000 to organise an events-based approach to developing cross-curricular education about rainforests. They had a year to carry out the project and make a full written report about it. The two case studies that follow are based on projects that took place in Lees Brook Community School and Eltham Green School.

Rainforests OK

CHRIS DURBIN

INTRODUCTION

This is an account of the planning and preparation of the event which we came to call 'Rainforest OK' (held between 5–9 March 1990) and of its various spin-offs. The stimulus for this event came from the rainforest itself. It came from a desire to go to a rainforest and learn more about this important environment a long way from home. The fact that Living Earth had invited me to join in this project merely coincided with my own increasing interest in tropical places – nine months before, I had been to Kenya, the first time I had been to the tropics.

I became concerned that we were portraying these remote places in a simplistic way, as poor, underdeveloped and riddled with social and environmental problems. From my experience as a teacher, I realised that there was a need to redress this balance – many young people easily 'switch off' when presented with problem after problem – and to raise awareness about 'solutions'. In addition, media coverage of the rainforest issue seemed to be encouraging some of the myths that surround the rainforest environment. I felt it was my duty as a teacher to raise the quality of the debate and show young people that these issues are not simple.

The Midlands group that formed part of the Rainforest Education Programme included a number of staff from Lees Brook Community School, which enabled me to co-ordinate and plan the event. The event was considered to be an important means of increasing understanding about rainforests by applying the enquiry process to the subject, so that young people could acquire a sense of the rainforest environment, understand the issues that it raises and respond in ways they feel appropriate.

Once Living Earth had given us the go-ahead and the funding to design an event, school circumstances dictated the potential audience. Year 7 had already experienced an event at Lea Green, a residential centre, in November; Year 11 would be winding up for examinations; Year 10 had completed a section on rainforests for their Geography GCSE. That left Years 8 and 9. The Year 9 tutors had already planned a variety of extra-curricular experiences for the year, which ruled them out. We nevertheless felt that this age group would benefit enormously from this event: they had, in the previous year, had an enormous success with a local environment project in the school grounds. We would be able to build on this.

PLANNING THE EVENT

Once we had also been given the notional go-ahead from the headteacher, the staff involved in the Rainforest Education Programme met as a team with no agenda other than the questions, 'What are we going to do?' and 'How are we going to do it?' The agenda that arose from that meeting was as follows:

- What do the children know about the rainforests?
- What do they need to know?
- What do they feel about doing an event?
- When shall we do it?
- How shall we involve staff, and whom shall we involve?
- What are we going to do?
- How shall we fund it?
- Can we involve children in the planning?

This brainstorm was divided into tasks that were to be solved outside the meeting and tasks that were to be solved in the course of the meeting. In the meeting, we decided to:

- hold the event between 5–9 March 1990 (having consulted the school calendar and individuals' diaries);
- approach individuals and make general announcements at briefing meetings;
- use the £1000 that Living Earth had contributed to resource the event.

At the time of the meeting we were unsure about including pupils in the preparation of the event. We agreed that Joe Shaw, a Year 8 teacher, should raise the first three of the questions on our agenda with his group and that we should look at what his pupils wrote in reply to these questions before deciding whether to involve them in the planning and what structure to give the event. As it turned out, involving the pupils earlier would have saved considerable planning time, since they identified concerns and interests which caused us to revise our thinking.

The question of how to structure the event became one of what to do in the course of the event. The illustration opposite indicates our first, and rather confused, ideas on the subject.

We took fright at some of the more experimental aspects of this plan, which involved looking at 'conflict', 'health', 'beliefs' and 'communications'. Instead, we decided to concentrate on 'perceptions', a subject more appropriate for our target group.

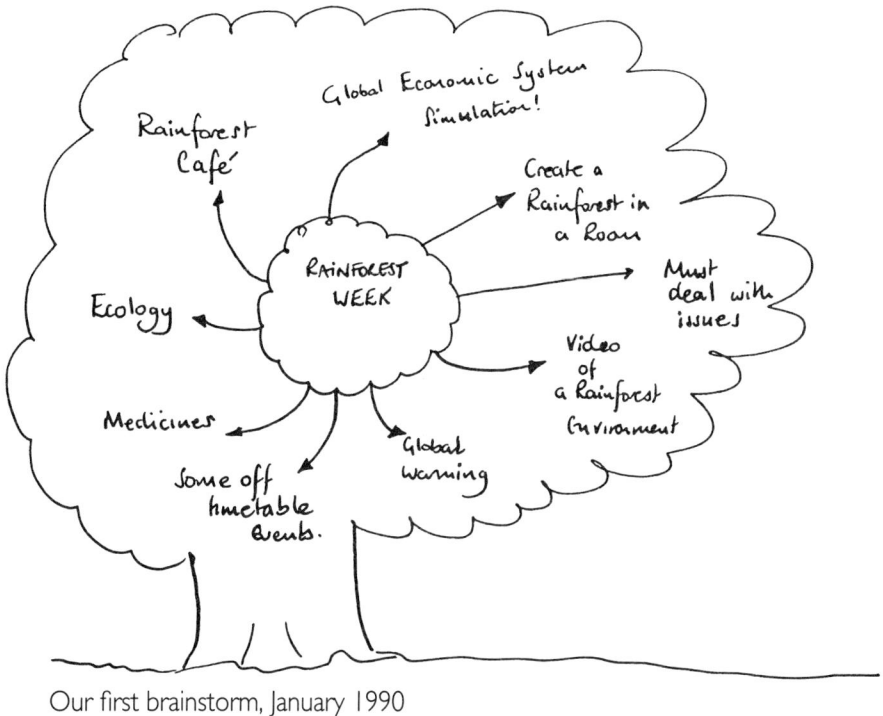

Our first brainstorm, January 1990

INVOLVING THE PUPILS

The next meeting discussed the responses of the pupils. There were three feelings which were commonly expressed in these responses which we found interesting:

- Apathy – why should we bother about rainforests? They're far away and nothing to do with me.
- Confusion – ranging from a misunderstanding of complex global issues to not knowing what a rainforest is at all.
- Jealousy – Year 7 pupils had been away for three days. This event was seen as a replacement for that residential session for the Year 8 pupils.

We drafted an outline of events to show young people that the events could be fun, to persuade them that they did need to bother and to take them out of their confusion. We needed to assume nothing and design activities for all abilities. The first plan was drafted at that meeting and is shown overleaf.

INVOLVING THE STAFF

Our planning group represented key curriculum areas, but we needed to involve others. If we were to involve all Year 8 teachers, we would next need to involve the curriculum teams. With this in mind, we agreed to inform the Year 8 pastoral team about the event. We also proposed to allocate rooms for the activities and asked a member of the team to investigate the implications of this.

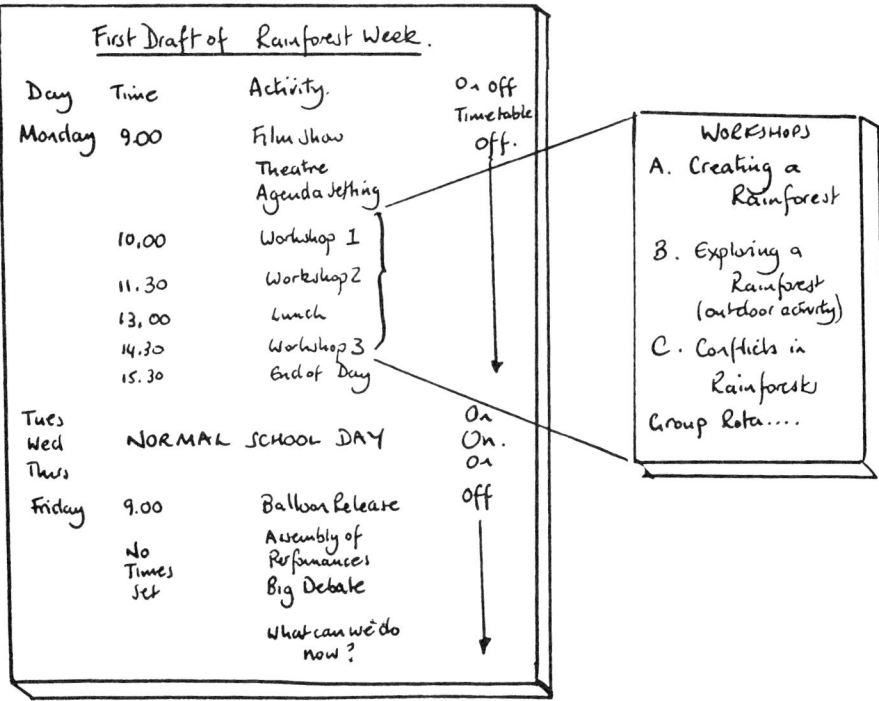

The programme we agreed for the first day of the event

Unfortunately, members of the group failed to understand that they should go to their own curriculum areas, talk to their colleagues and work out how they could benefit from the week. The delegation *did* work in one curriculum area – Maths – where the team used their curriculum meeting to plan what they were going to do together to involve all Year 8 teachers. The Art teacher, who was on the planning group, organised her own activity but didn't filter it down to members of her curriculum team. There was no member of the Technology department on the planning group, and that area became intensely complex since a circus of different subjects operated in a ten-week cycle. Other subject areas failed to co-operate at all.

This experience made us cautious, but we decided that enthusiastic innovative teachers were more important than 'whole coverage' of all subjects in the curriculum. We discussed the need for an impetus – something to remind us of rainforest issues and the environment and to galvanise our own enthusiasm. With this in mind, we set aside an afternoon to receive this kind of stimulus from a recent visitor to the Peruvian rainforest, Anna Culwick.

PREPARING THE FIRST RUNNING ORDER OF EVENTS

Towards the end of this planning stage, we realised that an outdoor stimulus was not going to prove possible on the first day of the event (Monday) and that we needed to seek a new time. In addition, we had limited time to prepare something creative, and we decided that this would need to come *after* the event, not as part of it. The main thrust of this planning involved negotiating with other members of staff for the release of staff to take full part in the two 'off-timetable' days. To smooth this, two supply teachers were employed each day, funded by a curriculum development fund designated by the headteacher.

Meanwhile, the curriculum areas were feeding back information about their lessons, and we started to produce publicity.

It became apparent that the Achilles heel of this structure was the cross-curricular links involved in the course of the Tuesday–Thursday section. It was difficult for us to find time to plan together and to share our ideas for this stage. We did ask what each subject was most effective in contributing to an understanding about rainforests. However, we failed to brief people properly and to enable them to find resources. A notable weak point was the

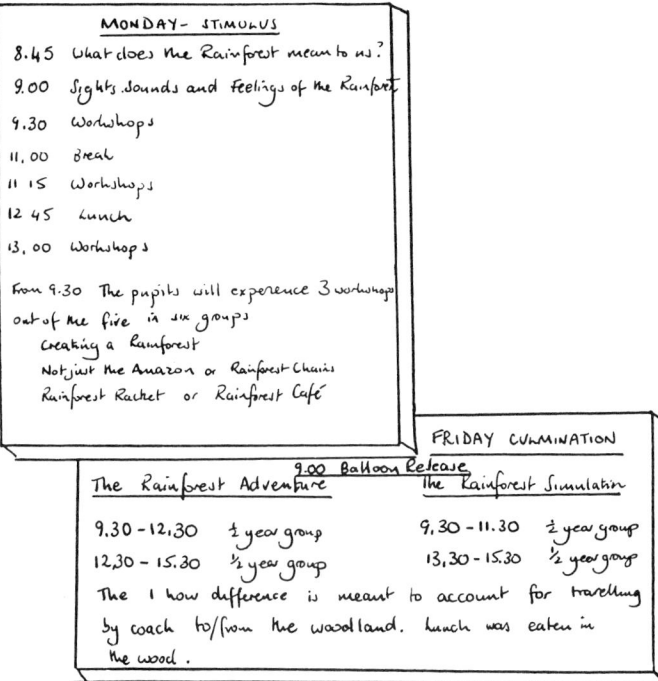

Humanities area where I, as co-ordinator, had taken on too much both to develop workshops for the stimulus day and prepare the work done in the Humanities area. Much of the creative work took place in our own time, in the corridor on the run, in the staff room over a cup of tea. These problems, in retrospect, could all have been avoided if we had been more open from the start and invited people to take part in the initial stages of the event's planning. In addition we had assumed, wrongly, that people had enough knowledge about the rainforest to enable them to plan a lesson or two related to the subject.

PREPARING STAFF AND PUPILS

From this final outline, however, a programme (see opposite) was released for circulation, together with a letter about the rainforest adventure. This stimulated more interest in the staff, some of whom asked, 'What can we do?' Many last-minute spontaneous activities arose in curriculum areas that had been slow to react, often, sadly, too late.

We decided that it would be a good idea to use a skit of Smith and Jones, 'What does this rainforest mean t'us?', in the week before the event, to start the pupils thinking about the issues. So Joe Shaw and I performed it during the Year 8 assembly, where it went down less well than it did later in front of some older pupils. This session encouraged more positive responses from pupils, who asked 'What are we doing?' and 'Where are we going?', etc.

The team rallied round to collect all the resources, prepare each of the assigned rooms and enabled me to relax and enjoy the weekend ahead.

THE EVENT ITSELF

The purpose of this article has not been to focus on the events themselves so much as to indicate the planning that went into them and, importantly, the mistakes that were made. However, it would give a false picture of the events if a brief account of what took place was not to be included, and the following description is intended to put some (minimal) flesh on the bones of the programme given on page 297. There is not enough space to include details of the subject-specific work that formed the basis of the activities for Tuesday, Wednesday and Thursday, so these notes only cover the cross-curricular activities of Monday and Friday.

Monday: Exploring the sights, sounds and feelings of the rainforest

A Science lab was set up to imitate a rainforest; the temperature was raised to 26°, boiling kettles were used to produce a humid atmosphere, and the pupils sat and watched a slide sequence in silence, while a tape of rainforest sounds played in the background (in this instance, 'Rainforest Requiem', National Sound Archive/Mankind Music, although there are many other suitable recordings available). From this introduction, the pupils broke up into their workshop groups with an assigned teacher for the day: this involved a practical exploration of what they had just witnessed.

Workshop 1: rainforest café
Pupils experienced examples of the rainforest's products and designed and produced a

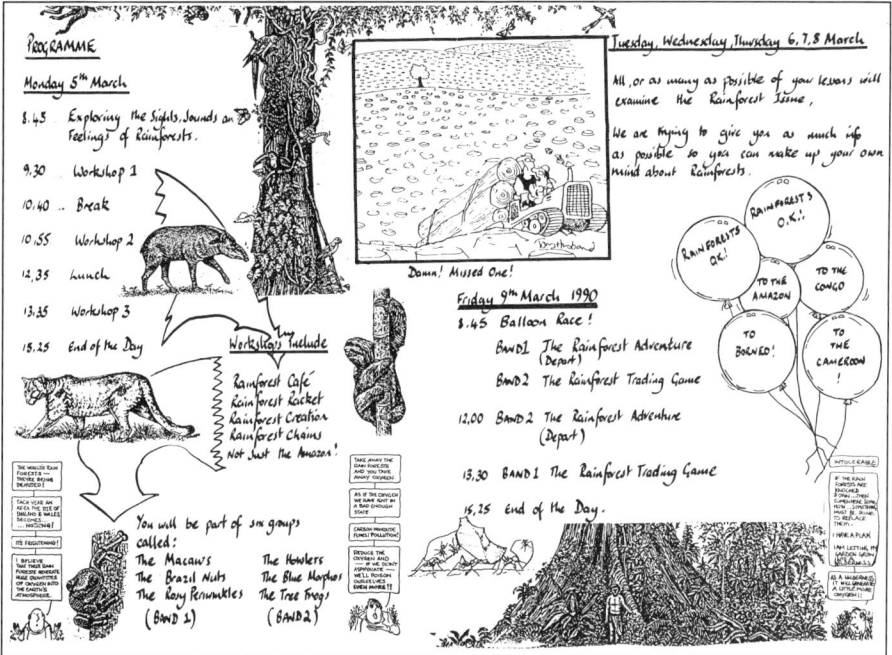

The programme for circulation

recipe for the rainforest café, producing and designing a menu to accompany this. This was very much enjoyed by the pupils, whose awareness of the range of products that originated from the rainforests was considerably enhanced in the process.

Workshop 2: rainforest racket

Pupils devised music to form part of the rainforest creation, drawing on the aural stimulus of the introductory session. While this was partially successful, it would have resulted in even more striking work had they had more equipment at their disposal and had there been preliminary activities which, for example, helped them to isolate the other senses by blindfolding, forbidding exploration through touch, etc.

Workshop 3: rainforest creation

A room had been prepared for this workshop, with blank white and grey paper covering the walls, cardboard on the floor, etc. Resources were provided in the form of standard art materials, cut up pages from *The Rainforest – a celebration* and cardboard tubes. Given such scant resources, the pupils came up with some fantastic displays of trees, leaves and wall friezes (with 3D branches sticking out of them!).

Workshop 4: rainforest chains

Pupils engaged in a number of activities designed to show the interrelationships of rainforest animals and plants and the way in which human actions can interrupt this carefully evolved interdependence. One of the ways of doing this was to allocate roles to pupils (bees, orchids; macaws, red fruits; harpy eagles, spider monkeys; etc.), each role being given a different piece of coloured wool; it was left to them to discover the connections and to see how the whole complex web may be maintained – or destroyed.

Workshop 3

Workshop 5

Balloon race

Rain forest adventure

Workshop 5: not just the Amazon!
This workshop took the form of a 68-piece jigsaw of the world, which pupils had to piece together, use to locate the tropical rainforests and, from there, to discover what lives in the rainforests, what threatens that life and what the threat to this life means to the lives of the pupils. The final product was to be a poster to convey information about one of the rainforests that they had been learning about in the session.

Friday: indoor and outdoor events

Friday: balloon race
The day started with the release of balloons carrying messages about the rainforest and instructions for those who found them to write and tell the school (one balloon reached as far as Melton Mowbray!). This was a publicity stunt to show pupils how to use the press to raise awareness of issues in the wider community. It was also a way of raising the status of the event in the eyes of the pupils.

Friday: the rainforest adventure
This was an outdoor simulation activity. We used a wood 30 minutes away from the school, which was in a valley of the local major river with a factory nearby. Groups of pupils were assigned various roles (shareholders, rubber-tappers, world bankers, forest dwellers, burger manufacturers, etc.). There were three groups in the imaginary rainforest, each of which had to behave in the forest as their role suggested. The Yanomami were hunting and gathering food and medicinal plants. The rubber-tappers identified 'rubber' trees and labelled them. The timber prospectors identified timber trees and made calculations of the quantity of timber available to them. We used species of Derbyshire plants and trees to represent rainforest species.

Using the 'bush telegraph', news was then spread that the ranchers were coming with their bulldozers. Each group had to come up with their reasons for not wanting the rainforest to be cut down and to formulate a plan of action. This was a very effective means of giving the pupils an insight into the lives of the people of the Amazon.

Friday: the rainforest simulation
This took place in the school hall. The purpose of the event was to help the pupils to make global connections. Each group was assigned a role (shareholders, world bankers, forest dwellers) and, as a warming-up task, had to make something associated with the lives of those people: for example, rubber-tappers might have to make a bag with which to collect the rubber, timber prospectors had to examine how to record their finds, etc. An area of rainforest, represented by paper cups, was managed according to the decisions taken by each group. All pupils enjoyed this activity.

EVALUATION

With hindsight, the planning could have been organised much more successfully. For one thing, the planning group was divided in its perception of what an 'event' was, and we at no stage stated our aims. A weekend spent at an outdoor centre had fired us with enthusiasm for a notion, but nobody had asked, 'Why are we doing this?' – not even the headteacher. If I were to prepare the event again now, the question I would raise is, 'Is the notion of an event away from the everyday school timetable enough to take the young people's environmental education further?'

For another thing, there were significant omissions in our planning: we failed to consider, for example, how the event related to the curriculum around it. While this might have revealed the isolation of the event in the school life of an individual pupil, it would have been a barrier to the idea of 'doing something innovative'.

Having said that, the event was an undoubted success, and not just because pupils tend always to like activities that are a break from the normal routine of the timetable (although this may be behind the surprise of one teacher who commented, 'We've only had one discipline problem all day!'). The basic aim with which we had started – to raise the level of awareness about the rainforest issue – had already been achieved by the end of Monday: the learning that came afterwards was an unforeseen bonus.

The event has had other, longer-term, effects. The school has decided to repeat the experiment, but with the proviso that the event must this time be linked more closely to the day-to-day curriculum. The event has also led us to draw up a school policy on the issue of environmental education – since it revealed a general lack of expertise in environmental issues – and to instigate a programme of staff development. This programme will examine the school's, and the County's, policy on the environment and ensure that teachers learn by doing.

Pupils learned, and continue to learn, from the event. A group of ten pupils became so expert at 'reconstructing the rainforest' that they were able to carry the event to other areas of the county and make it possible for 5000 people (many of whom will never experience the real thing) to have a simulated experience of walking in a rainforest. Similarly, the work produced in the course of the week, and in the weeks following it, was sufficient to mount a display in the City library to which another 2000–3000 people came. This was a learning experience that informed the whole community.

Finally, the event led to the school drawing up a model which would be used for all events relating to cross-curricular themes. This model has since been adopted as a model for particular curriculum areas. This is a considerable achievement: it is unlikely that any amount of staff development time would change some teachers' outlook so quickly.

Chris Durbin trained as a geography teacher at Notingham University. After a period of teaching in schools, Chris worked in an environmental education centre in Derbyshire before becoming Head of Geography at Leesbrook Community School. He then became an advisory teacher in Derbyshire before taking up his current post in London as Humanities Education Officer at the BBC.

INDEX

Index

Note: Entries in *italics* are book titles unless indicated otherwise.

abbeys 89–91
Acid News (journal) 40
acid rain 240–4
Acid Rain 20
Acid Rain: the Silent Crisis (slide set) 74, 77
ACTIONAID 61, 62
Acts of Parliament 44, 50
aluminium cans, recycling 113
animals:
    books on 20
    in the classroom 42–4, 46, 49–53
    wildlife areas 280–4
Annual Review of Environmental Education (journal) 37–8, 40
Antarctica 246–9
Antonia's Rainforest 20
art 138–42
arts, *vs.* sciences 4, 6

Bats in the Garden 21
Bioenergy 19
Bird Studies for Primary Science 45, 48
birds:
    in the classroom 45, 51, 52
    software 30–1, 32
    videos 67
Bolsover 169–73
books 16–23
    action guides 21–2
    on animals and plants in schools 43–8
    on energy 18–19
    environment in literature 153–9
    general 16–17
    on greenhouse effect, *etc.* 19–21
    on historic sites and buildings 89–91
    on industry and the environment 110–11
    on population 18
    series 22–3
    TV-related 64–5
    on waste 19
    on water 18
British Broadcasting Corporation (BBC):
    videos 54–5, 57, 65–6, 69
    Wildlife magazine 64
British Gas, posters 80
buildings 89–91
business, and schools 112–17
    see also industry
Buy Now, Pay Later 21

Can You Find It? (software) 29, 31
Caring for Environments series 22
Central Television 64, 65, 67, 69
Centre for Alternative Technology (CAT) 125–6, 127
charts and posters 78–83, 85–7
Children Need Food 18
Chimpanzee Family Book 20
Choices for the Planet (packs) 56, 57
Civic Trust 126–7
Classroom Creatures 43–4, 47
Colsterworth School 285–91
computers:
    software 26–32, 33–4
    use of 25–6
conservation 6

INDEX

Conserving the Jungles 20
consultants, environmental education 133–5
Council for Environmental Education 37, 122–3, 127
cross-curricular themes 12
curriculum see National Curriculum

Decade of Destruction (pack) 56–7, 67
Development Education Centre 62
Dictionary of the Living World (software) 30, 32
Down the Plughole 18
drama 143–51
    Neptune and the sea people 144–8
    The wise wet–woman 149–51

Earthquest Explores Ecology (software) 33–4
Easter celebrations 228–31
Ecologist, The (magazine) 40
Ecology Watch series 22
Ecosoft (software) 26, 31
ecosystems 237–9
educational packages, TV 65–6
Elephant Family Book 20
emotions, and music 223–4
energy, books on 18–19
Energy and Power 19
English 152–62
    environment in literature 153–9
    environmental collage 160–2
English Heritage, Education Service 88–91
English Nature (magazine) 40
Environment, The (pack) 58
environmental co-ordinator, local authority 103
environmental education 1, 4–7
    enquiry approach 4, 6, 7–11
    and the National Curriculum 12–14
Environmental Education (journal) 36–7, 39
Environmental Impact 2000 (wallcharts) 79
environmental studies 6
equipment, for fieldwork 97–100
Europe and the Environment 17

Feeding the World 18
fieldwork 6
    English Heritage 88–91
    tools and equipment 97–100
    zoos 92–6
Focus on Castries – St Lucia (photographs) 60–1, 62
Food for Thought 18
Food for the World 18

Fragile Earth TV films 64–5
Friends of the Earth:
    posters 81
    School Friends 121–2, 127

Gaia Atlas of Planet Management 17
Gamelan 225–6
Garden for Birds 21
gardening, books on 21
geography 163–73
    historic town development 169–73
    Mobil Greensight Pack 164–8
    National Curriculum 14
George, Alan 104–8
Global Environment, The (video) 54–5, 57, 65–6
global issues 6
Global Warming 19–20
Green Earth or a Dry Desert (slide set) 75, 77
Green Guide to Children's Books 21
Green Issues series 17, 22
Green Teacher (journal) 38, 40, 126
greenhouse effect, books on 19–21
Greenhouse Effect, The 20
Greenhouse Effect, The (pack) 55–6, 57
Greening the Staffroom (pack) 57–8, 66, 76
Grounds for Change (video) 76
groups and organisations, environment and conservation 121–7
Grow Your Own 21

habitat, loss of 19–21
Heating up the Earth: the Greenhouse Effect (slide set) 74, 77
Hedgerow 20
Hillcrest School, Netherton 118–20
historic sites 88–91, 169–73
history 174–87
    historical event 182–7
    historical survey 175–81
    National Curriculum 14

Ian and Fred's Big Green Book 17
industry:
    and the environment 109–11
    –schools links 112–17, 118–20
    see also Unilever
information technology (IT) 188–96
    environmental newspaper 193–6
    presentation of global problems 189–92
Institute of Biology, publications 46, 53
International Centre for Conservation

INDEX

Education (ICCE) 67, 70
International Journal of Environmental Education and Information 40

Journal of Biological Education 40
journals and magazines 35–41, 64
Just Rubbish? series 19, 22

Kenya 271–9

Landmarks – the Rainforest (software) 30, 32
languages 207–18
　environment pollution 208–12
　renovation 213–18
Last Frontiers for Mankind series 22
Learning through Landscapes 124–5, 127
　Newsletter 40
Lees Brook Community School 293–302
listed buildings 89–91
literature, environment in 153–9
litter 265–8
　see also waste
Living Biology in Schools 46, 48, 53
Living Earth Foundation 1, 2–3
local authorities 101–3
Looking into the Environment (pack) 58

magazines 35–41, 64
Making Peace with the Planet (slide set) 75, 77
mathematics 197–206
　rivers 198–202
　town planning 203–6
media, mix of 72–7
Minibeasts 42–3, 47
Mobil Greensight Pack 55, 57, 164–8
multi-media packs 54–9
music 219–26

National Association of Environmental Education (NAEE) 36
National Association for Urban Studies (NAUS) 35
National Curriculum 1, 4, 12–14, 49, 65
New Journeys (photographs) 62
New Scientist, posters 80, 81–2, 84
newspaper, environmental 193–6
Noah's Choice 20
Norton School, Cleveland 270–9

Oak and Company 20
Only One Earth (pack) 55, 57

organisations, environment and conservation 121–7
videos 66–8
Oxford *Atlases* 17
ozone layer, books on 19–21

Pampagrande (photographs) 61–2
People Trap 18
photographs 60–2
Pictorial Charts Education Trust (PCET) 85–7
plants:
　books on 20, 21
　in the classroom 44, 53
population, books on 18
posters 78–83, 85–7
Precision Steel 118–20
publications see books; journals and magazines

questions, environmental enquiry 9–11

radio 64, 73, 76–7
radio programme, making a 222–3
Rainforest Education Programme 292–302
rainforests:
　books on 19–21
　software 30, 33–4
rap 220–2
recycling:
　aluminium cans 113
　books on 19
religious education 227–35
　Easter celebrations 228–31
　responses of religions to environmental problems 232–5
Renewable Energy 18
Repairing the Damage series 22
resources:
　books 16–23
　journals and magazines 35–41
　living animals and plants 42–53
　mix of media 72–7
　multi-media packs 54–9
　photographs 60–2
　software 26–32, 33–4
　television and video 63–71
　wallcharts and posters 78–83, 85–7
　see also fieldwork
rhythm 224–5
rivers 198–202
Royal Society for the Prevention of Cruelty to Animals (RSPCA),
　publications 46, 48, 49–52

305

INDEX

Royal Society for the Protection of Birds (RSPB) 67, 70
rubbish see waste

Save Our Earth series 22
School Garden Company 21–2
School Library Services 23
science 236–44
    acid rain 240–4
    ecosystems, chemical change and weather 237–9
    National Curriculum 14
Science and Plants for Schools (SAPS) programme 44, 47
sciences, *vs.* arts 4, 6
series, books 22–3
Shell Education Service, posters 80, 82, 83
Sky Hunter (software) 30–1, 32
slide packs 73–5, 77
software, computer 26–32, 33–4
Some People Don't Eat Meat 21
Spaceship Earth series 22
Spaceship Earth (software) 27, 31
special needs education 245–54
    Antarctica 246–9
    Third World 251–4
Stimulus Video Project 76, 77
strategies, teaching and learning 4
Streetwise (journal) 35–6, 39
Survival series 22

Take One: Rubbish 19
Teacher Placement Service 113–14, 116
Teaching Environment: the Management of a Cross-curricular Theme (pack) 58
technology 255–68
    litter 265–8
    outside school environment 256–63
television 63–5, 73, 76
    see *also* videos
Television Trust for the Environment (TVE) 64
Third World 251–4
Threshold of Change (video) 75, 77
tools and equipment, for fieldwork 97–100
town planning 169–73, 203–6
    see *also* local authorities
Tree of Life 20
'Tree for Life' Project 285–91
trees, books on 20

Understanding British Industry (UBI) 113, 116

Understanding Our Environment (pack) 57
Unilever plc 1, 3, 104
    Education Liaison Manager, Alan George 104–8
Urban Ecology: a Teacher's Resource Book 45–6, 48

vegetarianism, book on 21
video 72
videos 65–8, 75–6, 77
    multi-media packs 54–9
Viewpoints (software) 28–9, 31
volcano, and survival 182–7

wallcharts 78–83, 85–7
waste:
    books on 19
    litter 265–8
water:
    books on 18
    software 27–8, 31
    video 76–7, 77
Water Connection, The (video) 75–6, 77
Water Cycle 18
Water Game, The (software) 28, 31
Water for Life 18
Water Pollution (software) 27–8, 31
Ways of Life (slide set) 75, 77
weather 237–9
Webster, Sally 128–32
What a Load of Rubbish 19
When the Bough Breaks (video) 76, 77
Why Waste It? series 19, 22
wildlife:
    areas 280–4
    books on 20
    films 63–4
    magazines 64
Wildlife in Danger (slide set) 75, 77
World Wide Fund for Nature (WWF):
    multi-media material 57–8
    Teacher Representative Scheme 124, 127
    videos 54, 66, 67, 69–70
    wallcharts 78–9, 82–3
Worldaware 123–4, 127

Young Green Consumer Guide 21
Young People's Trust for the Environment and Nature Conservation (YPTENC) 128–32

zoos 92–6

This book has been produced by Living Earth, Unilever and Hodder and Stoughton in partnership.

Planning is currently underway for an updated edition of ***The Living Earth - A Resource for Learning***. If you are a teacher, parent, or other interested party involved in environmental education and feel you would like to contribute, then we would like to hear from you.

You can contact **Living Earth** on
071 487 3661